Trailblazers for Whole School Sustainability

What does it take to prepare students, teachers, and school staff to shape a just and sustainable future? In *Trailblazers for Whole School Sustainability*, you will meet educators and school leaders who are on the front lines of re-imagining school through the lens of sustainability.

This book features inspiring stories from around the country, from urban and rural schools and districts, that highlight best practices and lessons learned from teachers, administrators, and students as they transformed their school communities for a just and sustainable future. These stories are structured around a practical framework that demonstrates how this work allows schools and districts to work smarter, not harder, by integrating sustainability and systems thinking into leadership; curriculum and instruction; culture and climate; and facilities and operations.

While each school and district's story in this book is different, the passion that drives each one to embrace sustainability in everything they do, from operations to curriculum, remains the same. *Trailblazers for Whole School Sustainability* shows what is possible when educators resolve to blaze a trail to re-imagine K-12 education for a just and sustainable future.

Jennifer Seydel is Executive Director of Green Schools National Network and editor of the *Green Schools Catalyst Quarterly*, the only peer-reviewed journal for the K-12 green schools community. She has been an educator for over 40 years.

Cynthia L. Merse is a freelance writer and editor based in Knoxville, Tennessee. She also serves as assistant editor for the *Green Schools Catalyst Quarterly*.

Lisa A. W. Kensler is the Emily R. and Gerald S. Leischuck Endowed Professor for Educational Leadership at Auburn University, USA.

David Sobel is Professor Emeritus of Education at Antioch University New England, USA. He consults and speaks widely on child development and place-based education.

Other Eye on Education Books Available from Routledge
(www.routledge.com/eyeoneducation)

Teaching Practices from America's Best Urban Schools: A Guide for School and Classroom Leaders
Joseph F. Johnson, Jr., Cynthia L. Uline, and Lynne G. Perez

Creating, Grading, and Using Virtual Assessments: Strategies for Success in the K-12 Classroom
Kate Wolfe Maxlow, Karen L. Sanzo, and James Maxlow

Leadership for Deeper Learning: Facilitating School Innovation and Transformation
Jayson Richardson, Justin Bathon, and Scott McLeod

Get Organized Digitally!: The Educator's Guide to Time Management
Frank Buck

Rural America's Pathways to College and Career: Steps for Student Success and School Improvement
Rick Dalton

Bringing Innovative Practices to Your School: Lessons from International Schools
Jayson W. Richardson

A Guide to Impactful Teacher Evaluations: Let's Finally Get It Right!
Joseph O. Rodgers

A Guide to Early College and Dual Enrollment Programs: Designing and Implementing Programs for Student Achievement
Russ Olwell

The Strategy Playbook for Educational Leaders: Principles and Processes
Isobel Stevenson and Jennie Weiner

Unpacking Your learning Targets: Aligning Student Learning to Standards
Sean McWherter

Strategic Talent Leadership for Educators: A Practical Toolkit
Amy A. Holcombe

Becoming a Transformative Leader: A Guide to Creating Equitable Schools
Carolyn M. Shields

Working with Students that Have Anxiety: Creative Connections and Practical Strategies
Beverley H. Johns, Donalyn Heise, Adrienne D. Hunter

Implicit Bias in Schools: A Practitioner's Guide
Gina Laura Gullo, Kelly Capatosto, and Cheryl Staats

Trailblazers for Whole School Sustainability

Case Studies of Educators in Action

Edited by

Jennifer Seydel
Cynthia L. Merse
Lisa A. W. Kensler
David Sobel

Routledge
Taylor & Francis Group

NEW YORK AND LONDON

Cover image: © Getty Images

First published 2022
by Routledge
605 Third Avenue, New York, NY 10158

and by Routledge
2 Park Square, Milton Park, Abingdon, Oxon, OX14 4RN

Routledge is an imprint of the Taylor & Francis Group, an informa business

Library of Congress Cataloging-in-Publication Data
Names: Merse, Cynthia L., 1981– editor. | Seydel, Jennifer, 1956– editor. |
Kensler, Lisa A. W., editor. | Sobel, David, 1949– editor.
Title: Trailblazers for whole school sustainability: case studies of educators in
action / edited by Cynthia L. Merse, Jennifer Seydel, Lisa A.W. Kensler, David Sobel.
Description: New York, NY: Routledge, 2022. | Includes bibliographical references.
Identifiers: LCCN 2021036706 (print) | LCCN 2021036707 (ebook) |
ISBN 9780367710644 (hardback) | ISBN 9780367716028 (paperback) |
ISBN 9781003152811 (ebook) Subjects: LCSH: Educational leadership—
United States—Case studies. |
Sustainability—Study and teaching—United States—Case studies. |
Place-based education—United States—Case studies. | Experiential learning—United
States—Case studies. | Environmental education—United States—Case studies.
Classification: LCC LB2805 .T64 2022 (print) | LCC LB2805 (ebook) |
DDC 371.2/011—dc23
LC record available at https://lccn.loc.gov/2021036706
LC ebook record available at https://lccn.loc.gov/2021036707

ISBN: 978-0-367-71064-4 (hbk)
ISBN: 978-0-367-71602-8 (pbk)
ISBN: 978-1-003-15281-1 (ebk)

DOI: 10.4324/9781003152811

Typeset in Optima
by codeMantra

Contents

Foreword

Timothy Baird

Why Savvy School Leaders are Adopting Whole School Sustainability Plans (Spoiler Alert: It is Not Just to Save the Planet)

It had been a tough 15 months. Sharon had only been in the superintendent's chair for a little over a year before the COVID-19 pandemic hit. Suddenly, everything was turned upside down. Schools were closed. Remote learning was rushed into place. Teachers were panicked and parents were upset. Now, in the past month, things had started returning to normal. However, normal for a superintendent was still a challenge.

Recently, her chief business officer shared that although one-time federal and state dollars helped with this year's budget, next year was going to be a financial mess. Her facilities director had revisited their maintenance plan with her. Most of the district's school buildings needed modernization. One area of the district was in sore need of a new school due to an influx of students, while other areas were losing students. In fact, there had been a steady decline over the last few years because an increasing number of students were choosing to attend charter and private schools. This trend only accelerated during the pandemic. Parents were concerned about student safety when it came to resuming in-person school. To alleviate some of their concerns, teachers started taking students outside for lessons. This created requests from teachers for gardens and outdoor learning areas to accommodate this type of learning. Not too long ago, students from the high school environmental club met with her to ask why their school did not offer an AP Environmental Science class and green job pathways in their career technical education (CTE) courses. Sharon needed a plan. And even if she came up with a plan, how could she work on so many things at once?

Fortunately, Sharon had some help. She recently met with the Green Schools National Network (GSNN) team. Sharon was initially drawn to GSNN because she wanted to integrate more environmental science into the district's K-8 curriculum. After seeing how a neighboring district had worked with GSNN to create a whole school sustainability plan, she realized that their systems-based approach could help her address many of the issues that were besieging her district. First, however, she needed to gain her school board's approval to move forward. Here are the five reasons Sharon used to convince her board that this was the right approach.

Save Money

Many people think that implementing sustainability practices can be expensive. This is partially true. Large projects, such as installing solar panels or modernizing buildings with more efficient heating and air condition systems, can cost millions of dollars. However, these types of projects can save district general fund operating dollars, which pay for energy bills, while paying for these projects from one-time funds such as school bond measure dollars or capital facilities accounts. This can create immediate savings in critical ongoing operation budgets. California's Encinitas Union School District used bond dollars to implement this strategy. Starting in 2011, they began to modernize their schools based on the district's sustainability plan. They installed solar panels and solar tubes at all schools. They built outdoor learning spaces and upgraded many windows and HVAC systems to be more efficient. The net result was an estimated $800,000–$1,000,000 in annual general fund dollars. The money saved was used to expand the district's technology programs and support enrichment programming for students.

Smaller sustainability projects such as installing water timers, rain barrels, and energy-efficient lighting have one-time costs, but the return-on-investment timeframe is short and most of these types of facilities changes pay for themselves and save money. Other sustainability initiatives are cost neutral and simply require a change in practice. Going green does not have to break the bank. It often can create district cost savings.

Create Healthier and Safer Schools

Everyone wants their children to learn in a safe and healthy place. Environmentally sound practices such as reducing or eliminating harmful chemicals in cleaning supplies and reducing car exhaust fumes at student drop-off areas create healthier spaces and are inexpensive to implement. Indoor air quality is also critical. Upgrading HVAC systems, preventing mold, and addressing asthma triggers, among other strategies, all contribute to good indoor air quality and occupant wellness. This leads to another key point. Highlighting these as health and wellness initiatives rather than environmental ones is an easy way to obtain buy-in from stakeholders.

Increase Student Learning and Engagement

School districts exist to teach students. Everything schools do is in support of this overarching goal. Yet, many districts face challenges posed by disengaged learners and lagging student learning. Implementing teaching practices around educating for sustainability can improve student learning opportunities in many ways. Most students are deeply engaged when learning about local ecosystems and humans' impact on them. It is a topic of interest for all learning levels and ages. This engagement increases when students are taught how to apply this learning in meaningful ways. Students recognize the purpose for the learning, and when the learning is geared toward solving environmental issues in the classroom, the school, the district, the community, or even the world, students see their actions connected to real-world work. This is powerful stuff.

Sustainability projects can be found everywhere in a school setting. For example, facilities changes, such as installing solar tubes or planting a garden, can become learning projects in the hands of a skilled teacher. These projects can also be used to teach reading, math, science, and many other parts of the curriculum. Engaged learners, real-world projects, and students making a difference through applied learning add up to academic success for all students, especially those who may not thrive in a traditional classroom setting.

There are other benefits to helping students acquire the skills to become sustainability-minded citizens and learners. One of the most important benefits is future employment. The International Labour Organization estimates that there may be a need for 24 million new jobs globally in the green industries sector (International Labour Office, 2018). This has prompted many school districts to redesign their CTE pathways to showcase green industries, such as renewable energy, and show how existing career pathways are shifting to a more environmentally responsible model. Green job growth will dictate a need for training in these areas, which schools can provide.

Improve Community Connections

School districts recognize the power of engaging with their community to support student learning. Not only does this practice connect students and teachers with real-world professionals and experts, but it also builds increased community support for the district when community members interact with students, teachers, and schools on a regular basis. How does a district purposely make this connection? One easy way is through project-based learning (PBL). Our communities have engineers, architects, farmers, politicians, scientists, and many other experts who are willing to share their knowledge and work with students. Community-based sustainability projects, such as managing stormwater runoff or using biomimicry to design tiny homes for the homeless, often explore focus areas that teachers may know little about. These are great times to take students to experts or bring experts to students, either in person or online. These relationships are further enhanced when students and experts work together to solve problems.

Build a Positive District Brand

School districts work extremely hard to share their successes with parents and the greater community. However, school leaders know this is a real challenge since a lack of knowledge about the district in the community can lead people to think that schools are not as successful as they are. This lack of knowledge can subsequently lead to negative impressions of the district, which have real consequences. Communities that are not connected to their school district may not pass bonds, support school projects, or even send their children to district schools. A focus on sustainability practices can greatly improve a district's branding and messaging, even in places that may not exhibit strong support for environmental goals.

Districts that are savvy about messaging around their sustainability practices and PBL can highlight success indicators, tailored for different audiences. For many community members, simply showing the district cares about the environment and is teaching students to care about the environment is enough. Many people will resonate with this message and support it. Real-world sustainability projects that result in student work or actions are great opportunities to have students speak and interact with the public. Community members tend to support schools and districts more when they connect with impassioned students sharing their work. This can result in better district press coverage, increased financial support, fewer students disenrolling, and overall greater community goodwill toward the district, its schools, and students.

People are also usually supportive when they hear their schools are safe and healthy places for children and adults. Small changes can support student and staff health in many ways. For some community members, highlighting the cost savings achieved through sustainability programs is the message they want to hear. Showcasing that the district is a good financial steward is important to many community members who do not have children in district schools.

School leaders are always looking for a great story to tell. In Sharon's case, her district's new whole school sustainability plan is her favorite story. She worked with GSNN, her team, and the community to write the plan. Implementing it went smoothly. Part of the plan involved successfully passing a new facilities bond. Parents and community members started talking about all the positive things happening in the district. Students began re-enrolling in the district, and this provided a significant boost to the budget. The solar and facilities upgrades gave schools a modern look and saved money. Most importantly, students and staff were heavily engaged in several sustainability projects across the district. This increased student attendance and performance metrics. The district received their state's Green Ribbon award and school districts from around the nation came to tour their schools and see their work. Sharon recognized there was more to do. But her district's whole school sustainability plan had done so much more than to help save the planet.

Timothy Baird, Ed.D.
Director of Partnerships
Green Schools National Network

Works Cited

International Labour Office. (2018). *World employment social outlook 2018: Greening with jobs*. Retrieved from: https://www.ilo.org/global/publications/books/WCMS_628654/lang--en/index.htm

Preface

Some might say it started with a young woman named Greta. Greta Thunberg, to be exact. In 2018, Greta, then 15-years-old, started to skip school on Fridays to protest for climate action outside of the Swedish parliament. Her actions, and subsequent TED talk, sparked a global youth movement to 'strike for the climate' (Georgiou, 2019), also known as Fridays for the Future. The largest of these youth-led climate strikes took place on September 20, 2019, drawing an estimated four million participants worldwide (Sengupta, 2019).

The climate strikes are just the tip of the iceberg. Climate activists like Greta are inspiring a new generation of young people to demand climate action and take a stand for a just and sustainable future. That is just for starters. Young people are rallying for change across issues as diverse as gun control, racism, immigration, and sexual harassment. They are engaging with policymakers and community organizations to advocate for policies and programs that improve the environment and their communities. They are rolling up their sleeves and tackling ambitious projects, from tree-planting campaigns and community garden installations to founding nonprofits to address racial injustice and environmental justice issues.

While youth activism is by no means a new phenomenon, today's climate feels different. There is a palpable hunger among youth in their fight for justice and change that is both striking and inspiring. They are tired of sitting idly by and feigning ignorance. They are tired of waiting for adults to get their act together. They understand what is at stake and are not afraid to raise their voices and take action.

This energy and passion for activism did not materialize out of thin air. More often than not, someone lit a spark along the way to ignite their passion and fanned the flames of their advocacy and activism. Often, that person was an educator.

What is a Stake: A Call for Whole School Transformation

There is a movement in K-12 education to make school more relevant to students' lives, more engaging and immersive than traditional curriculum built on rote memorization and endless testing. Teachers and school leaders are expanding the definition of school to include the community. They are providing students with opportunities to identify real-world problems, come up with meaningful solutions, and present them to authentic audiences. They are encouraging students to ask hard questions, to think deeply and critically, and to be creative in their search for answers. They are bringing excitement and enthusiasm for learning back into the classroom while equipping students with the tools, knowledge, and mindsets to become engaged, informed, and compassionate citizens.

As educators, activists, and advocates ourselves, we share a passion for preparing students to co-create a just and sustainable future. This work is deeply personal for us. Jennifer has over 40 years of experience as an educator and, as Executive Director of Green Schools National Network (GSNN), is a leading proponent of whole school sustainability. Cynthia began her career at the U.S. Environmental Protection Agency as part of the Schools Chemical Cleanout Campaign. Since 2006, she has expanded her focus to include a holistic look at school environmental health. Lisa has more than two decades of experience in learning and teaching about systems thinking and sustainability, including how leadership plays a key role in transforming schools into more socially just, ecologically healthy, and economically viable communities. And David has been a leading voice in place- and nature-based education and educating for sustainability for over four decades.

We also share a deep concern for the future of our planet and society. Simply put, life on Earth and humanity's quality of life on this planet are at stake. In October 2018, the United Nations Intergovernmental Panel on Climate Change issued a stark warning about Earth's future in their special report *Global Warming of 1.5°C*. The authors asserted that the global community must take drastic and unprecedented action within the next decade to reverse the impacts of climate change to prevent warming from exceeding 1.5°C. Warming beyond that level will significantly heighten the risk of extreme weather – more frequent and severe storms, fires, droughts, and heat waves – and pose profound impacts for humans. Rising temperatures and sea levels, drought conditions, and natural disasters may lead to mass migration, hunger, illness, and poverty, especially among underserved populations. Then there is the environmental toll, which is almost unimaginable.

Tackling this complex, wide-ranging challenge can feel downright overwhelming. As educators, we choose to focus our attention on what we can do in the K-12 community. Not just what is happening in one classroom in a school, or one school in a district. We are talking about whole systems transformation across all 14,000 school districts in the United States, impacting every child, in every classroom, in our country. This might seem crazy to some, or close to impossible. But is it? We argue that this work is not optional, but essential to co-creating the future we all want – a healthy, sustainable planet and a just and equitable society.

Yes, the stakes are high for our children, their children, and future generations. But we have hope. Why? Because, to paraphrase Greta Thunberg, action breeds hope. And this generation of engaged, passionate, and civically-minded students gives us a lot to be hopeful for. They are ready for change and are willing to commit to the hard work that is necessary to restore balance to our society and the planet.

A Road Map for Whole School Sustainability

It is these students, and the educators who support and encourage them, who inspire our work in whole school sustainability. Whole school sustainability is a living systems approach that integrates sustainability into all facets of a school's design, operations, curriculum, and culture, while responding to the learning needs of students. It is about creating the conditions so that all day, every day, everyone who works, learns, and plays in a school building or on its grounds benefits from attending a healthy, equitable, and sustainable school. It prioritizes teaching, leading, and managing for making a positive difference on social and environmental issues, most of which are interdependent. Students learn that they can act with confidence to make their schools, communities, and the world better places for humans and all life because they see the adults managing schools for that purpose and they experience a curriculum that honors the same.

The path to whole school sustainability has been paved over the last 40 years by leaders and educators engaged in the field of environmental education. Their efforts and persistence have resulted in a multitude of environmental magnet and charter schools. More recently, the architecture and engineering fields have shown us it is possible to build more sustainable and efficient buildings for the same cost as conventional buildings, leading to advances in net-zero school design. The convergence of these fields led GSNN to launch the Green Schools National Conference (now the Green Schools Conference) in 2010. In 2013, the Center for Green Schools at the U.S. Green Building Council convened a group of forward-thinking thought leaders and practitioners to create a *National Action Plan for Educating for Sustainability*. This document outlined a pathway for transforming K-12 education so every student in the U.S. graduates with the knowledge and skills to co-create a sustainable future.

That call to action did not fall on deaf ears. Many who contributed to the National Action Plan remain engaged and continue to pave the way for schools and districts to do the systems transformation work needed to achieve that vision. Their efforts, along with resources like the Green Schools Conference and the peer-reviewed journal, *Green Schools Catalyst Quarterly*, have inspired the creation of a framework for how to do this necessary and critical work. These best practices are captured in GSNN's latest iteration of its GreenPrint for healthy, equitable, and sustainable schools. The GreenPrint is a road map that provides many pathways to begin the journey toward holistic transformation, as well as "mile markers" of what to look for along the way. It is structured around four key, interrelated systems that drive holistic transformation in schools:

1. **Leadership:** Leaders communicate the vision, create policy, establish budgets, and hold others accountable for implementing what is said or written.
2. **Curriculum and Instruction:** Curriculum and instruction reflects what is taught in schools and how. It includes the design or adoption of

curricula, instructional philosophy and methods, professional learning, and the structures that sustain learning for all students over time.

3. **Culture and Climate:** Culture and climate shape and influence behaviors and mindsets within the school community.

4. **Facilities and Operations:** Facilities and operations oversee the purchase, design, construction, and maintenance of the physical spaces and resources needed to operate healthy, equitable, and sustainable schools. Facilities and operations also influence how members of the learning community use those spaces.

A Book for Educators, By Educators

This book is for educational leaders who believe that the actions we take and the choices we make each day shape the future – for our students, communities, and the planet – and are committed to deeply engaging in the work to make a just and sustainable future possible. We structured the book, like the GreenPrint, around the four key systems for holistic transformation in schools. In each section, you will find four case studies that explore aspects of these systems in-depth through real-world examples of schools and districts that are walking the walk and talking the talk. Section 1 features stories of schools and districts that are using visionary leadership to shape their approach to whole school sustainability. Section 2 focuses on schools and districts that are leveraging curriculum and instruction to promote health, equity, and sustainability. Section 3 includes stories of schools and districts that are putting systems and structures in place that promote a positive culture and climate. And Section 4 features schools and districts whose facilities and operations practices are models for reducing costs and environmental impacts and serving as teaching tools for real-world learning. Every case study concludes with a "Learning from..." section where you will find actionable tips, recommendations, and best practices for taking those initial steps toward becoming a healthy, equitable, and sustainable school or district.

These case studies are authored by a diverse set of leaders and educators, so no matter who you are – superintendent, curriculum and instruction leader, facilities and operations leader, school sustainability officer, or classroom teacher – you will see yourself represented in the following pages. The visionary leaders and educators you will meet come from urban and rural schools and districts, in red and blue states. Their inspiring stories show how this work is enabling them to work smarter, not harder, by integrating sustainability and systems thinking into everything they do. While each story is different, the passion that drives them and their school communities to embrace sustainability is the same. Our hope is that you will be inspired by their experiences and take away a sense of possibility that you too can create the conditions at your school or district that will allow you to shift away from the status quo and blaze a trail to reimagine K-12 education for a more just and sustainable future.

Works Cited

Georgiou, A. (2019). Greta Thunberg says Friday climate strike will go on for 'as long as it takes' to stir world leaders into action. *Newsweek*. Retrieved from:https://www.newsweek.com/greta-thunberg-friday-climate-strike-world-leaders-1464823

Sengupta, S. (2019). Protesting climate change, young people take to the streets in a global strike. *The New York Times*. Retrieved from: https://www.nytimes.com/2019/09/20/climate/global-climate-strike.html

About the Editors

Jennifer Seydel is Executive Director of Green Schools National Network (GSNN) and editor of the *Green Schools Catalyst Quarterly*, the only peer-reviewed journal for the K-12 green schools community. In her role at GSNN, Jennifer has developed a reputation as a leader in bringing together thought leaders in sustainability and education to gather, synthesize, report, and generate evidence-based resources to support healthy, equitable, and sustainable schools in the United States and beyond. Through GSNN, she has convened a network of over 300 schools and school districts that are engaged in documenting and evaluating the impact of their sustainability initiatives to inform how healthy, equitable, and sustainable schools are having an impact on student health and well-being, social and emotional development, equity, and college and career readiness. Prior to her work with GSNN, Jennifer was a Curriculum Specialist and School/District Coach for Expeditionary Learning, a nonprofit education reform organization specializing in closing the achievement gap through embedded literacy instruction and project-based learning. She served as Director of the S.A.G.E. Project at Springfield College in Springfield, Massachusetts, where she designed a graduate degree in Education and Counseling to prepare teachers with the full range of knowledge and skills needed to work in urban schools. Jennifer has authored articles and chapters for various educational journals and books over the past 25 years on topics ranging from adventure education to leadership development and urban education.

Cynthia (Cyndy) L. Merse is a freelance writer and editor based in Knoxville, Tennessee. Her areas of focus include education for sustainability, clean energy, water conservation, and food systems. She also serves as assistant editor for the *Green Schools Catalyst Quarterly*, a peer-reviewed journal published by Green Schools National Network. Prior to her freelance career, Cyndy worked for the U.S. Environmental Protection Agency where she gained experience in research, data analysis, communications and outreach, and program development. She worked on several high-level, national scale projects that concerned children's environmental health and healthy school environments, including the Schools Chemical Cleanout Campaign, a voluntary program that promoted responsible chemical management in K-12 schools, and heading an effort to develop a set of guidelines and a model program for state school environmental health programs. Cyndy obtained a BE in chemical engineering from Vanderbilt University and an MS in Environmental Policy and Planning from Ohio University.

Lisa A. W. Kensler is the Emily R. and Gerald S. Leischuck Endowed Professor of Educational Leadership in the College of Education at Auburn University. Her original training in ecology continues to fuel her love of systems thinking and the challenges located at the intersection of human and nature's systems, particularly as they appear in PK-12 schooling. She has engaged in learning and teaching about systems thinking and sustainability for more than two decades, in PK-12 schools as a secondary science teacher and in higher education as a professor of educational leadership. Lisa's research over the past decade has focused on green schools and the leadership and learning required for transforming schools into more socially just, ecologically healthy, and economically viable communities that engage intentionally with the global sustainability movement. She has published peer-reviewed articles and book chapters related to democratic community, systems thinking, trust, teacher leadership, and whole school sustainability. In 2017, she and Cynthia Uline co-authored *Leadership for Green Schools: Sustainability for Our Children, Our Communities, and Our Planet*, and in 2021, they published *A Practical Guide for Leading Green Schools: Partnering with Nature to Create Vibrant, Flourishing, Sustainable Schools*. In 2018, the University Council for Educational Administration recognized Lisa as one of its "Hidden Figures – behind-the-scenes giants in the field whose work cannot be ignored."

David Sobel is a Professor Emeritus in the Education Department at Antioch University New England in Keene, New Hampshire. He consults and speaks widely on child development, place-based education, and nature-based early childhood education. David has served on the editorial boards of *Encounter, Community Works Journal, Orion Afield*, and *Green Schools Catalyst Quarterly*. He has authored nine books and more than 80 articles focused on children and nature for educators, parents, environmentalists, and school administrators in the last 30 years. Some of David's books include *Nature Preschools and Forest Kindergartens, Place- and Community-based Education, Place-based Education: Connecting Classrooms and Communities, Childhood and Nature: Design Principles for Educators,* and *Mapmaking with Children*. His articles and essays have appeared in *Orion, Encounter, Sierra, Sanctuary, Wondertime, Green Teacher, Play Rights, Harvard Education Letter, Yes!,* and other publications. He has also contributed chapters to *Father Nature, Education, Information and Transformation, Stories from Where We Live-The North Atlantic Coast, Place-based Education in a Global Age,* and *The Child: An Encyclopedic Companion.*

Leadership

Meaningful, lasting change does not happen overnight. It takes consistent, focused, and visionary leadership and sustained, collaborative effort. This is no different in the case of whole school transformation. Creating a healthy, equitable, and sustainable school is a multi-year endeavor that requires the guiding hand of one or more committed, forward-thinking leaders. Such leaders embrace a shared leadership model and routinely engage the school community in carrying out the school's vision. They recognize all members of the school community as learners and leaders and empower them to play a role in the school's sustainability practices. Such leaders create a culture of community and belonging. They prioritize diversity, equity, and inclusion and make sure every individual who enters the school feels welcome, safe, respected, and valued. Such leaders foster strong school–family–community partnerships and actively seek out ways to engage families and community organizations in the school's sustainability work. Reciprocally, they seek out ways to support families and community members in need.

This section features four case studies that illustrate how visionary leadership shapes whole school sustainability at the school and district levels.

"The Philadelphia Sustainability Story: Drivers for a Large Urban Public School District's Sustainability Plan" describes how the School District

DOI: 10.4324/9781003152811-1

of Philadelphia leveraged visionary leadership and community partners to create a districtwide sustainability plan, called GreenFutures. You will learn about some of the district's early successes under GreenFutures and how partnerships with community organizations have contributed to the plan's success.

"Leadership and Autonomy Drive a Sustainable Future at Encinitas Union School District" describes how Encinitas Union School District adopted a shared vision for sustainability across nine schools, each of which adheres to a different instructional model. You will learn how the district created systemic change across its operations, culture, and curriculum by engaging the entire school community – school leaders, teachers, staff, and students – and focusing on three Gs: green teams, garbage, and gardens.

"Teaching Our Cities: Place-Based Education in an Urban Environment" describes how Common Ground High School is creating a model for urban place-based education that is culturally relevant and student-centered. You will learn how school leaders engaged the school community in developing a four-year progression of authentic learning experiences that, while rooted in core academics, allow students to follow their passions and interests and be introduced to some of the experiences and programs that students engage in over the course of their time at Common Ground.

"Food Waste Inspires a Shift to Whole School Sustainability at the School of Environmental Studies" describes how the School of Environmental Studies used the issue of food waste to kick start its shift to whole school sustainability. You will learn how the school's principal overcame a series of barriers to implement a schoolwide, student-led food waste reduction project, and how this project provided the momentum to develop a sustainability strategic plan that further embeds whole school sustainability into the school's operations, culture, and curriculum.

The Philadelphia Sustainability Story

Drivers for a Large Urban Public School District's Sustainability Plan

Francine Locke

School District of Philadelphia

Location: Philadelphia, Pennsylvania

Eighth largest public school district in the nation

Number of schools: 340 schools

Number of students: 200,293

Student demographics: 52% Black/African American; 21% Hispanic/Latino; 14% White; 7% Asian; 6% Multiracial/Other

2017 U.S. Department of Education Green Ribbon District Sustainability Awardee

---

A buzz of excitement perfumes the air outside of Philadelphia's City Hall. A crowd gathers and a hushed chatter rises and falls. It is May 16, 2016 and the occasion is a press conference to kick off a new chapter at the School District of Philadelphia. The district is announcing its commitment to implement an

DOI: 10.4324/9781003152811-2

ambitious sustainability plan, called GreenFutures. The plan, three years in the making, would ultimately lead the district to be recognized as a 2017 U.S. Department of Education Green Ribbon District Sustainability Awardee for its efforts in working toward the three pillars of sustainability: reducing environmental impacts and costs; improving occupants' health and performance; and increasing sustainability literacy. In the years since that recognition, the School District of Philadelphia has received additional accolades for GreenFutures and its sustainability work, including the 2018 Pennsylvania Governor's Award for Environmental Excellence and the 2019 Project Green Schools Green Difference Award. The district also established an Office of Sustainability in 2019 following the hiring of a Director of Sustainability and Green Schools.

How did the district get here? It took a superintendent with vision and individuals in key roles who were open to new ideas, collaboration within and outside the district, opportunistic timing, and perseverance.

Challenges or Opportunities

Like any school district found throughout the country, Philadelphia's schools face a number of challenges. Many of these challenges can be summed up by three overarching themes: health, infrastructure, and operations.

Health

Nationally, asthma is the leading cause of student absenteeism due to chronic illness and evidence shows that asthma affects academic performance (American Lung Association, 2009). Nearly 30% or more of students in Philadelphia are diagnosed with asthma (Pennsylvania Department of Health, 2015).

Infrastructure

According to an independent facility condition assessment of Philadelphia public schools (Parsons Environment and Infrastructure Group, Inc., 2017), there is a $4.5 billion need to bring all building systems into a state of good repair. The district's building stock is deteriorating, with an average building age of over 70 years, and there is inadequate funding to renovate building systems at a pace needed to ensure high-quality facilities.

Operations

An enormous public school operation and building portfolio carries a weighty footprint, with over 23 million square feet of building space, 1,300 acres of land, and over 150,000 free meals served daily at district schools. Energy consumption was benchmarked at 1,809,266,665 kilowatt British Thermal units (kBTUs) in 2016, and district- and contractor-owned buses consume fuel and emit pollutants daily while transporting thousands of students to and from public, private, parochial, and charter schools.

Taken together, these challenges presented an opportunity for the district to instill a culture of sustainability in its operations and to measurably impact environmental, fiscal, and social change.

The Path to GreenFutures – Visionary Leadership and Partnerships Drive Creation of Sustainability Plan

Dr. William Hite joined the School District of Philadelphia as its new superintendent in June 2012. Dr. Hite's leadership team was innovative, data-driven, and open to new evidence-based approaches to improve student academic performance. His team of curriculum writers, strategic planners, and educators designed a framework for student success that would ultimately catapult a variety of other successful initiatives, including a fiscal stability plan that resulted in a balanced budget and improved credit rating and a Read by 4th student literacy campaign.

A key driver for the district's sustainability success was a laser-focused Superintendent's Action Plan, which created a stable, results-oriented culture with a focused, shared vision: "Every child can learn, and every school can be great." The district's Office of Environmental Management &

Services interpreted "great" as "green." The plan was not formally approved by the School Reform Commission (now Board of Education) but was Dr. Hite's pronouncement of how to move the district forward. The action plan consisted of three consecutive versions: the first (2012) focused on stabilizing the district; the second (2013) started to look forward; and the third (2015) focused on repairing, building, and improving the district.

Although student literacy was the primary desired outcome of the action plan, the district leadership team recognized that various interventions were needed to accomplish this outcome, in addition to excellent instructional and curriculum interventions. For the district, this was the perfect time to introduce a framework for green, healthy, and sustainable schools, given that peer-reviewed research and data indicated that these environments were where children learn best (Okcu, Ryherd, and Bayer, 2011). Dr. Hite and his team welcomed the guidance because there was a clear connection between green, healthy, and sustainable schools and student academic achievement.

In May 2013, a new Chief Operating Officer, Fran Burns, joined the district leadership team. Ms. Burns was open to new ideas, and some of those ideas included addressing indoor air quality; creating healthy, clean, and welcoming school environments; creating more green spaces

Photo 1.1 Children at the William Cramp School's green schoolyard ribbon-cutting ceremony. Credit: The Trust for Public Land, Jenna Stamm.

at district schools; offering nutritious and appealing food; and engaging in energy conservation initiatives. While attending a professional development course at Harvard University's School of Public Health in March 2014, the district's Environmental Director learned how an organization's environmental department staff was uniquely qualified and positioned to lead sustainability performance improvement. A subsequent meeting with Ms. Burns green lighted the development of a districtwide sustainability plan.

The School District of Philadelphia was not a stranger to sustainability before adopting GreenFutures. A variety of green initiatives were underway as the sustainability plan took shape. All were incorporated into the plan to support its focus areas. Some of these initiatives included:

- Innovative energy procurement, energy benchmarking, utility bill auditing, and demand response programs that saved millions of dollars (Lee, 2012).
- Pilot recycling programs at 87 schools (by 2020, recycling had been implemented at all 220 schools).
- Construction of green stormwater infrastructure and outdoor learning spaces.
- The purchase of a fleet of environmentally friendly buses.
- Harvest of the month and farm-to-table programs.
- A district wellness policy.
- An indoor environmental quality program with an emphasis on asthma trigger prevention based on the U.S. Environmental Protection Agency's Indoor Air Quality Tools for Schools program.
- The construction of eight LEED-certified school buildings, including the first LEED Platinum public high school in the nation and a LEED-certified Existing Building.

In spring 2014, the district's Operations team held internal meetings to discuss how all departments were connected through sustainability. A "silo busting" exercise was conducted where Transportation, Food Services, Capital, Facilities, and Procurement leads shared ideas about how each department contributed to the district's overall environmental and fiscal footprint and how each department impacted the others. One example was breakfast in the classroom. When breakfast in the classroom was initiated by Food Services as a districtwide program, a huge increase in trash required Facilities to provide more cleaning services to respond to spills. Although Food Services was given federal funding for the breakfast program, an increase in funding for Facilities response services was not included. Further, milk and juice cartons were measured at 20% of the district's waste stream but were not accepted by its waste hauler as recyclable (This changed with the selection of a new vendor later). Another example was the purchase of bulk inventories of cleaning, maintenance, and science chemicals. Although the unit cost was usually significantly less when purchased in bulk, oftentimes, these chemicals remained on shelves for years only to be disposed of as hazardous waste through the Environmental Department at a cost that exceeded the purchase value. Clearly, it was time to connect the dots.

The next step was hiring a dedicated district sustainability staff member who could focus their time on developing relationships with partners who could mentor the Environmental Department's staff about sustainability. Megan Garner was hired as a consultant in spring 2014 to assist with this effort and was formally hired as the district's Sustainability Project Manager in 2017. Garner connected the district with local sustainability-minded partners who were immersed in initiatives that aligned with the ideas and plans the district was beginning to envision. The City of Philadelphia's Office of Sustainability, whose sustainability plan, Greenworks, has made significant measurable improvements in greening Philadelphia through infrastructure and social and cultural mindset changes, jumped at the opportunity to mentor the district's Environmental Department staff. The office also connected the district with dozens of partners who contributed their time, expertise, in-kind donations, and resources toward developing the sustainability plan and implementing its actions.

With its partners, the district formed five subcommittees, each dedicated to developing a mission, goal, actions, targets, and metrics for each of the plan's five focus areas: Education for Sustainability; Waste and Consumption; Energy

Photo 1.2 Children at the William Dick School examine native plants in their outdoor classroom. Credit: The Trust for Public Land, Jenna Stamm.

and Efficiencies; School Greenscapes; and Healthy Schools. The subcommittees researched other school district and higher education sustainability plans and incorporated their findings into the district's framework. The committees adopted the name "GreenFutures" to represent hope for a sustainable future where the students of today are the educators, innovators, environmental stewards, and global citizens of tomorrow.

Implementation and Impact of GreenFutures

GreenFutures officially launched in May 2016. The final plan included a framework that defined five focus areas, five targets, and 65 measurable actions to make every Philadelphia public school a green school by 2020, using existing resources, in-kind offerings, donations from partners, and district-funded initiatives. Interwoven throughout these focus areas were five guiding principles: education, efficiencies, engagement, environment, and equity. GreenFutures also created a framework for communicating clear goals for sustainability, establishing targets, and tracking specific actions needed to attain those targets. Annual reports, a GreenFutures website, and social media accounts communicated progress.

School District of Philadelphia GreenFutures Sustainability Plan

Focus Area	Target	Evidence
Education for Sustainability	100% of schools and administrative offices will show evidence of Education for Sustainability within five years.	The district implemented a GreenFutures Teacher Professional Development Series in 2016 that has reached teachers at 119 schools, creating a learning community of district educators. The series included three consecutive Climate Education Series Workshops. This program was conducted in partnership with The Franklin Institute, Fairmount Waterworks, the National Wildlife Federation's Eco-Schools USA program, and Arizona State University. In 2018, the district initiated a student-led energy education program that empowered students to identify and follow through with operational changes within their schools and promoted behavior changes among students and staff. The program is now implemented as part of all district energy retrofit projects. There are over 75 registered Eco-Schools in the district. Six of these schools have received program awards: Cook-Wissahickon Elementary School, George W. Childs Elementary School, Penn Alexander Elementary School, George Washington Carver High School, Lankenau High School, and Northeast High School.
Waste and Consumption	Increase waste diversion rate by 10% within five years.	In 2020, the district's average waste diversion rate was 12%. This exceeded the 2016 GreenFutures' target of 10%. A novel waste reduction program was completed at Southwark Elementary School in 2018 and the district's Office of Sustainability is planning to replicate the program at other schools when funding becomes available. Southwark's program repurposed outdated and discarded school furniture to create a functional and beautiful outdoor space at the school. The City of Philadelphia's Mural Arts "Restored Spaces Initiative," in collaboration with the Spanish trash-focused artist collective "Basurama" (which translates to "Trash-o-rama"), worked with the school community to design and produce the furniture. In 2021, the district plans to work with the City of Philadelphia to develop urban composting sites, so organic waste can be collected from schools. The district also plans to adopt a green procurement policy that will reduce waste at its source.

Energy and Efficiencies	Reduce energy consumption by 20% over five years.	Although the district has seen a slight decrease in its energy consumption since 2016, it has not reached its target of a 20% reduction. Much more work is needed to improve energy efficiencies in school buildings. One project that is contributing to this work is a pilot program with Energy Services Company. The district invested $24 million on this pilot, which was launched to take advantage of return on investment incentives provided by the Guaranteed Energy Savings Act. In 2019, the district completed deep energy retrofits at three schools. Upgrades were made to ventilation systems, light systems, and the building envelope. Seven additional projects are underway at district schools. Energy savings from these projects will be used to fund future energy efficiency projects at district schools.
School Greenscapes	Increase green schoolyards by five per year over five years.	Since 2016, the district has constructed over 30 large-scale green stormwater infrastructure projects, many with outdoor classroom features and play spaces. The district continues to grow the number of outdoor learning spaces, play areas, and green stormwater infrastructure components at its schools. Thanks to the William Penn Foundation, a Green Stormwater Infrastructure Manager was hired in 2019 to manage the operation and maintenance of each site that contains green stormwater infrastructure components and ensure the district receives public utility credits for diverting stormwater from municipal sewers.
Healthy Schools	Every school will be healthy. Thirty schools per year will receive a healthy schools baseline report.	The Healthy Schools focus area has morphed into three subcategories: hydration and nutrition, active transport, and healthy buildings. Highlights include: • Bottle filling hydration stations are present in every school, with at least four units per school. • Fresh fruits and vegetables are the norm on school menus as part of harvest of the month and farm-to-table programs. • The district partnered with Safe Routes Philly to identify solutions for making walking to school safer and more appealing. • The district is undergoing major environmental health upgrades related to the removal of legacy toxins such as asbestos and lead paint. The University of Pennsylvania donated $100 million over ten years to assist in this effort.

Funding partners played a significant role in bringing GreenFutures to fruition. A $50,000 donation was provided by the district's waste and recycling hauler for green initiatives within the plan's first year. By 2020, the amount of donations exceeded $170,000. Two additional resources have proven critical to funding GreenFutures. The Commonwealth of Pennsylvania's Educational Improvement Tax Credit (EITC) program allows businesses to donate to GreenFutures at a nominal out-of-pocket cost, while benefiting from a tax credit of up to 90% of the contribution. The district also has "the Fund," an independent 501(c)3 nonprofit organization that serves as a fiscal intermediary between the private sector and the district. The Fund aligns the investments of partners – private foundations, corporations and businesses, community organizations, and individual donors – with strategies that impact the success of students attending district schools. When GreenFutures launched, the Fund immediately started to identify funding for the plan's initiatives. To this day, the Fund continues to seek EITC funding on behalf of GreenFutures and the district's Office of Sustainability, based on proposals that are submitted to the Fund for consideration.

Other partners helped the district achieve its goals by providing resources and professional development to teachers and staff who were responsible for implementing programs and influencing behavior change across the district. For example, the National Wildlife Federation's Eco-Schools USA program, Fairmount Water Works, Keep Philadelphia Beautiful, and the Pennsylvania Horticultural Society helped the district develop a GreenFutures Professional Development Series for its teachers. Session topics align with GreenFutures' five focus areas and highlight the importance of creating school-based teacher teams to promote knowledge sharing and collaboration on lesson planning. By 2020, more than 30 professional development programs have been provided to educators.

Local partners have played a significant role in providing resources to carry out the plan's initiatives. The Philadelphia Water Department supported GreenFutures on multiple levels, from offering green stormwater infrastructure grant opportunities to running student-led drinking water promotion campaigns. Keep Philadelphia Beautiful, RecycleBank, and the

Photo 1.3 George Washington High School students organized a CLEANfutures Litterati Contest to reduce waste in their school's cafeteria. Credit: Venus Cataldo.

City of Philadelphia's Recycling Office provided free recycling bins, waste audits, and classroom trainings and reviewed the district's goals for reducing waste and increasing recycling. The Pennsylvania Horticultural Society offered a program for educators called Green City Teachers, which covered topics such as basic horticulture, composting, and school habitat gardens. The Philadelphia Zoo partnered with the district to host the UNLESS Contest, a year-long, project-based learning program that challenges students to come up with real-world solutions for environmental issues. Local universities, including Drexel University, provided guidance on how to develop an energy savings program through student-led energy education and facility improvements. Also instrumental were other local school districts that had already made advancements in sustainability, including North Penn, Upper Merion, and Garnet Valley School Districts.

Lessons Learned

GreenFutures owes much of its success to visionary leadership and the power of partnerships. Dr. Hite's visionary leadership made it possible for the district to develop a sustainability plan that aligned with its action plan and districtwide goals. In the process, he unified departments across the district, breaking down silos between those that would not normally work together, such as Facilities and Curriculum, to meet a common goal. Dr. Hite also opened the door to free thought, a change mindset, and creativity throughout the district. For example, Food Services implemented meal programs to introduce students to new and nutritious produce. Transportation initiated a bus anti-idling program to reduce asthma triggers and carbon emissions, and a route-reduction program to cut down on carbon emissions and fuel consumption. The leadership team used evidence-based research as the gold standard to support new initiatives, which led to "go-aheads" for trying new ideas, like outdoor classrooms, that would improve children's learning and achievement outcomes.

Contributions of partner expertise, services, and funding have transformed GreenFutures from a plan into a movement. Key to this success has been perseverance and collaborating with partners to develop realistic and attainable goals that are measurable and equitably shared with all schools.

 ## Learning from the School District of Philadelphia: Leveraging Visionary Leadership and Strong Community Partnerships in Your District

Dr. Hite's leadership and commitments from community partners played a key role in bringing GreenFutures to life. Here are a few ways your district can foster visionary leadership and strong community partnerships in support of sustainability efforts.

- **Create a clear leadership vision that can be shared with everyone in the organization.** The School District of Philadelphia's clear vision was that every child could learn, and every school could be great. This allowed for an organizational culture that supported diverse and creative ideas, even when those ideas were not traditionally academic, or curriculum based. When an entire organization commits to the same vision, real change is possible.

- **Map out your district's departments to find internal stakeholders who are already working to support sustainability.** For example, Food Services may already have a farm-to-table program or a composting plan. Capital may already have energy savings projects in the works. These are great launching points for sustainability that show early successes in the process of developing a plan.
- **Identify stakeholders who want to contribute to your district's sustainability initiatives and will consistently take the time to be involved.** Invite them to play a role in creating or carrying out your district's sustainability plan. For example, a community design nonprofit may already be raising funds for a school garden and have an implementation-ready design. A representative from this group could serve on the school's greenscape committee.
- **Coordinate with local government sustainability efforts.** The School District of Philadelphia is aligning its 2021 GreenFutures update with the City of Philadelphia's Greenworks to strengthen its impact on reducing carbon emissions.

Synthesis

GreenFutures created the conditions needed to make the School District of Philadelphia a sustainable organization. It has also shed a positive light on Philadelphia's public schools and the communities they serve. A great example is Bright Solar Futures, the first solar installation program at a public high school in Pennsylvania. Bright Solar Futures was funded by a $1.25 million award from the U.S. Department of Energy's Solar Energy Technologies Office. Introductory training was provided to 70 high school students in partnership with the Philadelphia Energy Authority, Solar States, the Energy Coordinating Agency, F.A.V.O.R., and the Philadelphia Education Fund between 2017 and 2019. Twenty trainees were eventually placed into paid internships in the clean energy sector. Sponsorship by PECO made this program possible. Other

Photo 1.4 Bright Solar Futures students receive recognition for their participation in the solar installation program. Credit: Megan Garner.

partners stepped up, inspired by the goals set forth in GreenFutures and willing to invest in greening Philadelphia's public schools. As a result, a new Solar Energy Career and Technical Education program was launched for tenth-graders in fall 2020 at Frankford High School. Students will receive 1,080 hours of content to be delivered between tenth and twelfth grades, making it the most advanced solar training of its kind in the nation. They will graduate with field experience, internship experience, and industry certifications and will receive job placement support. Thanks to GreenFutures, Philadelphia's students have become green career pathway leaders.

The next iteration of GreenFutures will be released in 2021. Whether its launch is marked by a celebratory event or not, it does not really matter. The outcomes, the greenhouse gas emissions reduction efforts, the student-led energy education projects, the construction of outdoor natural classroom spaces, and the improvement of indoor environmental quality are what make the real difference.

June 2012: Dr. William Hite becomes superintendent of the School District of Philadelphia

Fall 2012: Dr. Hite creates Superintendent's Action Plan with a focused, shared vision – "Every child can learn, and every school can be great."

May 2013: New Chief Operating Officer (COO) joins district team: open to innovative ideas that support action plan's anchor goals

March 2014: Environmental Director attends Harvard School of Public Health course: learns Environmental Office is positioned to lead sustainability efforts

Spring 2014: Consultant hired to work on sustainability plan and connect with partners

Spring 2014: Environmental Office given green light to spearhead sustainability plan / Office forms working group to identify sustainability connections

2015: District collects baseline data for trash/recycling, farm to table, energy consumption, and green stormwater management projects

May 2016: GreenFutures officially launches with an event at Philadelphia's City Hall

2017: District hires Sustainability Project Manager

2017: District recognized as 2017 U.S. Department of Education Green Ribbon District Sustainability Awardee

2018: District receives 2018 Pennsylvania Governor's Award for Environmental Excellence

2019: District establishes Office of Sustainability after hiring Director of Sustainability and Green Schools

Figure 1.1 School District of Philadelphia Timeline.

Works Cited

American Lung Association. (2009). *A national asthma public policy agenda*. Retrieved from: https://www.lung.org/policy-advocacy/healthcare-lung-disease/asthma-policy/national-asthma-public-policy-agenda

Lee, M. (2012). Cost savings in utilities for dummies [Presentation]. *School District of Philadelphia*. Retrieved from: https://www.epa.gov/sites/production/files/2016-04/documents/cost_savings_in_utilities_for_dummies.pdf

Okcu, S., Ryherd, E., and Bayer, C. (2011). The role of physical environment on student health and education in green schools. *Reviews on Environmental Health, 26*(3), 169–179.

Parsons Environment and Infrastructure Group, Inc. (2017). *School district of Philadelphia facility condition assessment*. Retrieved from: https://www.philasd.org/capitalprograms/wp-content/uploads/sites/18/2017/06/2015-FCA-Final-Report-1.pdf

Pennsylvania Department of Health. (2015). *Asthma prevalence report*. Retrieved from: http://www.health.pa.gov/My%20Health/Diseases%20and%20Conditions/A-D/Asthma/Documents/2015%20PENNSYLVANIA%20ASTHMA%20PREVALENCE%20REPORT%20UPDATED%20FEB%2023%202016.pdf

Relevant Websites

GreenFutures. Retrieved from: http://www.philasd.org/greenfutures

School District of Philadelphia. Retrieved from: https://www.philasd.org/

Leadership and Autonomy Drive a Sustainable Future at Encinitas Union School District

Amy Illingworth

Encinitas Union School District

Location: Encinitas, California

District is home to the nation's first certified organic school farm

Number of schools: Nine schools

Number of students: Approximately 5,400 students in grades K-6

Student demographics: 68% White; 22% Hispanic/Latino; 6% Multiracial/Other; 4% Asian

2014 U.S. Department of Education Green Ribbon District Sustainability Awardee

As the sun sets over the Pacific Ocean, eight elementary students stand before the Encinitas City Council, presenting their waste audit findings. Passing the microphone from one small hand to the next, the students from Ocean Knoll Elementary School, in the Encinitas Union School District (EUSD), passionately share their research, the "shocking" discoveries they made, and their recommendations. One of the biggest waste culprits these students found was the plastic-wrapped spork and napkin that came with each school lunch. An average of 105 plastic sporks were sent each day to the landfill from Ocean Knoll, a school that serves 600 students. "That

DOI: 10.4324/9781003152811-3

means over 18,000 plastic sporks and wrappers go into the landfill each school year from one school! Can you believe that?" asked Kate, a fifth-grader. After their presentation, the council will vote on a proposal to ban single-use plastic at public city events.

These students were articulate AND persuasive. After sharing a similar presentation with EUSD's Board of Education, the board agreed to implement a pilot program at Ocean Knoll that involved the purchase and use of real silverware and individual napkin dispensers at lunch – no more single-use plastic! This story is not unique to Ocean Knoll. Similar stories are playing out across EUSD each day, thanks to our district leadership's steadfast commitment to sustainability and environmental stewardship. What started as a leader-driven initiative has trickled down and engaged every member of the EUSD community.

Creating a District Vision for Environmental Stewardship: Where Do You Start?

You can say that sustainability is in Dr. Timothy Baird's DNA. Dr. Baird, who served as EUSD superintendent from 2001 to 2019, brought to his role the belief that sustainability must be integrated into every aspect of the district's operations and culture. An ambitious vision to be sure, but especially for a district as distinct as EUSD, where each principal has autonomy over how their school functions and each school has its own identity and personality.

Encinitas Union School District Schools and Instructional Models

Capri Elementary School – Dual Language Immersion/Global Communication

El Camino Creek Elementary School – Civic Learning

Flora Vista Elementary School – Civic Engagement and Environmental Science

La Costa Heights Elementary School – Leader in Me

Mission Estancia Elementary School – School of Wonder

Ocean Knoll Elementary School – International Baccalaureate

Olivenhain Pioneer Elementary School – Science, Technology, Research, Engineering, Art, and Math

Park Dale Lane Elementary School – Collaboration of Teachers and Artists

Paul Ecke Central Elementary School – Dual Language Immersion/ Garden Science

Dr. Baird understood that, to fulfill his vision of integrating sustainability into the fabric of every EUSD school, he would need to gain buy-in from not only the nine school principals but also from the schools' teachers, staff, students, and families. He needed to create and emulate a shared vision that everyone would embrace and uphold. A key step in this process involved defining four Pillars of Distinction (Figure 2.1) to guide EUSD's goals. These pillars – Academic Excellence, 21.5 Century Learning, Health & Wellness, and Environmental Stewardship – were adopted by EUSD's Board of Trustees in 2010. The pillars serve as common threads that tie together the varying instructional models adopted by EUSD's schools.

Figure 2.1 Encinitas Union School District's four pillars of distinction. Credit: Encinitas Union School District.

It is easy to say that your district supports environmental stewardship and sustainability. But implementing a comprehensive sustainability program across an entire school district? Not so easy. Creating change at the district level is hard. Systemic changes need to be implemented slowly to allow for stakeholder input and buy-in. Educational programs and teaching pedagogy need to be shifted. Culture needs to be created and supported. Operations need to be adjusted. These efforts require careful coordination and active involvement across the school community.

At EUSD, we were fortunate to have an eager and supportive school community that was willing to put in the work to build a foundation for sustainability within the district. This work did not happen overnight. It took years to develop and implement a consistent set of sustainability initiatives (Figure 2.2) across all nine EUSD schools. Some of these initiatives required district funding and installation, while others required more of a cultural shift over time. All practices are now common throughout the district, regardless of each school's unique identity. To get to this point, however, we needed to start somewhere. That starting place was a focus on three Gs: green teams, garbage, and gardens.

Systems Change Starts with Three Gs

In 2009, Dr. Baird formed a district Green Team that included himself, the facilities director, the food service director, and representatives from every district school. Each school also formed a Green Team of staff, parents, students, and community members to carry out the district's sustainability initiatives on campus. At the district level, the Green Team's task was fairly straightforward: how could the team help the district reduce its environmental footprint? To achieve some early success, the team started with small wins that were easier to implement and that people could see. Which brings us to our second G, garbage.

One of the first sustainability initiatives the district Green Team set its sights on was studying the amount of lunchtime waste. Waste audits conducted during the 2010–2011 school year found that many schools were creating 15–16 bags of trash at lunch. Very little was recycled or diverted. The team's findings led to the creation of a waste management plan and a SCRAP (Separate, Compost, Reduce, and Protect) Cart. Introduced in 2012,

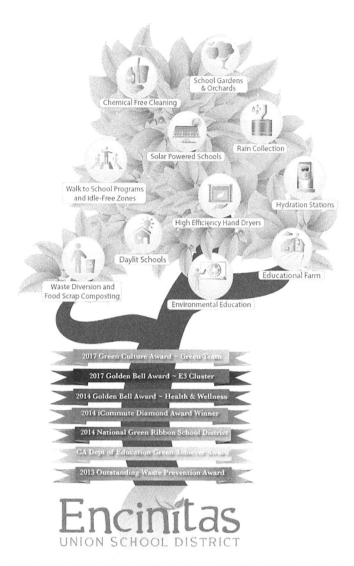

School Gardens & Orchards

Chemical Free Cleaning

Rain Collection

Solar Powered Schools

Walk to School Programs and Idle-Free Zones

Hydration Stations

High Efficiency Hand Dryers

Daylit Schools

Educational Farm

Waste Diversion and Food Scrap Composting

Environmental Education

2017 Green Culture Award ~ Green Team

2017 Golden Bell Award ~ E3 Cluster

2014 Golden Bell Award ~ Health & Wellness

2014 iCommute Diamond Award Winner

2014 National Green Ribbon School District

CA Dept of Education Green Achiever Award

2013 Outstanding Waste Prevention Award

Encinitas
UNION SCHOOL DISTRICT

Figure 2.2 Encinitas Union School District's sustainability initiatives. Credit: Encinitas Union School District.

the SCRAP Cart divides waste into landfill, recycling, and composting bins and is used to teach students how to properly sort lunchtime waste. A comprehensive recycling and composting plan followed, reducing lunchtime waste by 83% the first year. Since then, lunchtime waste has been reduced at each school by over 80%, saving EUSD over $40,000 every year.

In 2010, EUSD passed a $44 million school bond that invested heavily in green upgrades. Over the next seven years, we installed solar panels on every campus. We replaced electric lighting with solar tubes, which bring natural light into classrooms and provide a better environment for student learning. We installed rainwater collection barrels at each school to conserve water and decrease runoff pollution. The collected water is stored and used as needed for irrigation, and the barrels serve as educational tools for our school community. Every school has high efficiency hand dryers and hydration stations to encourage less paper and plastic waste. Our maintenance staff adopted a green cleaning system that uses chemical-free cleaning products. All over EUSD, changes like these helped us reduce our environmental footprint and save an estimated $800,000–$1,000,000 in utility costs.

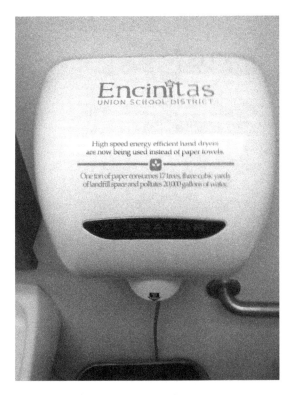

Photo 2.1 Hand dryers were one of the first districtwide green initiatives implemented at EUSD schools, eliminating the need for paper towels. Credit: Dr. Timothy Baird.

Despite these successes, something was missing. Sensors could turn lights off, but they did not change people's understanding of why lights need to be turned off. More and more, we realized that systems change alone would not create the type of sustainability we desired. This could only be done by directly involving students in the process.

Experiential environmental education is essential for nurturing behavior change and environmental stewardship. This is where our third G comes in: gardens. Gardens are powerful environmental education tools that can be used to deliver lessons and experiences that empower students to develop healthy behaviors and mindsets when it comes to food, nutrition, and food systems. All nine EUSD schools maintain at least one garden and several have orchards. One of the first site-based garden projects took place at Mission Estancia in 2013. The challenge posed to students – how could they grow food in a small space? The students responded by working with parents and community partners to create a hydroponic garden in a small area of their back playground. Their first crop was butter lettuce, and each grade level was assigned a slot to grow their own lettuce. The lettuce was sold as a fundraiser, and leftovers were donated to families in need. Now, students grow a wide variety of produce in their hydroponic garden for use at school and in the community.

Photo 2.2 Students and parents at Mission Estancia Elementary School work in the hydroponic garden. Credit: Heather Hutgren.

At La Costa Heights, students in each grade level adopt an outdoor area at the school, which becomes their habitat. Students research their habitat, design and care for the nature that lives there, and use eco-literacy skills to label their habitat so others can learn from them. Students maintain responsibility for their habitat throughout the school year.

In addition to school-based gardens, EUSD is home to the Farm Lab DREAMS Campus, a ten-acre, district-owned organic crop production farm and interactive learning center. As the nation's first certified-organic school farm, the Farm Lab DREAMS Campus inspires students to grow, choose, and eat local, fresh, and nutritious food. All EUSD students visit the Farm Lab DREAMS Campus and rotate through grade-level lessons. Hands-on experiences in the field and in food, science, and maker labs help students develop a rich understanding of the connection between our actions and our health, economy, and the environment. The primary intent of Farm Lab's DREAMS curriculum is to integrate design, research, engineering, art, math, and science into experiences that increase student understanding, analysis, and application in these critical areas. Lessons align with Next Generation Science Standards and Environmental Literacy, combine high-tech and low-tech activities, take place indoors and out, and center around real-world problem-solving. The agricultural backdrop provides opportunities that reinforce students' appreciation of organic food production and its direct benefits to air and water quality as well as healthy nutrition habits.

Sample Farm Lab DREAMS Grade-Level Lessons

First Grade: First-graders participate in a daylong learning experience where they examine how plants are useful to humans and develop an understanding of their role in sustaining life. Students consider several plants with properties that improve physical or emotional health (e.g., aloe vera, lavender, ginger, and chamomile) and make a sachet of dried herbs and flowers. They are introduced to top, middle, and bottom growing fruits and vegetables and then find and pick them during a nature hunt. They learn why our farm is organic and plant marigolds and calendulas to keep insects away naturally. As a culminating activity, students use maker-style materials to design, build, and code a robot that uses sound and motion to scare pests.

Sixth Grade: Sixth-graders participate in a five-day, two-strand unit focused on entrepreneurship and water resources. During strand one, students work together to create an organic salad dressing company. They complete market studies, design bottle labels, write a mission statement, and create a dressing recipe, among other tasks. On day five, students present their product to a panel of judges – complete with a taste test! During strand two, students learn about the water footprint and how much water it takes to grow a variety of produce. After reviewing drought patterns in California, students see a need for alternate fresh water sources and collaboratively design and build a desalination model. After calculating fresh water collection totals, they create a second iteration of their model to see if they can increase the amount of fresh water collected.

Photo 2.3 The EUSD Farm Lab educational component focuses on DREAMS! Credit: Julie Burton.

Implementation and Impact of the Three Gs

EUSD's systems change-driven sustainability efforts may have started with district leadership; however, it was the school community's buy-in and enthusiasm for the shared vision that ensured environmental stewardship would endure as a pillar for the district. Because EUSD's nine schools abide by different instructional models, how sustainability and environmental stewardship are implemented and modeled at each school is driven largely by the school's unique identity as well as leadership from its principal, teachers, and staff. Students have a role to play, too. In fact, student engagement, inside and outside the classroom, has turned out to be the not-so-secret ingredient in advancing our sustainability initiatives. Much of their early involvement occurred through school-based Green Teams, where student members helped conduct waste audits and care for school gardens.

A two-time Civic Award of Distinction winner, Flora Vista connects civic engagement with the United Nations Sustainable Development Goals and Next Generation Science Standards. Students select goals to focus on, research current events, and take action when necessary. Examples include creating public service announcements to educate the community on pollution issues, collecting canned food for San Diego Food Bank, fundraising for Friends of La Posada Homeless Shelter, and developing budgets and proposals for the school board to conserve energy in classrooms, replace plastic and cardboard lunch supplies, recycle markers, and reduce paper.

One of the district's earliest student engagement efforts evolved from a science experiment conducted by fifth-graders at Paul Ecke Central Elementary School. These students had partnered with undergraduates from the University of California, San Diego to measure the air quality in front of their school before and during parent drop-off. Their findings resulted in a student-led anti-idling campaign, which eventually led to anti-idling campaigns at all EUSD schools. The fifth-grade air quality study was a game changer for student engagement across the district. Our students saw they could make a real difference and realized that their voice could be a powerful tool in improving the environment. This led to greater student engagement in tackling environmental issues at the school, district, and community levels. In addition to Green Teams, most EUSD schools have student energy teams who work to identify energy conservation measures that go beyond the use of solar panels and solar tubes. Their findings have resulted in additional districtwide systems changes (e.g., reducing the number of sensors used to turn lights on in a room) and behavior changes (e.g., open the solar tubes and turn off the lights). Students have played active roles in purchasing practices, water use, and even some district construction projects and have created campaigns and public service announcements to educate peers on topics such as the benefits of walking to school, recycling, and composting at home. Their involvement in lunchtime waste audits led several EUSD campuses to institute Waste-Free Wednesdays and was instrumental in the Ocean Knoll students' push to eliminate single-use plastic during lunch. The pilot program, introduced earlier, has been successfully implemented at Ocean Knoll, and plans are in the works to expand to additional district schools during the 2021–2022 school year.

Upper-grade students at El Camino Creek participate in Film Guild, an enrichment activity where students learn how to make films. With support from their Film Guild mentor teacher, students have created films focused on EUSD's green initiatives, such as "The Green Team," "Helpful Hydroponics," and "Take the Pledge to Never Pollute." The films have won local and state awards and serve as public service announcements for the school community.

After completing a waste audit, Park Dale Lane students noticed that class birthday parties were generating a lot of excess waste. So, they created a proposal recommending every class have its own reusable supplies for class parties. The principal and PTA partnered with students to create a party box for each class, which includes reusable decorations, silverware, plates, and cups that can be taken home to be washed after a party. The idea was shared with all nine PTA presidents for future use at other EUSD schools.

Student engagement in sustainability initiatives is further nurtured through authentic learning experiences in the classroom. Our district-created Next Generation Science Standards units of study integrate environmental stewardship and environmental literacy across the curriculum. EUSD's school gardens and Farm Lab DREAMS campus, described earlier, exemplify how educators bring environmental education to life for students. However, environmental education opportunities extend beyond the garden to include topics such as water and energy conservation, waste diversion, litter prevention, composting, and environmental advocacy. A prime example is EUSD's involvement in the Storm Water Pollution Prevention Plan (SWPPP) Internship Program.

A year-long program, the SWPPP Internship Program trains students to observe, test, and analyze stormwater runoff on campus and develop solutions to prevent runoff from carrying pollutants downstream to the ocean. Students cap off the project by drafting a stormwater pollution prevention plan for their school that meets industry standards and is presented to the school board for approval. Students also prepare a multimedia presentation that showcases data collected throughout the year. The program

Photo 2.4 Student interns analyze stormwater runoff as part of the Storm Water Pollution Prevention Plan (SWPPP) Internship Program. Credit: Camille Sowinski.

started in 2013 with teams of fifth- and sixth-graders at La Costa Heights and El Camino Creek Elementary Schools. Students applied for jobs on their school's team and then interviewed for their positions. Those who were selected as SWPPP interns eagerly got to work, giving up recess and devoting time before and after school to check drains, test water samples, and write reports. Tours of the local wastewater treatment plant and interactions with professionals employed in related industries grounded their work in a real-world context. That first year, the SWPPP interns came to their board presentations ready to defend their plans and advocate for better stormwater management at their schools. Needless to say, these students were hooked.

By 2014, EUSD had established SWPPP Internship Programs at all nine schools. In 2016, EUSD was awarded a California Drought Response Outreach to School grant, which provided close to $700,000 for SWPPP teams to begin work on larger scale stormwater management best practices, in addition to the small-scale practices, like cleaning out or reducing waste around drains, they were already implementing. Students play a role in every phase of the projects that move forward: collaborating with EUSD's business and facilities departments, working with architects, writing bid specifications, conducting job walks with contractors, and ultimately helping the district install bioswales, replace drains, and make other pollution reduction improvements. One such improvement project took place at Olivenhain Pioneer Elementary School in 2018, when SWPPP interns participated in an effort to install permeable pavement in the school's parking lot. SWPPP interns are eager to share their work and have presented before a wide range of audiences, from the PTA and county board of supervisors to professionals in water and water pollution fields at state and national conferences.

Capri students designed a seascape mural made out of recycled bottle caps for an area of their school garden called Capri Commons. The school community collected plastic bottle caps in various colors, washed them, and created lunchtime activities to complete the mural. Students learned about recycling and the importance of using reusable bottles throughout the project. They shared their final product at a green conference, using global communication skills to present their work.

Photo 2.5 Students at Capri Elementary School designed an ocean-themed mural using recycled plastic bottle caps. Credit: Dr. Andree Grey.

Lessons Learned

A shared vision on paper is different than a shared vision in action across nine unique school campuses. Over the last decade, EUSD has upheld its commitment to environmental stewardship as a district value. We have maintained a district Green Team with representatives from all school campuses, a facilities department that supports the work of reducing our environmental footprint, and an educational services team that supports environmental literacy in and outside of classrooms. An important element in sustaining this work has been our process for onboarding new team members. Since 2016, we have welcomed new leadership at the administrative level, in our educational services and maintenance departments, at the Farm Lab DREAMS campus, and in our farming partners. Each interview process includes questions or tasks related to our sustainability initiatives, and our staff orientation includes training and support to help new hires learn about our initiatives, goals, and history.

Implementing our shared vision for sustainability has presented some challenges over the last decade. The first involves funding districtwide projects. While grants are available to begin sustainability work in schools, the challenge lies in securing ongoing funding. At EUSD, we are fortunate that our Board of Education supports our environmental stewardship goals and continues to fund ongoing projects across the district. Their support has ensured all schools have common green elements, such as solar panels, rain collection systems, SCRAP Carts, and gardens. However, once these elements were added, some community members questioned why the work needed more funding, why EUSD was focusing on sustainability over literacy, and why we needed a Farm Lab. We have found that the best way to address these questions is to continue telling the story of our district's four pillars, using student voices whenever possible. Each pillar is represented in our strategic plan and has various funding sources attached to action items that accompany each goal.

Photo 2.6 Students present ideas for a zero-waste solution to recycling sports equipment. Credit: Jodi Greenberger.

The second challenge involves supporting autonomous school site goals. Our nine school principals must find ways to connect the district vision with their school's unique instructional model. Maintaining Green Teams and including a Green Team representative on each school's PTA provides consistency and support within each school. Taking time to discuss sustainability initiatives during routine meetings with our superintendent and assistant superintendent of educational services serves as a valuable learning opportunity. Our principals also collaborate in triads, which are led by a district administrator. During triad meetings, three site leaders and their district representative visit school sites to see curriculum, instruction, and sustainability in action. These visits provide opportunities for idea-sharing and highlighting site-specific initiatives.

Learning from Encinitas Union School District: Bringing a Shared Vision for Sustainability to Your District

District and school leadership, community support, and student input are critical elements for turning a shared vision for sustainability into a reality, no matter which instructional model(s) you adhere to. Here are a few ways your district can leverage a shared vision in support of sustainability.

- **Establish a district Green Team and school Green Teams.** Green Teams should include representatives from across the school community to ensure multiple voices are heard and engaged in your sustainability initiatives.
- **Identify a set of champions to support your work at the student, parent, staff, and community levels.** For example, parents and community activists can keep sustainability front and center by speaking at public events, writing for newsletters, and sharing ideas with their school's principal and their school and district Green Teams.
- **Involve parents and community volunteers as partners.** Giving them a stake in the work will go a long way to earning their trust, support, and continued engagement.

Photo 2.7 Students work in the school garden at Ocean Knoll Elementary School. Credit: Julie Burton.

- **Connect and collaborate with other districts that are invested in the work of sustainability.** EUSD found partners by attending conferences, networking events, and webinars and through professional journals.

Synthesis

What started as a shared vision for environmental stewardship has morphed into a culture of sustainability that is wholeheartedly embraced by EUSD's school community, top-down and bottom-up. We are proud to be a district focused on educating and inspiring environmental stewards. We are inspired by our schools' efforts to implement sustainability initiatives, based on their unique identities, and the passion expressed by our teachers, staff, students, and community. And for anyone who asks, "How can elementary school students make a lasting impact on their community and the environment?" look no further than the Encinitas City Council, who *did* vote to support the ban on single-use plastic at city events

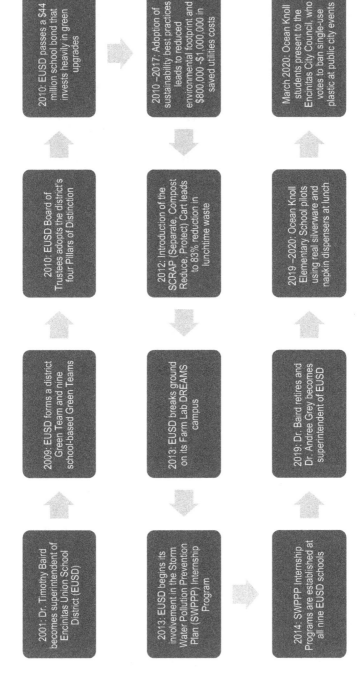

Figure 2.3 Encinitas Union School District Timeline.

after hearing from the Ocean Knoll students. If fifth-graders can make an impact at age ten, imagine what they can do to change the world over the next 90 years?

Thank you to Dr. Timothy Baird for his contributions to this story and for all he did to create sustainable (pun-intended!) green initiatives at Encinitas Union School District.

Relevant Websites

Encinitas Union School District. Retrieved from: http://www.eusd.net/

Teaching Our Cities

Place-Based Education in an Urban Environment

Joel Tolman

Crystal Fernandez had lived in the Hill neighborhood of New Haven, Connecticut for three years when she first walked into my classroom at Common Ground High School. I was new to the city, having moved there three weeks before. It was fall 2003, and I was co-teaching a class about New Haven's neighborhoods with Liz Cox – a gifted educator who retired as Common Ground's school director in 2020.

DOI: 10.4324/9781003152811-4

It sounds ludicrous, in retrospect: a first-year teacher, new to New Haven, teaching a class about the city to students who had called that place home for much or all their lives. It felt a little ludicrous, too. Crystal and her classmates knew I was a new teacher and treated me with a mix of "okay, prove it," and incredible generosity. Liz's coaching as an experienced co-teacher made an enormous difference, too.

Still, when Crystal, Liz, and I look back on what worked in that first, wobbly class, a few things stand out. A visit to Dixwell Plaza, the historic heart of New Haven's African American community. Walking to Katherine Brennan Elementary School once a week, where our students – some struggling readers themselves – taught reading strategies, wrote New Haven storybooks, and read aloud with second-graders. Gathering stories of people and places from our neighborhoods and publishing them in an anthology called "Pass It On." Crystal's contribution was a carefully researched piece about the renewal of a multi-ethnic Catholic congregation and its role in revitalizing her Hill neighborhood.

However tender and in need of tending, a seed of something powerful was planted in these experiences: a way of thinking about how students and teachers in urban public schools relate to each other and to the cities they call home.

Urban Schools Can Be Our Best Schools – When They Embrace Their Urban Environments

Put "urban" in front of "education" and something strange happens. The word "urban" is sometimes used to talk about schools that serve Black and Brown students as well as those that teach students living in poverty, without addressing racism or income inequality head on. Couple this with other tired stereotypes of urban public schools – achievement gaps, politicized bureaucracies, high dropout rates, and a mix of underprepared teachers and worn-out veterans – and it is easy to get stuck in a toxic narrative that seems to relegate students of color and low-income students to schools that do not support their success. This narrative – and the realities and illusions it contains – is one manifestation of the systemic racism and oppression built into our education systems.

Because "urban" often stands in for these negative narratives in public education, many urban public high schools turn their backs on their cities. Schools fortify themselves with locked doors and police officers. They cancel field trips and outdoor experiences and double down on test prep. They elevate and celebrate standards and ways of communicating that are remote from students' experiences outside of school. They forget that their cities are full of educators who may not hold teaching credentials – students' family members, local artists, and community gardeners, for instance. They mimic the cultures of wealthy suburban districts or fancy private schools because this is what "good schools" look like. They tell students the only path to success is to leave their families, neighborhoods, and cities behind.

What if we could turn this dynamic on its head? What if we recognized that cities are filled with things that make learning possible – people with talents and passions to share, problems to be solved and questions to be asked, organizations ready to provide the supports and opportunities students need, places where students can learn and grow? What if urban public schools embraced their cities and rooted themselves in their urban environments?

Building a School That is Rooted in Place and Helps Students Take Control of Their Educational Journeys

This is the destination that Crystal, Liz, and I were striving toward in that 2003 class we shared: an education that grew out of the city our students called home. We knew from experience that the richest learning happens when students do real work, with a public audience and a real purpose, grounded in the local environment and community. A belief in the power of active, authentic, place-based learning has always been at the core of Common Ground's approach. That is what our school's founders – mostly public school teachers and local environmental activists – set out to create when they reclaimed 20 acres of abandoned city park land and built a new school from the ground up.

This vision came to life in team-taught, interdisciplinary block classes – like the one Liz and I taught about New Haven's neighborhoods, which combined English and social studies. Crystal joined me for another block class in the spring trimester called POWER – team taught with math professor and former black panther Eddie Rose – which focused on using mathematics and social science to understand power in all its manifestations: energy and energy policy, political power, exponential equations, and the power of mathematical problem-solving.

While these block classes often contained magical learning experiences, Common Ground in 2003 was not the model of relevant, rigorous, and responsive learning that our students deserved. Back then, every student took three block classes a year – one each trimester – alongside their advisory and a handful of more traditional courses. What students experienced in one block class was often disconnected from the content and skills they encountered in a subsequent trimester. At times, these courses reflected the passions and lived experiences of the teachers more than those of the students. We were not doing enough to help students build the reading, writing, problem-solving, and leadership skills they needed to succeed beyond high school.

The results were what you would expect. Some teachers struggled to engage students, and school culture was rocky. Test scores were low. Many students struggled to make the leap to college and fulfilling careers. What we needed was a more integrated four-year high school experience – one that gave students room for real choice in following their passions, that leveraged the whole city to help them succeed, and that ensured they graduated ready for college and careers, leadership and life.

In 2005, Crystal left to study African American, Latinx, and Urban Studies in college and to launch a career in youth development. Liz and I remained at Common Ground, working with colleagues, students, and families to build an educational model that more fully met our students' needs. Between 2003 and 2014, our school community took the following steps together:

- We developed a schoolwide motto – POWER – that defined our approach to student leadership and built traditions for recognizing students as they grew into POWERful leaders for a just and sustainable world.
- We – at first reluctantly, and then with full commitment – embraced standards-driven curriculum and used data to guide instruction. We came to recognize that you cannot compromise between rigor, relevance, and responsiveness if you want to build a school that works for all students.

- We created a portfolio system that challenged students to curate their most significant environmental leadership experiences and made it a graduation requirement for students to defend their portfolios.
- We added new staff positions focused on connecting classes to our site and city.
- We built teacher capacity to use our site and city as a learning laboratory – getting out into our city, inviting community residents to lead professional development, and engaging in work to confront implicit biases and how systems of oppression showed up in our school.
- We invested in indoor and outdoor learning spaces and strengthened partnerships that enabled students to take on green jobs, college courses, field experiences, and programs beyond our site.
- We found and learned from peers – through Green Schools National Network and by building a regional network of urban public schools that shared our commitment to Teaching Our Cities.

We saw evidence that our students were thriving with each step we took and that made us want to deepen and accelerate the changes we were making. Between 2007 and 2014, the percentage of students demonstrating proficiency in reading and mathematics on state tests more than doubled, and we went from a school in need of improvement to a Connecticut School of Distinction. Our students were graduating at rates above state average – in 2015, our four-year graduation rate was 100%. Close to 100% were earning admission to college, as well. One hundred percent were also meeting our requirement to successfully defend their portfolios to graduate.

Reimagining the Four-Year Common Ground Experience

We made a lot of progress at Common Ground by 2015. Yet, when we looked around, we still saw areas where we fell short. Our students were getting into college, but many were not matriculating and persisting. The SAT was now the state accountability test (replacing a test that set a relatively low bar), and many of our students were not earning college-ready scores. While many pieces were in place, they were not coalescing into a coherent, four-year experience.

Most importantly, our students were telling us what was not working. In spring 2015, a group of students kicked their teachers out of their classrooms and led discussions in each of our advisory groups. The notes they brought back were eye-opening. Students had chosen Common Ground based on the promise of learning outside the classroom, and we were not delivering. They felt disconnected from their peers and the larger community. Students said that their teachers did not consistently welcome who they were – their racial identities, their lived experiences – into the classroom.

That student feedback – and our own reflections on the work ahead – led our school community to ask: how can we build a progression of active, authentic learning experiences over the course of four years at Common Ground? How do we root students in shared core academic experiences, while granting increased freedom for students to follow their own paths?

We knew our students, their families, our teachers, and our New Haven neighbors needed to be at the center of the design process. So, we started by soliciting their feedback through surveys. We asked foundational questions – what, how, and where our students should learn – and received rich answers. Input in hand, we sat down with these stakeholders to develop plans for integrated units that would make up the core of our ninth- and tenth-grade curricula. Students played a leading role in creating the vision for our four-year road map and worked with teachers and community partners to plan new courses and units of study. Teachers defined foundational building blocks of teaching and learning and developed Common Core-aligned skill progressions in reading, writing, and problem-solving. Many of the stakeholders who helped build our ninth- and tenth-grade core experiences returned as guest teachers. We followed a staged approach to implementation – starting with the ninth-grade experience as the foundation and building a new aspect of our four-year experience into each subsequent year. We repeated the cycle as we created new electives and internships for our eleventh- and twelfth-graders.

What follows is a snapshot of the four-year Common Ground experience that resulted from this work.

Starting Close to Home: Core 9

Ninth-graders spend four mornings each week in Core 9, which combines math, English, science, and social studies in ways that encourage students to think about who they are, what Common Ground is, and how they can contribute to our community. The interdisciplinary nature of Core 9 presents plenty of opportunities for place-based learning. For instance, Core 9's first unit explores food, how we sustain ourselves, and Common Ground's farm. In math and science, students research and calculate the nutritional value and productivity of different crops. In social studies and English, students examine the cultural and historical significance of the vegetables grown in our gardens. Based on their research, students present advice to our farm team on what they should grow in subsequent years.

Each unit builds toward real performances or products for public audiences and deepens students' connection to our place. On the last day of the food unit, for instance, students organize a family night where they present family food stories, share the science and history of food, and communicate findings from their math analysis. Over time, students build relationships with the people who comprise the Common Ground community – site managers, environmental educators, fellow students – so they can successfully navigate and improve our place over their four years of high school.

Photo 3.1 Ninth-graders circle up on Common Ground's urban farm as part of the first unit of the ninth-grade core, focused on "feeding ourselves." Credit: Joel Tolman.

The City Is Our Classroom: Core 10

Like Core 9, Core 10 brings together four classes – science, social studies, English, and a course called "interdisciplinary methods," which helps students build skills for academic success and integrate what they learn through the visual and performing arts. Each semester includes two units, each focused on deepening students' understanding of and agency in their urban environment. In unit one, students explore and document the stories of New Haven from the first peoples to the present. Unit two explores social and environmental justice (e.g., the school-to-prison pipeline, lead pollution, and housing segregation) and changemaking strategies that can address injustices. Unit three builds students' understanding of the science and political decisions behind the climate crisis. Unit four explores public health.

Common Ground's Teaching Our Cities commitment is central to the tenth-grade core. In each unit, students work with local artists to create products that demonstrate their learning. They create neighborhood photo essays; write and perform plays using Theater of the Oppressed methodologies; create and exhibit art about climate change; and make videos about community health. Community members also come and talk to students about how they influence and create change in the city. By the end of the year, tenth-graders have met four dozen community changemakers,

Photo 3.2 Students in the tenth-grade core take a break during a photo scavenger hunt of the New Haven green with local photographer Chris Randall. Credit: Chris Randall.

which creates opportunities to reflect on the kind of changemakers they want to be and builds connections they can revisit in later years. The Core 10 schedule (all afternoon four days a week and all day on Wednesdays) frees up space to go into the community without impacting other classes. These field experiences range from visiting parks to sample soil and hear from residents who are transforming vacant lots into greenspaces to taking walking tours and documenting how neighborhoods are gentrifying and changing.

Following Your Passions: Choice-Rich Eleventh- and Twelfth-Grade Experiences

During junior and senior years, students explore college and careers while pursuing individual passions and pathways. The "core" experience takes up less of a student's schedule than in ninth and tenth grades. Eleventh-graders take Junior Seminar, where they explore potential careers, prepare for the college application process, and continue work on their environmental leadership portfolios. By the end of junior year, each portfolio contains eight reflections – a "diary" of a student's high school career that explores experiences where the student grew as a leader. Twelfth-graders take a Senior Environmental Justice Capstone course where they write college essays, finalize their environmental leadership portfolios, complete a capstone project, and present senior defenses. Through their capstone projects, students learn how to conduct deep research, create changemaking strategies, navigate power structures, adapt to challenges, and build their own definitions of environmental justice. They also refine and follow their individual pathways – building competence as future educators, scientists, entrepreneurs, artists, and more.

Alongside core experiences and traditional academic courses, juniors and seniors can access opportunities not found in traditional schools. Through Green Jobs Corps, our year-round youth-employment program, students can work on Common Ground's farm, help run farmers markets, or restore habitat at city parks. They can participate in a credit-bearing internship where they may create a recruiting video or develop a proposal for school improvements. Eleventh- and twelfth-graders can also take electives that are co-designed by students and taught by nontraditional teachers. For instance, students can choose between a class on Race, Identity, and Justice; a course where students put on a Shakespeare play and earn college drama credit; and an outdoor leadership class taught by an educator from Common Ground's environmental center. Students work with their Guide – a teacher who acts as an academic advisor throughout a student's four years – to map out the combination of classes and nontraditional learning opportunities that are right for them.

Implementation and Impact of the Four-Year Common Ground Experience

At Common Ground, we are making the road by walking, as educator Paolo Freire would say. The four-year progression presented here may sound complete, but it is still a work in progress. We recognize that we need to keep deepening our answers to the questions that Liz, Crystal, and I explored back in 2003: How can we root learning in our students' lived experiences and in the city they call home? How can we challenge students to tackle real-world problems and perform for real audiences? How can we hold all students to high standards and let them follow their own paths?

We have seen signs we are headed in the right direction. The first students to take part in Core 9 – members of the class of 2021 – scored in the 99th and 90th percentile for growth in math and language usage, respectively, according to results of the NWEA Measures of Academic Progress. As sophomores, they made similarly significant progress. The class of 2021's reading growth rate was in the 99th percentile and language usage in the 93rd percentile. While these students' junior and senior years were impacted by COVID-19, they continued to demonstrate dramatic academic progress. Their growth between fall 2019 and winter 2020 was again in the 99th percentile nationally in reading and math. It has been incredible to witness their resilience and tenacity in the context of distance learning – and rewarding to see the joy on their faces as they begin to receive college admission letters.

These pioneering students have also demonstrated growth as leaders for a just and sustainable environment. For the past three years, the nonprofit evaluation group NewKnowledge (now Knology) has surveyed

Common Ground students. In 2017, the percentage of students who said experiences at Common Ground helped them grow into a leader, become someone who cares about the environment, and become committed to social justice doubled between ninth and twelfth grades. Our first group of Core 9 students grew more as environmental leaders than their predecessors, with 57% saying experiences at Common Ground influenced them to become someone who cares about the environment, up from 46% the year before. The percent of ninth-graders who consider themselves a leader because of experiences at Common Ground increased from 32% in 2017 to 50% in 2018. These students continued to show growth in leadership confidence and identity as they experienced Core 10 curricula. Between the end of ninth grade and the end of tenth grade, the percentage of students in the class of 2021 who say they are someone who cares about the environment grew from 57% to 80% and the percentage who say they are someone who creates social change grew from 48% to 59%. By the time students graduate, less than 5% disagreed with the statement, "Because of experiences I had at Common Ground, I am a leader."

Lessons Learned

Eighteen years have passed since Crystal, Liz, and I first shared a classroom, during which time there has been much room for mistakes, learning, and growth. A few critical lessons stand out in reflecting on this long arc of work to build a school that is responsive and relevant to our students and rooted in the city they call home.

School change work is human relationship work. Lasting progress has been possible because we have taken time to get to know each other and ensure we are rowing in the same direction. When we struggle, it is often because people feel left out of decisions that impact them. This is true for our teachers (for whom a co-creative process can sometimes feel like a loss of agency) and community partners (who naturally expect us to show up for their needs and causes, as they have shown up for us).

Anti-racism and anti-oppression work are a critical part of professional and personal development. Technical teacher training and an understanding of environmental issues matter, but they are not enough. Rooting students' learning experiences in their lived experiences and urban environments requires confronting implicit and explicit biases, understanding how systems of oppression manifest in our schools and relationships, and building skills to name and change these systemic patterns.

Stakeholders and their contributions have real value and should be treated as such. When we invite community members to co-design and co-teach with us, we pay them the same hourly rate we pay our teachers. We also pay students to join in curriculum design, and when we do not pay them, we award academic credit or community-service hours. We know that our community members' contributions have real value and want to signal that we see them as full partners and strive to undo dynamics where only those with accumulated privilege can join in school change.

Co-creation needs to be ongoing – not a moment or phase in the design process. New teachers join interdisciplinary teaching teams and need space to make curricula their own. New students enter our classrooms and bring a shifting set of passions and concerns. We need strong and reliable structures through which the school community can work together to redesign learning experiences, while staying grounded in shared design principles.

Photo 3.3 Teachers, students, parents, and community partners work together to design new integrated units of study for Common Ground's ninth-grade curriculum. Credit: Joel Tolman.

Learning from Common Ground High School: Leveraging Culturally Relevant Practices in Your School

Common Ground has been on the road to teaching our city for a long time. It often feels like we are still finding our way. Here are some steps to consider for schools that are getting started on their own journeys.

- **Identify your assets and strengths.** Akiima Price, an environmental educator and community changemaker whose work has been instrumental to Common Ground's approach, taught our students and staff to use a "surroundings survey" to identify the assets and problems, natural and social, in the area around our school. This simple process of community mapping gave us a powerful starting point for building new experiences for students.
- **Get to know your city – together with students, families, and neighbors.** Find ways to spend time in the urban environment and build relationships with the people who call it home. Some of our most valuable professional development experiences include walking around our immediate neighborhood with a student's parent and sitting down with students, families, alumni, and neighbors to sketch out plans for a new unit of study.
- **Design culminating performances and products first and scaffold backward from there.** At Common Ground, we started using a simple four E framework to design learning experiences rooted in place: What are the assets and challenges in the urban Environment that our students are exploring? What are the Expectations to which we are holding all students? What is the culminating Exhibition through which students will demonstrate their learning? What are the Experiences that will help students build toward this exhibition?
- **Find some traveling companions.** One of the most valuable things we did was to connect with educators and students from peer schools who are travelling parallel paths to ours. Participating in broad networks – like Green Schools National Network – and smaller, tighter ones – like the five urban, environmentally themed public high schools we bring together through Teaching Our Cities – is valuable. At an even

smaller scale, finding a few colleagues to read and share practices with through an informal accountability circle or book club can make a huge difference.

- **Talk with your students.** Ask them what they love and want to change about the city they call home, and where they see opportunities to make their school experiences more real and relevant and follow their lead.

Synthesis

Crystal returned to Common Ground in early 2019 and serves a leader on our student pathways team, which helps students map and travel their paths to college and career, leadership and life. This is the first time an alum has assumed a management role at the organization. In some ways, the school that greeted Crystal 15 years after she graduated was almost unrecognizable. In other ways, Common Ground is still rooted in the same earth as when Crystal was a student. Our vision is the same – the urban environment is a rich classroom for student learning, and students do their best work when they do real work for a real audience. Hopefully, we are more skilled at realizing that vision than when Crystal and I first shared a classroom – and hopefully, we keep improving at living into this vision.

Crystal's return to Common Ground is a real-life manifestation of a hope we hold for all alumni. By the time students graduate, we want them to be on their own paths – knowing what their passions are and how they are going to follow them. Whatever paths they choose, we want our students to be powerful environmental justice leaders, successful in college and careers, and leading happy and sustainable lives. Common Ground students are blazing new paths – some take them far away and some bring them back home to help us mobilize a city's worth of learning opportunities to help another generation of students thrive.

Relevant Websites

Common Ground High School. Retrieved from: https://commongroundct. org/

Food Waste Inspires a Shift to Whole School Sustainability at the School of Environmental Studies

Lauren Trainer

School of Environmental Studies

Location: Apple Valley, Minnesota

Home to the country's first student-led LEED Gold certification, achieved in April 2019

Number of students: 400 students

Student demographics: 77% White; 7.4% Hispanic/Latino; 6.2% Multiracial/Other; 5% Asian; 4.4% Black/African American

2013 U.S. Department of Education Green Ribbon School Awardee

"Wait, that's recyclable!" and "Hold on, you can compost that." Eleventh-graders McKenzie Mace and Harmonie Hokanson offer these daily reminders while manning the waste-sorting station in the cafeteria at the School of Environmental Studies. They volunteer their lunch time nearly every day to help their peers properly sort their lunch waste. "I do it because

DOI: 10.4324/9781003152811-5

it needs to be done," McKenzie says. Harmonie explains that having a student demonstrate how to use the compost, recycle, trash, and sharing table options is more powerful than having a teacher do so. "A teacher telling us where to put our stuff would make us feel like we *had* to do it. If a student stands here, it looks like we do it because we care."

In 1995, educators, parents, and community leaders got together and dreamed a dream about a little school that could make a big impact. Fast forward a quarter of a century and you have the School of Environmental Studies (SES), a public environmental magnet school for eleventh- and twelfth-graders that is located on the grounds of the Minnesota Zoo in Apple Valley, Minnesota. SES is recognized as one of the "pioneering schools" in environmental education, using an interdisciplinary, integrated curriculum to drive our theme. So, it may come as a surprise that, as recently as 2019, we did not have a whole school sustainability practice in place.

Photo 4.1 Students Harmonie and Piper volunteer their lunch time to help peers sort their waste. Credit: Lauren Trainer.

Opportunities and Barriers: Navigating the Path to Whole School Sustainability

A key driver in our shift to whole school sustainability is our students. Student voice and choice have been part of SES's fabric since its founding. While our student-centered focus has never wavered, the make-up of our student body has changed. When SES was founded in the mid-1990s, we were seen as an elite, competitive school that students needed to apply to get into. Since then, our demographics have diversified. We started to enroll more students who required special education services as well as students who felt disenfranchised at their current schools and wanted to go to a school where they felt there was more opportunity. Of course, we still enroll students who are attracted to SES's mission and want to become leaders in environmental and sustainability fields. However, the shift in student population necessitated a re-examination of who SES is, who we serve, and where we want to go as a school.

I assumed the role of SES principal during the 2017–2018 school year. From the start, I could see that SES was a special place and that its students were engaged in some heavy-hitting, impressive work, including attending United Nations climate conferences and obtaining LEED certification for our school building. However, I saw something else, too – a lack of opportunities for ALL students. What about the student who cannot afford to travel or the one who does not own a car or the one who holds an after-school job? I was determined to make it possible for all SES students to engage in rich environmental and sustainability experiences that not only support what they learn in the classroom but also contribute to sustainability at SES, throughout the school day. For a school with "environment" in its name, this was non-negotiable for me. So began my journey in whole school sustainability.

That journey got off to a bumpy start. While our teachers and staff agreed this shift to whole school sustainability needed to happen, there was some initial resistance to getting this initiative off the ground. The crux of the issue was time. SES teachers and staff work unbelievably hard. Many teachers put in a minimum of 60 hours per week, not just writing lesson plans and grading papers but also forging relationships in the community, sleeping in snow quinzees in 15-degree weather with students, and reading poems about winter while standing in a snowstorm on a frozen pond.

So, while our teachers care about modeling and facilitating daily environmental and sustainability opportunities for students, the question was, how do you remove the barriers, namely resources and time, to put in place a system they can follow?

For SES, the answer involved going back to the basics, in our case food waste, to set a course for the future.

Back to the Basics: Food Waste Sets the Stage for Systems Change

In January 2019, I received an email from our county's School Recycling Program Coordinator, Ali VanderCook. Dakota County (where SES is located) had been assigned a GreenCorps member to work with them on a food waste reduction project. Ali wanted to know if SES would like to participate by implementing a student-driven food waste reduction initiative. This offer was the opportunity SES needed to get our sustainability efforts off the ground without asking more of our teachers. I said yes.

Several weeks later, I met with Ali and Hannah, the GreenCorps Assistant, to learn about the project. Joining me were two teachers, Brooks Autry and Kim Colburn-Lindell; our food service manager, Lisa Germond; and our building chief, Sam Firpo. According to Ali, students would conduct a food waste audit and, using the audit's results, make recommendations for how to reduce the waste we were creating. Lisa was skeptical at first. She was worried we would find that we were wasting fruits and vegetables, explaining there is a requirement for students who receive free and reduced-priced lunch to take certain items, even if they do not intend to eat them. Hannah and Ali put Lisa at ease, explaining they were there to help with ideas and education and not to stand in the way of a school's guidelines and requirements. With approval from Sam and Lisa in hand, we were ready to proceed with our food waste program.

Our program kicked off in March 2019. Ali, Hannah, and their team brought in the equipment we would need to facilitate the food waste audit. As promised, we met to discuss results and co-create realistic goals. The Dakota County team walked us through the process of a food waste audit, and we learned we were wasting approximately 17.5 pounds of food each day. Obviously, we had some work to do!

Kim took the reins when it came to student involvement. Kim teaches an AVID course, which is a student-centered curriculum designed to help students acquire the skills they need to be successful in college. AVID includes a community service component, and Kim decided to focus her class's community service on educating the school community about food waste. Students in Kim's AVID class created posters and gave presentations to their peers on the issue of food waste. They worked with food service staff to identify which items students are required to take when they go through the lunch line and created signs to help their peers make smart decisions so they do not end up throwing food away. Dakota County provided SES with a share table where students could put unopened food for others to take and a "flavor station" where students could literally spice up their food to make it more to their liking. We were also the first school in our district to receive a bulk milk dispenser. The "steel cow," as it is called, gives students autonomy over how much milk they take and reduces milk carton waste, as students drink milk out of reusable cups. These new initiatives were overseen not by faculty but by Kim's AVID students. These students even volunteered their lunch time to stand at our waste-sorting station to help their peers identify what is recyclable, what is compostable, and what goes to landfill. Overall, our new food waste program was proving to be a success. Every SES student, every day was interacting with a system unique to our school that demonstrated our commitment to sustainability. They got to participate regularly and build sustainable habits they could take home. We dismissed for summer patting ourselves on the back.

Then came the start of the 2019–2020 school year. Our partnership with Dakota County on the food waste initiative had ended in the spring, and it was up to us to sustain the work ourselves. Kim remained dedicated to the cause, and with a new group of AVID students in her classroom, she worked hard to facilitate opportunities for her students to better understand what individuals can do to address food waste. One such opportunity involved a collaboration with a group of gardeners who run a community garden on campus. They agreed to allow students to place uneaten fruits and vegetables in their compost bin. However, participation and enthusiasm were waning. We only had two students, Harmonie and McKenzie, who regularly volunteered to spend their lunches at the waste-sorting station. Both girls saw room for improvement. They reported that students were not taking the time to slow down and sort, even with them standing there. They also wished more students volunteered.

Photo 4.2 Kim Colburn-Lindell, teacher-leader of SES's food waste reduction initiative, works with students to finish waste sorting after lunch. Credit: Lauren Trainer.

Kim was concerned that we were losing the momentum we had worked so hard to establish the previous school year. She brought her plea to a faculty meeting where she asked her colleagues to stand with the student volunteers at lunch and help model the waste sorting. She passed around a sign-up sheet, and it came back with fewer than half of the blanks filled in. Simply put, people were tired. They needed their lunch to plan and have something to eat. Further, SES teachers, by contract, are entitled to a 30-minute, duty-free lunch. Even as principal, I cannot make them give up lunch to help supervise, lead, and guide how students sort their food waste. The stall in momentum was real and it seemed there was little I could do about it.

In winter 2020, I received another email from Dakota County about a $10,000 grant they were offering to support sustainable practices in schools. Kim, Brooks, and I submitted an application where we requested additional recycling bins for classrooms and reusable silverware for the cafeteria. SES was awarded the grant and soon after, Ali and her partner for this project, Megan, arranged a meeting to discuss how we would use the grant money to accomplish our sustainability goals. Once again, I invited Sam and Lisa to join us. Both voiced concerns when it came to the reusable silverware. Sam and his custodial staff were already volunteering their time to help Lisa and her partner, Monica, wash reusable cups after lunch. The kitchen lacked sufficient space to store the silverware, and students were throwing away their reusable cups and trays. It was becoming increasingly clear: SES did not need a $10,000 grant to buy things – we needed funding to put a sustainable infrastructure in place that everyone in the school community could buy into.

With this in mind, I reached out to Ali with a proposal to use our grant funds to hire a facilitator who could work with a group of SES representatives to develop a sustainability strategic plan. The plan would lay out a clear and feasible pathway to sustainability that was not dependent on staff time and funding and would include actions that could be accomplished during the school day. Initially, we received some resistance from the county – the money was intended to purchase equipment to support waste reduction and recycling programs. I pled my case: how could we begin to use the equipment if we did not have a system in place to begin with? With Ali's help, the county relented and changed the parameters of the grant to allow SES to use some of our grant money to bring a facilitator and a group of stakeholders together to develop a sustainability strategic plan. Our shift to whole school sustainability was beginning to unfold in earnest.

A Work in Progress: Implementation of Whole School Sustainability at SES

Starting simple, in our case with food waste, was the secret sauce to ease SES's shift to a whole school sustainability mindset. With funding secured from Dakota County to build out our sustainability infrastructure, the real work could begin.

First, we identified a group of SES stakeholders to participate in the strategic planning process. This group included me, Lisa, Sam, teachers, and students. Starting in September 2020, we met for 90 minutes once a week, over the course of six weeks, to lay out a framework for our sustainability strategic plan. This process involved revisiting our vision statement (*A thoughtful community of leaders engaging with others to create a sustainable world*) and beliefs statement to create a plan that would embed a focus on sustainable habits into the SES student experience.

SES Beliefs Statement

Inquiry: An inquiry-based, interdisciplinary learning environment deepens understanding.

Student-Centered: Educational opportunities are shaped by the needs and interests of our students.

Leadership: Leadership is fostered by opportunities to lead, follow, question, plan, and act.

Community: Effective communities value collaboration, flexibility, and respect.

Academic Challenge: Every student deserves academic challenge.

Nature: Connections with nature are powerful and encourage responsible choices and actions.

Experience: Active, experiential learning is fundamental.

Systems Thinking: Understanding environmental systems and their interrelationships is essential.

Global Citizenship: Embracing diversity strengthens our ability to create compassionate global citizens.

True to our school's student-centered focus, students played an active role in the strategic planning process, lending their voice and perspective on the changes they would like to see. The strategic plan is intentionally structured to provide students with multiple access points for contributing to sustainability practices at SES. One access point is through representation on the school's green team, which includes seats for two juniors and two seniors. Students can participate in decision-making in other ways, too, such as determining the sustainability goals SES pursues each year. While our strategic plan identifies some general goals, the plan charges students with creating, monitoring, and executing data-driven goals, with adult mentoring, for sustainability projects – many of which are proposed by students.

Another access point for contributing to our school building's sustainability will be through curriculum. Beginning in the fall semester of the 2021–2022 school year, SES will offer a green building literacy course where students will work to maintain the school's LEED Gold certification. Students will examine data, learn how the building operates through a sustainability lens, and provide recommendations for improvements and new initiatives. The culminating product will be a comprehensive report that summarizes how well SES is doing across a range of sustainability metrics. The course is being developed with support from a U.S. Green Building Council staff member, who is also working to identify mentors in the community who can engage with the lead teacher and students in specific areas, like air quality.

Photo 4.3 Students took markers to poster paper to educate one another about the importance of reducing and sorting our waste. Credit: Lauren Trainer.

SES has also made a commitment to create and nurture partnerships with community organizations to provide students with an array of rich, real-world experiences to complement and deepen their classroom learning. One organization we are reconnecting with is the Minnesota Zoo. Despite being located on the zoo's grounds, and at one time being called the Zoo School, SES has not engaged with the Minnesota Zoo on a regular basis. So, starting with the 2020–2021 school year, our organizations have been working to build a mutually beneficial relationship. An immediate opportunity arose when the zoo received an endowment from a family to eradicate buckthorn from its 40-acre site. Instead of hiring an outside company to complete the job, the zoo approached SES and asked how they could involve our students in attacking this problem. Billy Koenig, Senior Environmental Science Teacher at SES, took the lead on this project and, working with the zoo, created a multi-pronged approach that ties into the curriculum and provides opportunities for students to acquire work skills and get paid by the zoo to do the manual labor. We are also building a partnership with a district elementary school that recently adopted an environmental theme. The goal is for SES students to serve as mentors to the younger students on topics related to environmental education and sustainability.

In addition to looking at our building and operations through a lens of sustainability, we are also exploring how we can shift our curriculum model to one that is more inclusive of sustainability. This is not entirely new territory. SES teachers already integrate the United Nations Sustainable Development Goals into the curriculum, and students participate in a half-day interdisciplinary course – led by a trio of language arts, social studies, and environmental science teachers – where they explore environmental themes through inquiry-based, experiential learning experiences. However, we recognize that we must take an honest look at the two-year student experience and determine what we want our students to learn and take away from their time with us. We also want to meet the needs of students who are showing a greater interest in environmental and social justice issues. As a first step, we hired a consultant through Green Schools National Network at the beginning of the 2020–2021 school year to conduct a curriculum review and work with our teachers to update their instructional practices with a focus on serving a more diverse student community. Despite an interruption in this work due to the COVID-19 pandemic, we noticed the addition of elective classes to our schedule has allowed us to tackle more of the sustainability issues we care about during the school day. We scored an early win in November 2020 when our school board approved three new courses in green building literacy (mentioned previously), land management, and environmental justice, all set to launch during the fall semester of the 2021–2022 school year.

Lessons Learned

Shifting to a whole school sustainability mindset is a long-term commitment, and SES is in it for the long haul. I know the work ahead will not be easy. Our journey so far has been messy and imperfect. It is not the happy story of a school getting together and seamlessly implementing a powerful practice that is changing the world. But we are making progress, and I see signs that we are on the right track every day.

I have learned many things throughout this experience, but one lesson stands out above the rest. That lesson is you need to have courage. I believed from the start that SES could and should embody sustainability practices, from the building to the curriculum. I had the courage to follow through on this belief and persevere because I believed it was the right thing to do for our school, our students, and our community. The more I embodied this courage and built the confidence in my staff that whole school sustainability was possible, the more we were able to accomplish without letting dissent or pushback stand in our way.

I also had the courage to ask for what I needed to make things happen. We would never have gotten our whole school sustainability efforts off the ground without Dakota County's help and willingness to change the terms of their grant. If I did not have the courage to speak up, SES would have ended up with a stack of recycling bins. Instead, we received a facilitator who helped us write our sustainability strategic plan. As a bonus, Dakota County is sticking with the new grant model having recognized that giving people the "what" before they know the "how" is not helpful or sustainable. SES is proud to have influenced that change so other schools can benefit as well.

Photo 4.4 Students bring leftover food from lunch out to the compost bin SES shares with the community partnership garden. Gardeners use the compost created to fertilize their crops. Credit: Lauren Trainer.

Learning from the School of Environmental Studies: Bringing a Whole School Sustainability Mindset to Your School

Taking the time to slow down and take baby steps helped SES tackle the larger goal of moving toward a whole school sustainability mindset. Here are a few ways your school can follow our lead in support of whole school sustainability.

- **Start with the basics.** If you want students to have concrete evidence that they are contributing toward a sustainability effort, start with easy things like food waste or recycling. With foundational elements in place, you can begin to tackle larger, more complex projects.

- **Bring a comprehensive group of stakeholders to the table.** Miss a key stakeholder and you risk missing potential barriers and opportunities only they can surface. In our case, having the building chief and food service manager at the table when we started our conversations with Dakota County was huge. By empowering Sam and Lisa and including them early in our efforts, they felt respected and were willing to work with us to develop a feasible plan.
- **Involve students throughout the process.** Honoring student voice is critical, and students have a lot to contribute, if you let them. Give them a seat at the table during the strategic planning process, include them on your green team, and ensure they have multiple ways to contribute to building-wide sustainability goals.
- **Make whole school sustainability a priority.** Put it on your calendar and make a conscious effort to make things happen. Also, having a dedicated group of people who hold each other accountable to say this is a priority is vital. At SES, those who played a role in creating our sustainability strategic plan continue to stay involved and hold regular meetings. Bottom line: you must make time for whole school sustainability or it will not happen.
- **Network, network, network.** Make the time to get out and connect with others. The more conversations we have with outside organizations, the more unintended opportunities for students that arise. People want to give and be part of the work we are doing.

Synthesis

More than two years have passed since we began our journey to whole school sustainability at SES. Harmonie and McKenzie are now seniors. New students are taking up the mantle for sustainability by learning from Harmonie, McKenzie, and other green team leaders. It is now the norm for all 400 SES students to sort their waste each day. Celebrating one small barrel of garbage and two of recycling – and trying to beat yesterday's amounts – is part of our culture. Sure, we have room to grow, but I feel like we are on the right path. With our sustainability strategic plan in hand and support from our school community, I am confident that whole school sustainability will flourish at SES. We just have to take it one step at a time.

Relevant Websites

School of Environmental Studies. Retrieved from: https://ses.district196.
org/

Curriculum and Instruction

The content that schools teach shapes how students view their world and engage with the people, places, and ecosystems that surround them. Curriculum that addresses the challenges and issues that students are and will be facing will prepare them to lead and live in a just and sustainable future. Culturally relevant curriculum does just that because it is engaging, experiential, interdisciplinary, and purposeful. It builds student confidence AND competence in the knowledge and skills they need to be agents of change for social and environmental justice.

Leaders and educators who work at schools that practice whole school sustainability plan for and implement curriculum and instructional practices that focus on health, equity, and sustainability. This includes putting in place structures, such as professional development, strategic hires, and curriculum maps, that support and nurture an integrated approach to curriculum design and delivery. They also use instructional practices that include phenomena-, place-, project-, and problem-based learning to increase student engagement, deepen learning, and breathe life into standards.

This section features four case studies that illustrate how curriculum and instruction is being leveraged to promote health, equity, and sustainability, thus preparing students to be sustainability champions.

DOI: 10.4324/9781003152811-6

"Places, Projects, and Problems, Oh My! An Integrated Approach to Sustainability Curriculum at Prairie Crossing Charter School" describes how Prairie Crossing Charter School adopted an integrated approach to its curriculum through an increased focus on place-project-problem-based learning (P³BL) using a sustainability lens. You will learn how Prairie Crossing teachers adapted education for sustainability (EfS) standards for a K-8 setting and created grade-level units that incorporate P³BL and EfS, illustrated by specific grade-level examples.

"Planting Seeds for Engaged 21st-Century Citizens: Civic Education through Place-Based Education at The Cottonwood School of Civics and Science" describes how the Cottonwood School of Civics and Science has embedded civic education and engagement into their place-based education (PBE) program. You will learn about the steps that school leaders and teachers took to build an authentic PBE program and find examples that show how they are using PBE to teach civics across the grades.

"Student-Centered Assessment Empowers Students as Agents of Positive Change for a Just and Sustainable Future" describes how New Roots Charter School has implemented a student-centered assessment process using a sustainability lens. You will learn how New Roots developed a set of core practices for student-centered assessment that map with the school's educating for sustainability focus, and how these practices are being applied through student engagement in the Cayuga Wetlands Restoration Project.

"California's Plumas County Connects Students to Place through Outdoor Core Mountain Kid" describes how Plumas County Unified School District implemented a hands-on, outdoor place-based learning program called Outdoor Core Mountain Kid. You will learn about the program's origins, the structures that were put in place to ensure its success and sustainability, and the grade-level themes and experiences that students engage in as they progress from grade to grade.

Places, Projects, and Problems, Oh My!

An Integrated Approach to Sustainability Curriculum at Prairie Crossing Charter School

Naomi Dietzel Hershiser

Prairie Crossing Charter School

Location: Grayslake, Illinois

Number of students: 432 students in grades K-8

Student demographics: 68% White; 15% Asian; 8% Hispanic/Latino; 5% Multiracial; 3% Black/African American; <1% Native American

2012 U.S. Department of Education Green Ribbon School Awardee

2017 Best of Green Schools Award Winner

The air crackles with equal parts excitement and nerves as Megan Ottaviani's third- and fourth-grade students practice one last time for their school board presentation on the use of herbicides. A few giggles escape, their eyes dart nervously, but they are intent on mastering their presentation. They lean over, compare notes on index cards, and work through the final

DOI: 10.4324/9781003152811-7

details. That night, the students present in front of a room of adults including faculty, parents, and school board members from Prairie Crossing Charter School. They confidently deliver an impassioned plea for a policy change concerning the use of Round-Up on campus. Their effective planning pays off. The school board passes a resolution in favor of responsible chemical use.

The students' presentation was the culmination of weeks of work spent researching glyphosate's (Round-Up) impacts on the environment and human health and identifying healthy, economically viable alternatives. The issue hits close to home for these students. They can see many of the raised beds that are used to grow food on Prairie Crossing's campus outside their classroom windows. They use the food as ingredients in classroom cooking projects, enjoy it as part of farm-to-table lunches, and donate some of it to a local food pantry. The students also work in those gardens, digging their hands in the soil and caring for the plants. This personal connection motivated the students to learn and, ultimately, take action to make a positive change in their community.

The Round-Up project is a prime example of place-project-problem-based learning (P³BL), a pedagogical approach that Megan has embraced in her multi-aged classroom. In addition to Round-Up, her students have studied local food issues and used a cider sale to explore the economics of farming and commerce. Megan is not alone in her enthusiasm for P³BL – this integrated approach to learning has become the Prairie Crossing way to keep students engaged while learning rigorous academic content and important 21st-century skills.

A Shift in Pedagogy to Prepare Students for a Sustainable Future

Place-based education and outdoor learning have been central to Prairie Crossing's pedagogy since the school opened in 1999. An environmentally focused public charter school, Prairie Crossing was founded on the idea that nature is an important and powerful teacher and that learning in and from nature is key to developing environmental literacy and a sense of place. Our location within a nationally recognized conservation community has allowed our teachers to weave meaningful outdoor learning experiences into the curriculum, everything from solo sit-spots and nature journaling to phenology lessons, where students collect and analyze data related to seasonal changes.

Yet, as a faculty, we knew that we could do more to increase academic rigor and prepare students for the future they will inherit. This recognition led us to make two significant shifts to our curriculum in 2017. First, we expanded our environmental focus to include the other two Es of sustainability: equity and economic prosperity. Environmental degradation is a serious problem that goes hand-in-hand with social strife and economic instability. Because these issues are interrelated, students need to understand the importance and impact of all three to successfully navigate the future.

Second, we decided to adopt a more integrated approach to our curriculum by increasing our use of P^3BL units. Our teachers had witnessed how impactful this pedagogical approach could be through participating in several high-quality service-learning projects over the years. Their experiences, as well as our deepening engagement with like-minded schools through Green Schools National Network's Catalyst Network, inspired us to incorporate P^3BL units strategically and regularly across all grade levels.

Developing an Integrated P^3BL Curriculum Grounded in Sustainability

The first step we took in our curriculum transition was to set a goal – *Prairie Crossing Charter School demonstrates growth each year on all academic standards through an integrated curriculum grounded in education for sustainability, service learning, and place-project-problem-based learning (P³BL)*. Once our goal was in place, we formed a curriculum committee in late 2017. The committee was led by the Dean for Environmental Learning with faculty representatives from across all grade levels. Committee members researched and learned about P^3BL strategies and created rubrics to help teachers recognize and create high-quality P^3BL units. These rubrics provide guidance to ensure all units contain a challenging and authentic problem, standards-based learning, inquiry, student choice/voice, ample opportunity for reflection, and an appropriate product.

Next, the curriculum committee dove into the Cloud Institute for Sustainability Education's Education for a Sustainable Future: Benchmarks for Individual and Social Learning (EfS Benchmarks). Finalized in 2017, the EfS Benchmarks lay out the skills, applied knowledge, applications/actions, dispositions, and community connections that define the essential elements of EfS. The curriculum committee focused its work on the applied knowledge (i.e., content standards – the other elements were addressed as we worked to achieve our other goals). These include descriptions of what students should understand upon graduation in the following areas:

- Inventing the Future
- Laws and Principles that Govern the Physical and Biological World
- Strong Sense of Place
- Cultures, Traditions, and Change
- Many Ways of Knowing
- Healthy Commons
- System Dynamics and Change
- Responsible Local and Global Citizenship
- Multiple Perspectives
- Sustainable Economics

The committee's primary task was to convert these complex standards into teacher- and student-friendly language for use in a K-8 setting. In their original form, the standards are not broken down by grade level. This made it hard for our lower grade teachers to know what building blocks would be needed early on to achieve the desired understandings by the end of twelfth grade. The committee's solution was to develop a series of content standard summaries that simplified the original language. The teaching staff used these summaries to create a matrix of age-appropriate learning targets for each EfS standard, across all grades and subject areas. These tools have allowed us to modify and create units, one at a time, to fully incorporate P³BL and EfS into our curriculum.

A new third/fourth-grade economics unit provides an example of how teachers thought through this process. In 2017, Illinois released new social studies standards that included a greater focus on economics. This presented an ideal opportunity to address a gap in our curriculum while applying our newly adopted EfS-based P³BL approach. Teachers started with the learning standards ("Describe how goods and services are produced using human, natural, and capital resources" and "Analyze how spending choices are influenced by price as well as many other factors"). They examined the EfS standards to find relevant tie-ins, including ideas in the Sustainable Economics standard about true costs (and hidden ones!) and making informed consumer decisions.

Teachers wanted to ensure that this unit was grounded in place and provided opportunities to learn from the land and the community. They also wanted students to engage in a hands-on experience with economics and working with money. In the end, they decided that local food was an ideal vehicle for meeting the unit's goals. Students would assess the true costs of their food choices – on their pocketbooks, their personal health, and the local economy. Classes focused on local food production, the impact of food miles, and the movement to support local farmers and producers.

As part of their learning, students met with a local organic farmer who runs a CSA and farm stand. They learned about financial considerations for farming and seasonality that many had not considered before. Students also visited a local apple orchard and learned about the production, marketing, and sale of apple cider. The unit culminated in students hosting a hot apple cider sale at school. They budgeted and set prices – including a discount for BYO mug customers. They advertised their sale and organized the logistics of giving the entire school community an opportunity to participate. They even applied to the "bank" (school business office) for a loan to cover their expenses prior to earning any funds! After the sale was over and their loans were repaid, the students donated the proceeds to local charities, which were selected by the students.

This project was extremely engaging and checked all the boxes. It met content-area standards in social studies and incorporated math (budgeting and food miles) and ELA (research, writing advertising copy). It addressed several issues related to sustainability. It was very much based in place, used local community resources, and culminated in a student-run project. Students even contributed to the broader community through their donation after the project was complete.

An Integrated EfS-Based P³BL Approach in Practice

With a foundation in place and tools to guide them, our teachers felt more confident in their ability to incorporate EfS-based P³BL units into their curriculum. Starting in 2018, they began to transition to an EfS-based P³BL approach in earnest. Since then, across our entire K-8 scope and sequence, they have worked to modify, overhaul, or replace units to include components of P³BL and tie in EfS standards. The following examples illustrate some of the ways we are incorporating this approach throughout our curriculum.

Kindergarten

Starting in the 2019–2020 school year, our kindergarten teachers added a citizen science component to their weather unit using the GLOBE Observer app. In prior years, students studied weather and collected data daily to record patterns over time and practice their writing and communication skills. Now, students gather data such as cloud type and percentage of sky covered and submit it with photos via the GLOBE Observer: Clouds tool. The data is used by scientists to study changes in clouds over time. This citizen science component makes data collection more meaningful to students by involving an authentic audience and teaches them how citizen scientists play an important role in advancing scientific knowledge.

First/Second Grade

Every two years, first- and second-grade classes do a P³BL unit focused on our garden's produce. Some of the produce is used for cooking projects like making salsa. During the 2018–2019 school year, students were challenged to find a way to use up a large quantity of dried beans they grew and harvested. Their solution was to hold a soup-in-a-jar sale. Students worked in teams to create soup kits; set a budget; develop marketing materials such as posters, commercials, and informational videos; and distribute their product. They even planned and hosted a cross-promotional meal as part of our farm-to-table lunch program. Classes discussed local production and consumption and learned about ecosystem goods and services. At the same time, students learned about growing cycles and gardening techniques and used their writing and communication skills to market their soup. This unit is now a permanent part of the first/second-grade curriculum.

Photo 5.1 First- and second-graders add ingredients to mason jars to create their soup-in-a-jar products. Credit: Naomi Dietzel Hershiser.

Third/Fourth Grade

Third- and fourth-graders learn about Illinois history and the lives of native inhabitants from Cahokia through modern day as part of their social studies curriculum. This unit has a strong hands-on, place-based experiential component that includes visits from local Potawatomi who teach students traditional skills and help them understand current Native culture and issues. However, the unit did not contain a strong project/product element. So, during the 2020–2021 school year, our third/fourth-grade teachers decided to complete the P³BL approach to the unit by adding a Native Land Acknowledgements project. For this project, students researched Native Land Acknowledgements and then wrote one for Prairie Crossing. It is now used during school events and announcements and is on display throughout our campus.

Photo 5.2 Third- and fourth-grade students display first drafts of their Native Land Acknowledgement signs. Credit: Naomi Dietzel Hershiser.

Fifth Grade

A fifth-grade P³BL unit focuses on the study of pollinators. Students learn about interrelationships between plants and animals through in-person observations, reading, and watching videos. They connect with local partners such as Liberty Prairie Foundation and Prairie Crossing Farm to visit their sites and see how they care for and encourage pollinators. They also add pollinator plants, such as purple coneflower and bergamot, to our school's landscape each year. During the 2020–2021 school year, students learned about garden design and native plants and created garden plans for an area in front of their classroom building. A composite of their design won a grant from the Department of Natural Resources to fund planting materials for these garden areas, which were planted in May 2021.

Sixth Grade

Sixth-graders completed a hydroponics P³BL unit during the 2019–2020 school year that culminated in the installation of a hydroponic system on campus. Students researched hydroponic systems by reading articles and watching DIY videos. They gave presentations to each other on several options, including ready-made products and built designs, and selected Tower Gardens. They sought approval from administrators for a location, budget, and their design of choice and then installed the gardens themselves throughout the school year. As the project evolves, future focus areas will include fair distribution of greens to students, system maintenance, and choosing what crops to grow. Ultimately, these hydroponic gardens will help students make healthier eating choices and encourage consumption of local food.

Seventh/Eighth Grade

Seventh-graders learn about land use, change over time, and chemistry by studying water, air, and soil quality. Students learn to read and interpret Air Quality Index scores and test soil for acidity/alkalinity. They test water quality by conducting chloride, nitrate, and pH tests; look at turbidity; and determine a biotic index of water health by catching and identifying macroinvertebrates. They use this information to create written recommendations for the local homeowner's association, noting common pollutants they know or suspect might be in the water and what actions they might take.

Eighth-grade math classes study statistics, graphing, and data analysis using a sustainability lens. Students examine climate data, create and analyze graphs, and draw conclusions regarding impacts of climate change. They also analyze census data and make connections to the United Nations Sustainable Development Goals (SDGs). They compare census categories to the SDGs and discuss how census information can be used to measure progress in meeting the SDGs. Media literacy is woven into this unit, as students use examples from TV and print news to examine how the same data can be presented in different ways to convey different messages and impressions.

Photo 5.3 Middle school students catch macroinvertebrates to assess water quality. Credit: Naomi Dietzel Hershiser.

A Progression of EfS-Based P³BL Units at Prairie Crossing

Grade Level	Illinois Priority Learning Standards and EfS Standards	Place	Authentic Problem	Authentic Project
Kinder-garten	IPLS: Earth's systems – weather patterns EfS: Responsible Local and Global Citizenship; Laws and Principles that Govern the Physical and Biological World; Sense of Place	Students observe weather in their outdoor classroom.	How can students' observations help scientists and be used for authentic research?	Students keep a weather journal and serve as citizen scientists by entering cloud data in the GLOBE Observer app.
First/ Second Grade	IPLS: Economic decision-making and financial literacy; budgeting; plant life cycles; writing instructions EfS: Sustainable Economics; Sense of Place	Students plant, harvest, and care for bean plants in the school's raised-bed garden.	How can students use the beans they harvested from the garden?	Students make and sell soup-in-a-jar kits.
Third/ Fourth Grade	IPLS: Human geography; historical perspectives EfS: Cultures, Traditions, and Change; Many Ways of Knowing; Sense of Place	Students learn about previous human inhabitants of the land they occupy and participate in authentic Native skills and activities on and around campus.	How can students help Prairie Crossing acknowledge the original human inhabitants of our campus?	Students research and write Native Land Acknowledgements for use in school events and display on campus.

(Continued)

79

Grade Level	Illinois Priority Learning Standards and EfS Standards	Place	Authentic Problem	Authentic Project
Fifth Grade	IPLS: Interdependent relationships and transfer of energy in ecosystems; budgeting and aesthetics of garden design; writing for an audience; mapping skills EfS: Laws and Principles that Govern the Physical and Biological World; Responsible Local and Global Citizenship; Sense of Place; Healthy Commons	Students observe pollinators and plant native plants in the schoolyard and at home.	How can students increase local pollinator populations?	Students design a pollinator garden, submit a grant to fund it, and plant the pollinator garden on campus.
Sixth Grade	IPLS: Water cycle; research and present information EfS: Responsible Local and Global Citizenship; Sense of Place; System Dynamics and Change	Students think about food production year-round in our climate.	How can students grow food on campus year-round?	Students research and purchase hydroponic systems and grow lettuce throughout the year.
Seventh Grade	IPLS: Land use; change over time; chemistry/water quality; writing for an audience EfS: Responsible Local and Global Citizenship; Laws and Principles Governing the Natural and Physical World; Sense of Place; Healthy Commons; System Dynamics and Change; Inventing the Future	Students test water quality in local lakes within walking distance from school.	How can students use water quality data to learn about local lakes and make recommendations for water treatment?	Students write and present recommendations to the local homeowner's association about water quality in the lakes.

Grade Level	Illinois Priority Learning Standards and EfS Standards	Place	Authentic Problem	Authentic Project
Eighth Grade	IPLS: Data analysis and statistics EfS: Healthy Commons; Responsible Local and Global Citizenship, Inventing the Future	Students relate learning to current relevant news coverage of the census.	How can students relate news coverage of census and climate data to the SDGs?	Students create hallway displays of important data (with graphs/ visuals) and analyze it in written reflections.

P³BL units in kindergarten through sixth grade pave the way for students to complete culminating service-learning projects during their seventh- and eighth-grade years. Prior to graduation, each student, working alone or in pairs, tackles an environmental issue of interest to them. Students assess community needs, think about their passions and talents, and complete a project that involves a solution to a real-world problem. Past projects include installing butterfly gardens at the local library, removing invasive garlic mustard, teaching local preschool children about recycling, and holding electronics recycling drives. A foundation of P³BL throughout their years at Prairie Crossing gives students the skills they need to succeed with these more independent projects.

Impact on Students and Teachers

Although we are still in the early stages of our shift to an EfS-based P³BL approach, the impact on student learning and engagement has been significant. Megan, who oversaw the Round-Up project, shares, "These projects are authentic and un-siloed, so social studies and science can be interconnected with ELA. Students gain essential collaboration, communication, and critical-thinking skills as they identify solutions to real-world problems in creative ways. They get to be leaders in small groups and learn to function as a team" (Ottaviani, 2020).

Even more important is student motivation. Students learn "without even realizing they're doing work!" The classroom feels like a place where students have chosen to come, rather than a place where they have to be. "Students respect the process and the intentionality of P³BL units," Megan reports. "In traditional classes, they don't always understand why they're learning what they're learning. They appreciate having a context for their learning, and there's deeper learning because they're actively engaged, and because it has real-world relevance" (Ottaviani, 2020).

It is also worth noting that switching to an EfS-based P³BL pedagogy has changed Megan as a teacher, too. "I feel like I am part of the learning process with the students, rather than being their instructor" (Ottaviani, 2020). Just like her students, Megan is excited to come to school during these units and loves to see her students create and problem-solve. A happy and motivated teacher leads to motivated and successful students!

Lessons Learned

The Prairie Crossing community recognizes the importance of implementing EfS-based P³BL units and has made it a priority. As with any major change, the transition to teaching primarily EfS-based P³BL units has been a long-term process, and the work continues. Many challenges have arisen. However, as benefits are realized and classroom culture normalizes this type of learning, these challenges have become smaller and more conquerable.

One major challenge is teacher preparation time. Creating high-quality curriculum is time- and mind-consuming work! While a few in-service days are offered throughout the year, and most are dedicated to this work, other solutions are necessary, too. One solution is using school-day release time (i.e., hiring substitute teachers for half days) to allow teacher teams to collaborate and dedicate time to unit creation. Summer stipends are also available for curriculum work.

Another challenge is teacher comfort level. Different teachers have different tolerances for change as well as for the chaos that can accompany student-guided learning and problem-solving in student-centered classrooms. Collaborative grade-level teams who work together to plan and implement instruction have kept everyone moving forward together. The teams help less enthusiastic teachers feel supported and play a valuable role in identifying gaps and weaknesses the group can work on together. Administrative support, including a growth-oriented teacher evaluation system, is also imperative for increasing teacher comfort. If people are afraid of punitive responses to something that does not work perfectly, they will not be willing to try anything new!

A final challenge is staff turnover. It is important to onboard new teachers as they enter the school community. New hires are learning a thousand different things, from their co-workers' names and how the photocopier works to what the curriculum map includes and how the school day is structured. This is a challenge we still struggle with, but prioritizing the whys, hows, and whats of teaching EfS-based P³BL during new-teacher in-service days definitely plays an important role in getting them up-to-speed and ready to dive in. We have also started including this work as part of a mentoring program that takes place during a new hire's first two years of employment, since what is learned early on needs continual reinforcement or it will be lost to the daily challenges of being a new teacher.

Learning from Prairie Crossing Charter School: Implementing an Integrated EfS-Based P³BL Approach at Your School

A schoolwide commitment to adopt an EfS-based P³BL approach made it possible for Prairie Crossing to evolve its teaching pedagogy. Here are a few actions your school can take to begin incorporating EfS-based P³BL units in your curriculum.

- **Start with one unit (or one per grade level).** Trying to overhaul an entire curriculum at once is overwhelming, but one unit feels more achievable. A successful start will give teachers and students a sense of how engaging and worthwhile these experiences can be and will make it easier (and more enjoyable!) to develop subsequent units.
- **Make unit development a priority for professional development.**
  - Give faculty the time and resources to gain a full understanding of EfS and P³BL. This includes time to explore standards, rubrics, and examples that clearly show how standards are met through high-quality P³BL units that incorporate EfS standards. Having staff

participate (as students) in a mini-unit can show them the benefits, as can visiting a school that is already implementing an EfS-based P³BL approach.

- Provide time to collaborate and create units. Teachers are busy and cannot do this work during regular school days or on top of full-time responsibilities to themselves and their families.
- Have experts to turn to for feedback, advice, and ideas. A school instructional coach or curriculum leader can play an important role (assuming that they are motivated and interested in these pedagogies and have knowledge of them). Outside experts can also be invaluable. Our work has been facilitated by Green Schools National Network, whose experts provide fresh eyes, require accountability, and bring new resources and contacts to the table.
- **Create a culture that embraces collaboration and openness.** Give teachers plenty of opportunities and leeway to work in teams and individually to problem-solve, develop ideas, and help each other through challenges. The degree to which people embrace change is partially dependent on the institution's culture. People will not teach in new ways if they are not rewarded for doing so, or if the rewards are far greater for sticking with the status quo.

Synthesis

An EfS-based P³BL pedagogy is that rare thing everyone seeks – a win–win–win! When Megan's students worked to change our school's herbicide policy, her job as a teacher became more rewarding. The teacher wins because her students are motivated and engaged, and she can integrate multiple subject areas meaningfully into one unit of study. The students were excited to learn and make a change at their school. They win because they are invested in their learning and gain valuable citizenship skills while obtaining content-area knowledge. And the world wins because sustainable solutions to problems are enacted by school-age children and will continue to be in the future as these empowered youth become adult citizens.

Works Cited

Ottaviani, M. (2020). Personal communication.

Relevant Websites

Education for a Sustainable Future: Benchmarks for Individual and Social Learning. Retrieved from: https://cloudinstitute.org/efs-benchmarks

Prairie Crossing Charter School. Retrieved from: https://prairiecrossingc-harterschool.org/

Planting Seeds for Engaged 21st-Century Citizens

Civic Education through Place-Based Education at The Cottonwood School of Civics and Science

Sarah Anderson

Cottonwood School of Civics and Science

Urban, place-based charter school that uses the city as a classroom

Location: Portland, Oregon

Number of students: 205 students

Student demographics: 77% White; 9% Hispanic/Latino; 8% Multi-racial; 2% Black/African American; 3% Asian

DOI: 10.4324/9781003152811-8

A visit to Oaks Bottom Wildlife Refuge in Portland, Oregon reveals an urban sanctuary tucked between a city neighborhood and the Willamette River. Once the site of a sanitation landfill, the park is now a restored marsh and woodland teeming with wildlife. Oaks Bottom is an exploration ground for students at the Cottonwood School of Civics and Science. It is here where our students develop a sense of place through play, exploration, and learning.

When we benefit from a place like Oaks Bottom, the natural question for us to ask is, "How can we give back?" When we posed this question to the city ecologist who oversees the refuge, she offered the perfect answer: a compelling problem with a built-in project. The city had decided to remove the small culvert that connects the Oaks Bottom wetland to the Willamette River and replace it with a wider one to encourage spawning salmon to visit. What was uncertain was if the larger culvert would lead to less water in the refuge and how that would impact the waterfowl. Apparently, the city and other organizations were curious about this but did not have the capacity to launch a study. So, our seventh- and eighth-graders took it on.

For several weeks each fall between 2017 and 2019, students took the city bus and then walked the last mile to Oaks Bottom to collect data. Students worked in groups to monitor water and soil quality, identify plants and trees, observe human use of the park, and count birds. Despite bad weather and the tedium that can come with repeated data collection visits, students persevered to present their findings to the city ecologist. Her feedback provided them with an authentic experience as citizen scientists, and their research gave the city helpful information about one of their sites. This story is a great example of a field-science class. What may not be as obvious to some is that it is also a wonderful illustration of civics in action. Through direct engagement with cities, towns, and communities, place-based education (PBE) offers students insights and experience in how to collaboratively care for the places we call home.

The Importance of Civic Education

What is the responsibility of public schools in sustaining our democracy? Successfully preparing our young people means more than training them for high-tech jobs. Future citizens will need to be skilled problem-solvers, communicators, and collaborators to tackle crises such as climate change. They will also need to navigate and appreciate diverse perspectives. Schools can serve as fertile grounds for the next generation of citizens by infusing civic education into the bedrock of their curriculum.

The need for improved approaches to civic education has come to the forefront in the national discussion about the responsibilities of public education. Yet, many educators hold antiquated perceptions of "civics" as simply the study of government. Learning about government is not enough. According to the 2018 Brown Center Report on American Education: An Inventory of State Civics Requirements, "…interactive and participatory components of a civics education are not optional, supplemental, or 'extra' aspects of civics education that are nice to have. Rather, interactive and participatory practices are core components of a high-quality civics education" (Hansen et al., 2018, p. 17). The best way to prepare our children for a life of civic action is to give them the opportunity to practice civic skills in their classrooms, schools, and communities. At Cottonwood School, our place-based approach to civic education deeply connects students to the communities around us and offers hands-on experience with civic engagement.

Laying the Foundation for Place-Based Civic Education at Cottonwood School

Civic engagement and PBE have been embedded in Cottonwood School's vision, mission, and values since our founding in 2007. A group of parents wrote the original school charter after their neighborhood school was closed by the city. They experienced hands-on learning as they navigated the political system of establishing a charter school and decided that students should have similar experiences to help them learn about civic involvement and responsibility. They discovered PBE during this process and integrated the approach into the school's mission.

A critical responsibility of PBE is to honor the diverse human experiences that exist in one place. Only when students recognize the array of experiences and perspectives in their community can they effectively understand how best to help others and engage in the work. Community building is at the heart of PBE at Cottonwood School. We strive to build strong community in the classroom, with families, and with partnering agencies, organizations, and neighbors. We work with our partners to construct curricular projects that meet the needs of our community, thus integrating our students further into the "outside" world and making their work more relevant.

From the very beginning, we were committed to the idea that a child's world grows as they grow. Inspired by the work of David Sobel (2013), our students learn about and explore places that expand in concentric circles with each grade level: from home and family at the youngest age, to school, neighborhood, city, region, country, and world. Coordinating scope in line with a child's evolving understanding of the world allows us to create a developmentally appropriate approach to learning about place. But it was not until we added a half-time PBE coordinator to our staff in 2014 that we received the support we needed to build an authentic place-based program.

We took a multi-year approach to improve our PBE program. One of our first steps was to create a schoolwide curriculum map for our science and social studies units. Over two days, our teachers examined state and federal science and social studies standards, teased out the skills-based standards from the content-based standards, and used them as building blocks for our map. We used content-based standards to identify unit topics and placed them so that they grow and develop over a students' time at Cottonwood. For example, students learn about salmon and river health in first/second grades, they apply a wider lens to learn about watersheds in fourth/fifth grades, and they dive in-depth into ecosystems and sustainability in seventh/eighth grades. Skills-based standards were used to construct learning goals, assessments, and progress reports.

Next, we designed a curricular unit planning sheet to help teachers design their projects. Our PBE coordinator worked closely with teachers during this process and helped identify potential community partners. The coordinator met with partners to find projects that would be mutually beneficial to both organizations and coordinated logistics, like site visits, field trips, and guest speakers. After the first few years, it became easier to coordinate projects because we could rely on existing partnerships and unit plans. However, without the PBE coordinator, it would be much more difficult to be true to our mission.

A Grade-Level Progression for Place-Based Civic Education

Place-based projects at Cottonwood School are grounded in the history, environment, and people of Portland and the Pacific Northwest. Each trimester concentrates on key concepts anchored in social studies or science and sometimes both. Reading, writing, public speaking, art, and geography skills are heavily embedded into project work. Through an integrated approach, students go deep into a topic over an extended period of time. This allows them to learn the complexities of an issue while discovering how components naturally connect with other concepts. We apply the lenses of social justice and eco-justice to all units, and all units incorporate skills and content essential to civic education. As students advance from grade to grade, they not only develop a deeper understanding of their place but also learn and practice the skills needed for problem-solving, community collaboration, and advocacy.

Grades K-2: Learning Close to Home

In our youngest grades, students learn from each other and from surrounding neighborhoods to construct a rich understanding of family and community. These essential understandings, along with a few necessary skills, build the basis for civic literacy at Cottonwood School.

A kindergartener's sense of place is mostly limited to family, home, and school, which makes this a perfect time for students to explore who they are in relationship to others. This starts with fostering an appreciation for diversity and creating a classroom culture that allows students to authentically contribute and be heard. The beginning of the school year is spent practicing routines that solicit student participation and build an empowered sense of community. Students co-create the class agreements, practice problem-solving circles and small group mediations, and share individual and family experiences through class lessons and activities. These practices are built on and nurtured at every grade level.

As kindergarteners build confidence in their voice and identity, they create an exhibit for a class museum that includes artifacts that teach about their culture and/or identity. Drawings and other reflections are included,

Photo 6.1 Class agreements from Kimberley Bonder's kindergarten classroom. Students brainstormed and discussed what would be included in the agreements for several class periods before creating this poster. Credit: Sarah Anderson.

along with a paper "quilt" crafted from student family portraits. Family members, caregivers, and friends are invited to the museum, extending the learning into the wider community. Adults and children may not recognize this as "civic education," but it is. Learning about and from the people in your community is one of the most fundamental responsibilities of a democracy.

In first and second grades, the scope of "place" expands to include the local neighborhood. Students construct a classroom model of a neighborhood based on prior knowledge and research they conduct through field trips and reading books. Trips include a tour of a local apartment building and retirement home; visits to a bank, a fire station, a library, and a hospital; and travel on the Portland streetcar. As students visit various locations, they are asked to consider how institutions like banks, hospitals, and libraries help the community. Responses are recorded and added to an ongoing list that is posted in the classroom.

Photo 6.2 A brainstorm list of student responses in a first- and second-grade class-room. Students will come back to this list throughout the neighborhood unit to make revisions based on new experiences and knowledge. Credit: Nesa Levy.

Photo 6.3 First- and second-graders visit a Portland fire station. Credit: Chris Beckley.

As students build their model and create characters who live and work in the neighborhood, teachers introduce problems for them to solve. Where can residents find food if they are hungry? How can we fix traffic jams? Students work together to grapple with these issues and identify solutions to include in their model. Sometimes, students discover inconsistencies between their model neighborhood and the neighborhood outside our doors. Our model has a grocery store, but our neighborhood does not. Why is that? Our model includes a library, but we must travel downtown to visit the closest one. How come? Students ask these questions when community planners visit their classroom and the answers give them a glimpse into public discourse and the decision-making processes used by civic agencies.

Students wrap up the neighborhood unit by identifying a community need and proposing a solution they could implement. One year, students created a coloring book about the neighborhood for children moving into local apartment buildings. Another year, students worked with a partnering construction company to design and build a "Little Free Library," installed outside the school gates. In addition to these projects, other community partnerships are

Photo 6.4 Pancake Court, a neighborhood designed by Nesa Levy's class of first- and second-graders at Cottonwood School. The neighborhood includes a school, public parks, and an aerial tram. Credit: Sarah Anderson.

woven into the school year to strengthen the relationship between students and the neighborhood. For example, we developed a "Reading Buddies" program where students visit a nearby retirement home once a month to read with their resident "buddy" and we partnered with the city's Parks and Recreation Department so students can maintain an area of natural land near the school. These ongoing experiences with civic engagement and service help students construct a deeper understanding of community and how even the youngest community members have a role to play.

Grades 3–5: Exploring Regional Geography, History, and Indigenous Culture

In third- through fifth-grades, the scope of place expands across space and time to encompass a wider look at our region's history, environment, and people. At the same time, students deepen their civic engagement skills involving collaboration, public speaking, and navigating diverse perspectives.

For the past several years, third-graders have partnered with a local rocks and minerals museum to create learning materials for their display. One year, the class created a scavenger hunt that led visitors to learn more about the fossil collection. Another year, students assembled a timeline of the Earth for one of the exhibit rooms. The class also has a partnership with Portland State University's archaeology department and participates in their annual Archaeology Roadshow. This event brings together exhibitors from around the region who have a connection to public archeology and local history. Our students are the only ones below college level to host a booth. Presenting student-made materials to a partner agency or sharing with adult visitors at a public event takes learning to another level. Young people gain confidence in their ability to speak and present information publicly, skills often necessary for civic involvement.

During the spring semester, third-graders learn about native plants from the perspective of Indigenous cultures who have tended and harvested food plants since time immemorial. Students learn from Indigenous educators and see the relationship between Native people and the land as a present-day relationship, not something from the past. Students also learn how stewardship practices established by local tribes are being used today to restore health to Oregon's forests and waterways. For example, reinstating burns conducted by Native peoples to maintain oak savannas in the Willamette River valley and doing more to protect old-growth trees could help prevent devastating forest fires. Learning how to best help the community means being willing to learn from more than one way of knowing.

Building on the third-grade curriculum, fourth- and fifth-graders delve deeper into Oregon's people and geography. Over the course of two years, students investigate watersheds, regional ecozones, the ocean, and Oregon history from a place-based perspective. This means we explore the region's history from the standpoint of looking east, instead of the traditional view of "Westward Expansion." Students learn about Indigenous history and the tribes of today. Studying ongoing conflicts and injustices that have taken place between tribes and settler colonists leads to introductory conversations about federal and state policy and the nature of citizenship. Students read fiction and non-fiction, write poetry and research papers, and analyze primary sources to deepen their understanding of Oregon's peoples.

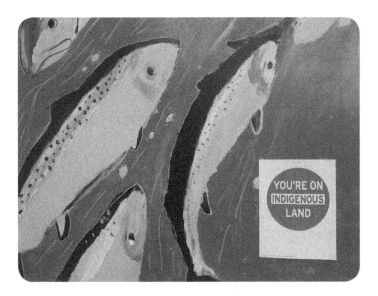

Photo 6.5 A land acknowledgement flyer posted by Fawn Morosky's third-grade class. This was part of a larger project exploring local Indigenous cultures and current events. Credit: Sarah Anderson.

Photo 6.6 Clifton Bruno (Confederated Tribes of Warm Springs) shares family stories and ecological knowledge with a group of students. Credit: Christine Bruno.

One year, as part of the watershed unit, students explored a local creek from its headwaters to its confluence with the Willamette River. Near the confluence, they found that a long, narrow culvert was preventing salmon and other fish from going up the creek to spawn. A local conservation group asked if our students would be interested in writing letters to their U.S. representatives in support of a bill that would replace the culvert with a highway overpass, providing more access for wildlife. Students learned how to format and write a formal letter, including how to make a claim and back it up with evidence and reasoning. We later learned that our students' letters had a profound impact on the congressional delegation, who voted to fund the project.

Grades 6–8: Making Local, National, and Global Connections

Our sixth- through eighth-grade curriculum introduces students to national and global topics while striking a balance with local connection. At this age, students are prepared to apply their knowledge and skills to real-world investigations and problem-solving.

One of our place-based goals at Cottonwood School is for students to better know their city and the people who live in it. In sixth grade, we teach the history of Portland's Black community, from the original state constitution which made it illegal for Black people to live in Oregon to ongoing issues such as police brutality and housing discrimination. The lack of racial diversity in Portland is directly linked to racist laws and policies established early in the state's history. Students study primary documents, watch documentaries, interview classroom speakers, and conduct field work to uncover Portland's history of redlining and segregation, while also learning about individual leaders, victories, and current events. This history has not traditionally been taught in Portland schools, but is necessary learning to help all residents gain a richer and more accurate understanding of the city's past and present.

For years, our seventh- and eighth-graders have engaged in Project Citizen, a program where students identify and research a community problem and then propose a policy-based solution which they attempt to enact. Students have investigated problems such as pet owners not picking up after their dogs, smoking in public parks, unpaved roads, the housing crisis, traffic congestion, and unsafe playgrounds. Classes have presented to city commissioners, testified at city hall, and explained their project to judges at the state house. Nothing raises the bar on student work more than preparing an oral presentation for commissioners at city hall!

As part of the process, students identify who has a stake in the problem. Who in the community agrees that this is a problem and why? Who disagrees? They do this again when vetting their proposed solution. Who would support our solution and why? Who would oppose it and why? This step may involve conducting interviews, writing letters, or giving surveys, all of which offer opportunities to teach essential literacy, math, and sometimes science skills.

Seeking out an issue's "players" and delving into their individual reasoning is enormously valuable for middle school students. It is easy to make assumptions about why someone disagrees with your point of view without taking time to ask questions and consider their answers. This research sometimes leads students to extend more understanding and empathy to their opposition. At the very least, it allows them to construct a stronger counter-argument. Either way, they come out of the experience with a better grasp of how to navigate the policy-making process within a diverse democracy.

Lessons Learned

Creating a place-based civics program is a continual learning process. As our program develops and grows, we adjust and sometimes scrap things altogether. Experience and trial and error are often the best teachers!

Our steepest learning curve has concerned Indigenous studies. Creating authentic connections between the classroom and Indigenous experiences requires time and intentionality. Supported by grant funding, our school is nearing the end of a three-year project to better incorporate Indigenous perspectives across our curriculum. The first year was dedicated to teacher professional development. We attended workshops led by Indigenous educators, visited significant cultural sites, and delved into books about local and national topics. Robin Wall Kimmerer's (2015) *Braiding Sweetgrass: Indigenous Wisdom, Scientific Knowledge, and the Teaching of Plants* was an excellent common text as we reevaluated how we taught science and history. We are currently creating an Indigenous studies curriculum map along with learning kits based on lessons from the state of Oregon and local tribes (mandated and funded by the state legislature in 2017 and implemented in classrooms in 2020). An essential part of this work involves reaching out to and building relationships with tribal representatives and educators. These relationships will guide us as we continue to reconsider and construct integrated studies that include Indigenous perspectives.

This professional development is already transforming our teaching practice. Several years ago, our third-grade study of local tribes was nested within a larger archeology unit, but the dangers of placing Indigenous experiences primarily in the past support the myth that Native Americans are extinct. We now begin our unit with current events and local issues. Partnerships with local groups, such as Confluence, help us bring Indigenous educators into the classroom and our students into the field.

Another important lesson learned is how instrumental partnership building is in PBE, and how much time it takes. This is where the PBE coordinator position is key. Teachers often do not have time to reach out to community organizations and agencies; nor do they have time to schedule and attend planning meetings and pre-project site visits. Some organizations have little experience working with schools or may not have the resources or capacity to work with a school or a group of students. Without a coordinator who can make contacts, screen potential partners, and identify project needs and goals, many of our projects would not happen.

Successful field work needs lots of scaffolding. Our teachers are no strangers to taking students into the community. In a typical year, our school leads over 100 field trips – so we have had lots of practice! Over time, we have strengthened the supports and structures around field work. Our students spend several weeks at the beginning of the school year practicing norms for such actions as walking on the sidewalk, crossing the street, and riding on the streetcar. They also practice how to prepare for and show appreciation to guest speakers. Teachers have created tip sheets for guest speakers to help them prepare and lead a session that everyone can benefit from. Just like anything else, the more we practice, the easier it gets.

Learning from the Cottonwood School of Civics and Science: Bringing Place-Based Civic Education to Your School

Cottonwood School prepares students for future civic success using a place-based lens. Here are some ways to create fertile ground for powerful place-based civic education at your school.

- **Establish routines to build classroom community.** Practices such as morning meetings and student-created community agreements lay the groundwork for having meaningful conversations and emotional safety.
- **Give students a voice.** Young people cannot become engaged citizens without practice. Nor can they be expected to have the confidence to add their voice to the conversation if they are not invited. Think about how you can add student voice to your classroom, from how you set "rules" to how you determine the curriculum. Learning about rights and responsibilities within a community is a key part of this.
- **Honor diverse perspectives.** This means more than acknowledging different points of view when they arise. It means seeking out diverse perspectives and experiences and teaching students how to navigate differences. It also means fostering an appreciation for our differences while recognizing our similarities.

- **Integrate civics into core subjects.** Civics does not need to be (and perhaps *should* not be) a stand-alone class, but a topic that is integrated into other subjects just as literacy and science are. Consider how you can weave questions about community, citizenship, and student action into novel studies or current events. How can your students take action on climate change or racial injustice at school or in the community?
- **Do not forget your local governments.** People primarily engage with government at the town, city, and county levels, so the more students know about how they work, the more confident they will be to engage with them. Do not leave out tribal governments; it is important to know that tribes are separate from local, state, and federal governments, reinforcing the concept of tribal sovereignty.
- **Start small.** You do not need a PBE coordinator to do place-based civics. Start by adding one or two place-based elements, like inviting a guest speaker or going on a field trip. Add something new every year, and eventually, you will be able to manage a more comprehensive project. It takes time and that is okay!

Synthesis

When our seventh- and eighth-graders visited Oaks Bottom to collect data, they were learning how to be scientists AND how to care for public land. When the students prepared a report for the city ecologist, they were practicing math and literacy skills and learning how to share their work with an official who makes decisions that could impact their community. When the students presented their findings, they honed their public-speaking skills and learned how to effectively communicate with government.

Part of our mission at Cottonwood School is to take down the walls between school and the rest of the world. It is vital that we allow our students to "do" civics – that is, engage in place-based civic education – rather than simply learn about civics. By bringing our school into the community and our community into the school, we give our students the best preparation for a future of civic engagement.

Works Cited

Hansen, M., Levesque, E., Valant, J., and Quintero, D. (2018). The 2018 Brown Center report on American education: How well are American students learning? *Brown Center on Education Policy at Brookings*. Retrieved from: https://www.brookings.edu/wp-content/uploads/2018/06/2018-Brown-Center-Report-on-American-Education_FINAL1.pdf

Kimmerer, R. (2015). *Braiding sweetgrass: Indigenous wisdom, scientific knowledge, and the teaching of plants*. Minneapolis, MN: Milkweed Editions.

Sobel, D. (2013). *Place-based education: Connecting classrooms and communities*. Great Barrington, MA: Orion Society.

Relevant Websites

Cottonwood School of Civics and Science. Retrieved from: http://www.thecottonwoodschool.org/

Student-Centered Assessment Empowers Students as Agents of Positive Change for a Just and Sustainable Future

Tina Nilsen-Hodges

New Roots Charter School

Location: Ithaca, New York

Number of students: 115 students in grades 9–12

Student demographics: 82% White; 11% Black/African American; 4% Asian; 3% Native Hawaiian/Other Pacific Islander

2021 U.S. Department of Education Green Ribbon School Awardee

2019 Best of Green Schools Awardee – Transformation category

"It was a profound moment when it hit me: everything we learned about how human activity impacts the environment was real! When I canoed around the wetland to test the water's chemical health, I experienced firsthand how the lake's health fluctuated with the weather and the seasons – but it wasn't until I stopped to reflect on my learning that it all came together."

DOI: 10.4324/9781003152811-9

This student reflection illuminates a core insight that has emerged from our experience at New Roots Charter School: student-centered learning anchored in meaningful, real-world experiences ignites powerful learning that restores connection with the natural world and taps students into their power, passion, and purpose. The practice of student-centered assessment – including such practices as projects of choice, mastery-based grading, goal setting, and self-assessment – is a catalyst for rendering these real-world experiences into impactful, relevant, deep, and long-lasting learning that helps students discover their own capacity as agents of positive change.

A Paradigm Shift: Teaching Sustainability through Student-Centered Assessment Practices

Authorized by the State University of New York, New Roots Charter School was established in 2009 as a pioneer in the movement to develop whole-school models of sustainability education that provide relevant, real-world learning to prepare students to become tomorrow's sustainability innovators and leaders. "Growing students for a just and sustainable future" has been our motto from the very beginning.

We based our curriculum framework on the Cloud Institute for Sustainability Education's Education for a Sustainable Future: Benchmarks for Individual and Social Learning (EfS Benchmarks). Our four-year scope and sequence begins by deepening student understanding of the relationship between human and natural systems and culminates with students exploring their roles as citizens, entrepreneurs, environmental stewards, and visionaries with the capacity to design and lead for a just and sustainable future. The EfS Benchmarks ground students in the fundamentals of systems thinking, natural laws, and ecological principles so that they develop an intimate understanding of the relationship between people and place.

The process of self-regulated learning is one of five essential elements defined in the EfS Benchmarks. It engages students in the practice of higher-order thinking skills identified as *mindful thinking*: metacognition, questioning, reflective thinking, and transference. Student-centered instructional practices allow students to take ownership of their learning and develop capacity for self-awareness and lifelong learning, both necessary to navigate life in a rapidly changing world. Student-centered assessment is an essential dimension of sustainability education. It develops core EfS thinking skills and dispositions of being and relating while reinforcing learning of applied knowledge and skills, such as building capacity, leadership, and collaboration.

Learning to teach the EfS Benchmarks through real-world projects and student-centered assessment practices was a paradigm shift for our teachers. We needed a long-term plan for deepening teacher learning that would guide implementation of these practices with students.

Establishing an Enduring Focus on Student-Centered Assessment through a Sustainability Lens

In our early days, we drew on the expertise and services offered by the Cloud Institute for Sustainability Education, the State Education and Environment Roundtable, and EL Education to provide professional development for teachers in EfS and student-centered practices. Since then, senior faculty members like New York State Master Teacher David Streib have worked with school leaders to develop and lead professional development to support our faculty's capacity in using student-centered learning and assessment practices. Our challenge was creating structures that would allow us to build and sustain a community of practice over time with this model, given the myriad demands of teaching and leading in a small independent charter school.

In 2017, we were thrilled to collaborate with Jennifer Seydel of Green Schools National Network on a three-year work plan, one firmly grounded in effective approaches to student-centered assessment like those articulated in Ron Berger's (2014) *Leaders of their Own Learning: Transforming Schools Through Student-Engaged Assessment*.

Jennifer facilitated a Sustainability Leadership Summit in October 2017 that generated the goals and parameters of our work plan. This set into motion a process to ensure that every course was explicitly mapped to the EfS Benchmarks as expressed in our curriculum framework. Our work plan called for teachers to develop and facilitate one interdisciplinary, community-based project per semester, and to assess for EfS content, skills, and sustainability mindsets on a quarterly basis. Atlas Rubicon curriculum mapping software helped us see the big picture of how we were assessing for EfS learning across the curriculum. Our work plan also calls for developing teacher capacity to use student-engaged assessment strategies, so we can be confident that the EfS standards are not simply being "covered," but are truly being internalized by students.

Our work plan supports teacher development in the following practices across disciplines, which serve as drivers of student learning and instructional planning:

- **Learning Targets:** Teachers develop clear statements of learning objectives for each unit and lesson using student-friendly language that guide lessons and provide a focus for projects and assessments.
- **Check for Understanding:** Teachers use formative assessment practices to assess student learning and adjust instruction, as needed.
- **Choice:** Assessments are designed to give students a range of choices for demonstrating how they meet learning targets, including choice of topics and mode of presentation. They also take a variety of learning styles and interests into account. Teachers emphasize opportunities for open-ended responses in class dialogue and in products of learning.
- **Self-Assessment and Goal Setting:** Students engage in self-assessment practices, including reflective writing and assessment of their work in response to rubrics and checklists, and assessments designed to raise awareness of their interests, passions, and learning styles. They actively engage in setting goals for their learning and growth, monitor progress toward those goals, and determine how to address gaps.
- **Peer Review:** Peer-review processes are designed to reduce self-consciousness so students can focus on the work. For instance, all students may write a piece anonymously, then form publishing committees who comment on other student pieces and determine whether they are ready for publication.
- **Mastery-Based Grading:** Mastery-based grading practices put assessment in the context of feedback, which is used by students as they work toward learning targets or goals.
- **Portfolios:** Students develop passage and graduation portfolios to demonstrate their learning in relation to our Schoolwide Outcomes (see sidebar).

- **Authentic Audience:** Students present their learning throughout the year to authentic audiences of peers, parents, members of the school community, and experts and partners from the wider community.

New Roots Charter School Schoolwide Outcomes

New Roots graduates will be:

- **Healthy Persons** who demonstrate physical fitness, emotional intelligence, practical life skills, and a healthy lifestyle.
- **Lifelong Learners** who demonstrate essential study and computer skills; scientific, mathematical, and creative problem-solving abilities; self-direction and self-evaluation; and interdisciplinary and systems-level thinking.
- **Communicators** who demonstrate competent use of the English language, another language, the language of mathematics, and the language of the arts for the purposes of understanding and expression and who understand the purposes and challenges of effective communication and conflict resolution.
- **Community Members** who demonstrate exploration of their vocation, an understanding of economics and entrepreneurship, social intelligence, service to their community, and action to transform their community toward sustainability.
- **Citizens** of national and global communities who demonstrate an understanding of human history and the current historical moment and who are prepared to be active as democratic leaders and citizens.
- **Members of Ecosystems** both regional and global, who demonstrate a scientific understanding of matter, life, and mind and a personal, conscious, and comfortable relationship with nature.
- **Visionaries** who demonstrate awareness of the vastness and interdependence of human and natural systems, development of an ethically based personal vision for themselves and their communities, and actions taken to realize this vision.

By establishing a set of core practices supported by our work plan, New Roots teachers create an environment that multiplies the effectiveness of these practices many fold, as students learn new habits and ways of learning across disciplines and take ownership of their learning. Teachers use data gathered via assessment tools to track student progress and modify their approach, as necessary, to help students gain a better understanding of concepts and knowledge in areas where they are struggling.

Cayuga Wetlands Restoration Project: Student-Centered Assessment in Action

The essential contributions of student-centered learning in achieving the goals of EfS are illustrated by student and teacher experiences with the Cayuga Wetlands Restoration Project ("Wetlands Project"), a four-year project funded by the New York State Department of Environmental Conservation. Launched in 2016, the Wetlands Project engages students in restoring and expanding the wetlands of the Cayuga Lake watershed through water quality monitoring and planting and caring for native wetland species, like cattail, calamus, and arrowhead. It is a real-world opportunity for New Roots students to take direct action to make their beloved lake healthier while acquiring deep understanding of the concepts and skills taught by David Streib in his upper-level science courses in the context of our four-year, interdisciplinary curriculum.

Photo 7.1 New Roots students and their mentors conduct an initial site evaluation along the Cayuga Lake Inlet. Credit: New Roots Charter School.

The following provides a snapshot of how our student-centered assessment process is carried out in relation to the Wetlands Project through David's eleventh- and twelfth-grade Chemistry and Environmental Science courses.

Learning Targets

The Wetlands Project uses the lenses of social studies, science, and math to examine learning targets related to Cayuga Lake's ecological and chemical health. The project addresses two primary New Roots learning targets:

- I can understand and describe the relationship between human and natural systems, and
- I can describe and implement practices that demonstrate how humans can restore a mutually beneficial and balanced relationship with the natural world.

Clear and explicit learning targets are essential to student-centered assessment. They serve as guideposts for students when noting learning outcomes relative to specific benchmarks. Learning targets also serve as building blocks for understanding, providing students with the opportunity to understand each facet of a complex whole, and helping teachers ensure all students are building this complex understanding.

In Chemistry, students tackle an aspect of the Wetlands Project related to chemical water quality. Students perform water quality tests; collect, interpret, and analyze water quality data; and present their findings to local scientists and community members. Doing so, they address learning targets related to the EfS benchmark Laws and Principles that Govern the Physical and Biological World, such as *I can use a periodic table as a model to predict the relative properties of elements based on the patterns of electrons in the outermost energy level of atoms*. This project requires students to identify atoms and ions and describe their properties and bonding behavior, a skill that can be taught through experiences like water testing and interpreting chemical water quality data. Presenting on local water quality to a real audience allows students to demonstrate their understanding of this learning target in a real-world context.

Photo 7.2 New Roots students analyze water quality testing data in the school lobby. Credit: New Roots Charter School.

In Environmental Science, students research, develop, and implement a plan to improve water quality and habitat at Cayuga Lake's southern end. Different solutions emerge every year, but two solutions remain constant: restoring the natural wetland and replacing invasive species with native trees to restore habitat for insects that are an important food source for migratory birds. Students write reflections on their plans, addressing how their actions mitigate human impacts on the natural world, and evaluate potential impacts of their ecosystem restoration work. In doing so, they address learning targets such as:

- I can use mathematical representations to support and revise explanations based on evidence about factors affecting biodiversity and populations in ecosystems of different scales.
- I can evaluate the claims, evidence, and reasoning that the complex interactions in ecosystems maintain relatively consistent numbers and types of organisms in stable conditions, but changing conditions may result in a new ecosystem.
- I can use a computational representation to illustrate the relationships among Earth systems and how those relationships are being modified due to human activity.

- I can design, evaluate, and refine a solution for reducing the impacts of human activities on the environment and biodiversity.

By addressing specific environmental problems through ecosystem restoration, the Wetlands Project enables students to demonstrate evidence of these learning standards through action, authentic assessment projects, and reflective writing.

Check for Understanding

We use a variety of tools and methods to check for understanding. For example, teachers ask students to complete "exit tickets" – questions that point to learning goals for that lesson – to generate a snapshot of what students are thinking and learning during class. This data informs plans for the next day's instruction. Tools like rubrics and checklists are used for student self-assessment and to evaluate how a team functioned on a task, project, or assignment.

Learning targets and exit tickets work in tandem to help students create the building blocks of understanding that contribute to their capacity to conduct water testing and analysis. For instance, David will ask his Chemistry students to work in small groups to test levels of phosphate and nitrate in creek water. After checking for understanding, students move to independent testing, comparing current and historical data. After establishing that students have these basic skills, David provides a variety of ways for them to apply core concepts and skills, from analyzing how human activity impacts water quality to how nutrients cycle through ecosystems. Combining the use of learning targets and exit tickets allows students to know what they need to know and to receive confirmation of the same, and for teachers to know how to tailor instruction so all students receive the benefit of this experience.

Choice

In Chemistry, students are challenged to explain and characterize (at the atomic level) a local and global case of water contamination throughout history. Students are introduced to example case studies, do initial research on others that interest them, and choose a case study to focus

Photo 7.3 Students use portable lab equipment to conduct water quality testing near the wetlands site. Credit: New Roots Charter School.

their research on. This autonomy allows students to choose case studies that catch their interest as well as what data to collect to answer the question, "Is our water healthy?" In this way, students are given the choice and freedom that naturally accompany the real scientific work of answering unknown questions.

Similarly, in Environmental Science, students are not assigned a particular problem or solution. Rather, by learning about the connection between human and natural systems and examining relevant case studies, students gain information that help them create a more informed plan regarding the local problem they wish to address and how they might go about solving it. In this way, students are given autonomy and choice in evaluating the information presented to them to make informed decisions about how best to tackle a local environmental challenge.

Peer Review, Self-Assessment, and Goal Setting

An example from Environmental Science demonstrates how student-centered assessment practices such as peer review, self-assessment, and goal setting work in concert. In this class, students address this learning target on carbon, nitrogen, and water cycling: *I can develop a model to illustrate the role of photosynthesis and cellular respiration in the cycling of carbon among the biosphere, atmosphere, hydrosphere, and geosphere.* To learn and demonstrate this standard, students engage in a two-week lesson cycle in which they build and explain an enclosed ecosystem (called an ecocolumn) capable of surviving in space. Students are given a list of materials the teacher can provide and a list of materials they can provide and are invited to create any design that will work, given the project's constraints and parameters. Once initial designs are complete, students use a peer-review process to compare and contrast their designs. Since each student creates something unique, there is much to learn from their peers' designs. After collecting data on their ecosystem's performance and comparing data with their peers, students write a self-reflection describing specific ways their ecosystem can be improved.

Students also complete peer assessments and self-reflection regarding decisions made throughout the duration of a project. They reflect on potential sources of error during data collection and comment on data they may have omitted that would have enabled a better outcome. They also reflect on the efficacy of their proposed actions. Because students are given choice in which data to focus on, the natural variation in their products is a tool for reflecting on and assessing their goals for chemically assessing local water quality (in Chemistry) or taking action to improve ecosystem health (in Environmental Science).

Photo 7.4 During a study of biogeochemical cycles, students designed and built self-sustaining ecosystems with living and nonliving components that would effectively cycle carbon, oxygen, nitrogen, and water while maintaining homeostasis for living organisms. Students compared the performance of their ecosystems to develop conclusions about which designs were the most effective at cycling the abiotic components necessary for life. Credit: David Streib.

Mastery-Based Grading

We use a mastery-based grading approach to shift the focus of evaluation to what students are learning and how they demonstrate their learning. While we do assign grades, we know that students learn far more from the assessment process when they understand how they performed relative to the lesson's learning targets. Students get as many opportunities to demonstrate their learning as needed. If a presentation does not go well, or an essay does not quite articulate what was intended, students are given constructive feedback and the opportunity to revise their work and present their findings again. In essence, mastery-based grading aims to ensure the grade a student earns accurately reflects the skills and understanding a student can demonstrate by the end of a learning cycle.

In practice, mastery-based grading requires continual feedback between teacher and student as well as peer feedback and self-assessment. To achieve mastery, students must be aware of the gap between where they are and where they want to be by the end of a learning cycle or a project. Mastery-based grading is at the core of assessment for the chemistry water quality project, which is scaffolded so students receive feedback during each step of the process. Students can revise each aspect of the project until they earn a score they are satisfied with. The score they earn is based on a rubric for content laid out by the New York State Disciplinary Core Ideas and the qualities of a scientific investigation laid out by the New York State Learning Standards Science & Engineering Practices, in reference to the EfS Benchmarks. Instead of focusing on the quantity of assignments completed, mastery-based grading requires teacher and student to focus on where the student's work is in relation to the content and skills they must show mastery of. In the end, mastery-based grading is informative for students and teachers because each piece of feedback a student receives guides them closer to mastery of specific course learning targets.

Mastery-based grading is a great system for teachers, too, because it ensures that daily tasks are purposeful and aligned to learning targets. In Chemistry and Environmental Science, every class activity and formative assessment is intentionally crafted to bring students to the goal of demonstrating mastery. For instance, giving a public presentation on water quality findings involves mastery of many chemistry concepts and skills, like asking scientific questions, collecting and analyzing data, designing experiments, and describing errors in measurement. Also implicit in this task are skills of understanding an audience, designing a presentation, and speaking publicly. Therefore, class activities are designed to build these skills and content knowledge, and assessments are designed to provide feedback about how students can improve (and where they stand) relative to these specific pieces of content knowledge and skills.

Portfolios

In tenth grade, students develop Passage Portfolios to demonstrate their learning in relation to our Schoolwide Outcomes. The Passage Portfolio experience prepares students for their senior Graduation Portfolios, which document the full scope of their learning and development across all four years of high school. These portfolios include student-selected reflections, project summaries, and other work products presented and evaluated through a descriptive feedback process in an atmosphere that celebrates the unique contributions each student makes to the school community. Some classes use portfolio development on a smaller scale to help students learn the process and develop the skills needed to think critically about how to demonstrate their learning in a particular area.

The Wetlands Project provides many students with an anchor experience to reflect on in their portfolios, particularly in reference to the Members of Ecosystems standard. By engaging in real-world projects that contribute to the Wetlands Project, students are in the field, collecting real data and seeing firsthand how human and natural systems are inextricably interwoven and influence each other. The portfolio development process encourages students to deepen their understanding of the broader significance of these and other science-based projects involving the investigation of healthy water and ecosystems and reflect on how this learning has impacted their personal growth and development.

The Wetlands Project, which was initially inspired by a senior capstone project, has catalyzed many subsequent senior capstone projects. Past projects include student-designed studies that analyzed the chemical composition of water inside of plants to understand the impacts of bioremediating plant species and remediation strategies developed in response to evidence of microplastic contamination. Another project was inspired by an exploration of the links between agriculture and phosphate contamination in a Global Environmental Studies class. These students investigated how local policies and political practices could be used to support a network of local farmers using sustainable practices, thus reducing the presence of glyphosate in the Cayuga Lake watershed. Their investigation inspired other students to explore how increasing the biodiversity of agricultural crops could improve water health.

Authentic Audience

New Roots students participate in one or more symposiums or exhibitions each school year, presenting their learning to an authentic audience of peers, parents, members of the school community, and experts and partners from the wider community. These experiences give students a reason to fully engage in formative assessment, peer feedback, and self-evaluation. The chemistry water quality project is a great example. While students are given autonomy and freedom of choice throughout the project, presenting to an authentic audience of scientists and community stakeholders encourages them to take responsibility for the quality of their choices as they relate to project outcomes. Also, and perhaps most importantly, the authentic audience gives students a platform to use what they have learned to benefit and educate the wider community, giving them a deeper reason to care about the quality of their work.

In April 2021, eleventh- and twelfth-grade students hosted a symposium entitled *Inventing our Future in the Cayuga Lake Watershed*. The symposium was based on science projects that students completed in fall 2020 related to mitigating human impacts on our local environment and the interdependence between human and natural systems. To prepare, students extended, deepened, and refined their projects and worked together to figure out the symposium's logistics. They invited special guests, including a leader from the Cayuga Nation, a university professor and assistant director of the Center for Native Peoples and the Environment at the SUNY College of Environmental Science and Forestry, a local permaculturist, and a local food systems activist. Students presented their projects and took questions and feedback from their invited guests. Symposium topics included original research on the impacts of glyphosate on food crops, the social and economic history of industrial agriculture in our region, urban food production at the New Roots Urban Farm demonstration plot, and the use of traditional ecological practices and bioremediation to restore impacted bodies of water. More than just research, these presentations were rooted in direct experience and hands-on work with the Wetlands Project and our student-initiated urban farm demonstration plot. They also served as a call to action, linking these learning experiences directly to real issues impacting the health of people and ecosystems in our region.

Lessons Learned

One challenge we encounter in using new student-centered assessment practices is the learning curve involved for teachers and students. New experiences take people out of their comfort zones, and it can be daunted to switch gears. To support the transition, we intentionally make time to teach new tools and practices as part of our professional development program and explain how they contribute to student learning through the lens of EfS. All teachers get opportunities to experience the value of these tools and practices firsthand, just as their students do in the classroom. They also have the option to develop portfolios demonstrating their learning to earn Education for a Sustainable Future certification status, a New Roots credential that provides opportunities for further professional advancement and income.

Another challenge involves finding time for interdisciplinary teacher teams to compile and develop shared tools, such as rubrics, that can be used to guide student understanding and practice across disciplines. One solution we have found to be helpful is to carve out dedicated time at the beginning and end of each school year to work on these tools as well as time for interdisciplinary curriculum planning teams to meet regularly throughout the school year.

Learning from New Roots Charter School: Implementing Student-Centered Assessment at Your School

Student-centered assessment is a team effort that takes time and patience to implement. At New Roots, we are still learning and evolving as we go. Based on our experience so far, here are some things you can do to ease the transition to a student-centered assessment process at your school.

- **Develop a repertoire of core assessment practices.** Tap into your teachers' expertise to learn what methods work best for them. Use these as a blueprint to develop a system of consistent tools and practices that can be used schoolwide, so students know what is expected and can become proficient in how they use these tools and practices to deepen their learning. Refine as needed over time.

- **Do not reinvent the wheel.** Teacher time is precious. Start with a core set of practices (like those listed under Establishing an Enduring Focus on Student-Centered Assessment through a Sustainability Lens) for teachers to respond to and adapt based on their experience in the classroom.
- **Make professional development an ongoing commitment.** It is critical to build in regular time for professional development throughout the school year. These sessions should immerse teachers in using the assessment tools they use with their students. Teachers are more likely to adopt assessment practices if they have personally experienced their value.
- **Leverage teacher team meetings.** Set aside time during teacher team meetings to review assessments and resulting student work to further engage teachers in self-assessment and peer review and deepen their learning around these practices.
- **Be flexible with release time.** Provide release time for teachers to serve as panelists for student presentations in other classes and to work with colleagues on assessment design. This gives teachers perspective on the student experience across disciplines, allowing them to create greater consistency and learn from one another.
- **Adopt an approach to changing assessment practices that anticipates the learning curve of students and staff.** Lay the groundwork for the change, communicate a vision and a plan, implement in a manner that establishes these new practices as part of your culture, and periodically review progress and analyze results.

Synthesis

Student-centered assessment encourages students to discover and develop agency and voice; to experience learning rooted in their own power, interests, and passions; and to make learning their own. It also provides students with structures and opportunities to connect the dots between the big ideas, applied knowledge, skills, applications, actions, and dispositions that comprise education for sustainability, so they can experience profound and powerful moments like the student in this story's opening quote.

Photo 7.5 New Roots students plant native cattail species to restore natural wetlands at 12 sites on the southern end of Cayuga Lake and its inlet. Credit: New Roots Charter School.

"Planting cattails," one student reflected, "I realized that I am not just healing the lake, I am healing myself." Students often feel powerless in the face of complex environmental problems like climate change. Student-centered assessment practices that teach EfS mindful thinking skills magnify the power of projects like the Cayuga Wetlands Restoration Project to restore our relationship with the natural world and empower students to act as agents for positive change. By giving students the experience of being a "leader of their own learning," they become the leaders our world needs.

Works Cited

Berger, R. (2014). *Leaders of their own learning: Transforming schools through student-engaged assessment.* San Francisco, CA: Jossey-Bass.

Relevant Websites

New Roots Charter School. Retrieved from: https://newrootsschool.org/

California's Plumas County Connects Students to Place through Outdoor Core Mountain Kid

Rob Wade

Plumas Unified School District

Location: Plumas County, California

Number of schools: 13 schools

Number of students: 1,760 students

Student demographics: 78% White; 12.6% Hispanic/Latino; 6.3% Multiracial/Other; 1.9% Black/African American; 1.2% Asian

Fourth-grader Maria was often off topic and energetically over the top. However, I saw another side of Maria when we went on a walking field trip to Boyle's Ravine, Quincy Elementary School's Learning Landscape. Her class was studying Boyle Creek as part of their Outdoor Core studies. Maria and her classmates were sitting on the creek bank, writing in their field journals in response to a sensory activity called sights, sounds, and smells. After 15 minutes, I checked in on the class's progress. Everyone was done but Maria. She was afraid she might be in trouble, but I assured her she was okay and offered to walk her through the activity. It was pretty straight-forward. I asked her what she saw (trees), what she heard (the creek), and what she smelled (the air). Next, I asked her to slow down, tell me a little

DOI: 10.4324/9781003152811-10

more about each, and then write down what she thought and felt. After the first two, I asked her to take a deep breath and really smell the air. I did the same and smelled the wood smoke filling the ravine. I asked her what she smelled. Maria looked up and said, "The air smells like...freedom."

Growing Pains: Bringing Place-Based Learning to a Rural Community

Place-based learning (PBL) seemed like a natural fit for Plumas Unified School District (PUSD). This is what I had in mind when I took a position as an AmeriCorps volunteer at PUSD in 1995, a year after moving to the area. Located in rural northeastern California, at the geographic nexus of the Sierra Nevada and Cascade Ranges, PUSD serves four mountain communities in the Upper Feather River watershed. Working and playing in the outdoors is a way of life in Plumas County. In my new position with PUSD, I envisioned creating a hands-on, broad-scope PBL program that fostered an appreciation for the environment students call home and showed why Plumas County is so special, all while making learning local, adventurous, relevant, and fun.

As a district in a rural area, I did not have a big budget to work with to bring my vision to life. What I did have was the incredible resources in the land and waters of the Upper Feather River watershed. These natural resources allowed me to create moving and engaging learning experiences that helped students shift from passive to active learners and take ownership in their learning with a sense of pride, place, and belonging. I had a clear vision and was settling into an equal mission with the help of some allies. Mike DeLasaux, University of California Cooperative Extension Forester, was my mentor. Other supporters from Feather River Community College, the U.S. Forest Service, and PUSD encouraged and guided me as a new arrival to a place I would come to love more than I could ever imagine.

I did not start entirely from scratch. I based PUSD's initial foray into PBL on the Adopt-a-Watershed framework I had been engaged with while living and working previously in the Lake Tahoe region. I started the watershed program at an elementary school in 1995. However, when the AmeriCorps funding ended, the program shrank dramatically and was only kept alive thanks to the dedication of a few committed teachers. It quickly became clear that outside partnerships would be essential to keep this type of program viable. Teachers needed sustainable resources and support to integrate hands-on, local exploration in their core lesson plans. So, I started to connect with "bright spots" – people and places in the community that were already tuned in to the value of connecting with nature as part of the learning process.

What developed from these connections was a residential outdoor school for sixth-graders at PUSD and in the broader county area. This sixth-grade program started in 1988 as a two-day, one-night experience. After taking over the program in 1995, it grew into a four-day, two-night residential outdoor school. A partnership with Feather River Community College's Outdoor Recreation Leadership Program allowed us to include whitewater rafting in 2000. In 2001, we embraced a year-long watershed theme that followed a local drop of water from the backyard peak, down past the school's tributary creek, and ultimately into the ocean. From the first week of school to the last, students studied their watershed through 36 weeks of travelling around the sun – from winter mountain snow to spring river flow, and the many uses of their Feather River water drop. Their watershed study culminated in a five-day, end-of-year rafting trip called "Plumas to the Pacific." This adventure transformed the sixth-grade year into a rite of passage, marking the shift between elementary and secondary education.

Photo 8.1 Sixth-grade students from C. Roy Carmichael Elementary School rest at the Old Juniper on their way to the summit of Kids Peak, located next to their school. Credit: Rob Wade.

As our sixth-grade program took shape, I interviewed teachers from across the district to learn what obstacles were keeping them from teaching outdoors. The feedback I received made it clear that teachers did not feel like they had access to good outdoor spaces. There were no easily accessible trails, no seating areas, and no science and exploration equipment to use. Also, many K-6 teachers did not have a strong science background and felt vulnerable when it came to developing experiences and lesson plans that used the natural environment as their main resource and focus. I took these concerns to heart as I considered my next steps for PBL at PUSD.

Learning Landscapes and Mountain Kids: Place-Based Learning Takes Root at PUSD

I knew from my teacher interviews that access to high-quality outdoor learning spaces would determine whether PBL at PUSD would sink or swim. Fortunately, I had an idea in mind that would help overcome this barrier.

In 2000, I became a founding board member for the Feather River Land Trust (FRLT). It was also at this time that I became PUSD's Outdoor Education Coordinator, a position that is funded by FRLT. As Outdoor Education Coordinator, I was tasked with coordinating partnerships, leveraging assets, providing support to teachers and staff, and demonstrating program efficacy to secure buy-in from stakeholders.

I soon found myself engaged in conversations within PUSD regarding how to expand the mission of PBL in the region. It became apparent to me that FRLT and PUSD shared some alignment in their missions and that a partnership might be in order to integrate land and learning across all grade levels. That partnership came to be known as Learning Landscapes. Launched in 2004, Learning Landscapes is a conservation and education program designed to improve access to outdoor learning spaces and support teachers in leading authentic outdoor learning experiences for their students. Through PUSD's partnership with Learning Landscapes, every district school had an outdoor classroom on their campus by 2010, all of which were designed and built with help from teachers and students. This partnership has also conserved 16 private and public off-campus properties within a 10-minute walk of every school to secure perpetual access for field-based learning. These sites support regular scientific inquiry, from long-term monitoring projects to gather and analyze data to stewardship activities that students design with local professionals. During the 2018–2019 school year, over 700 science-related walking field trips were independently led by teachers to their Learning Landscape sites.

Of course, we could not expect teachers to use these outdoor classrooms without the right training and equipment, both of which were identified as barriers to outdoor learning by PUSD teachers. So, the FRLT team assembled "field kits" that contained items such as binoculars and field guides which teachers could use with their classes to help students explore and learn about the natural environment. FRLT also developed and provided training in PBL and outdoor education to help teachers feel more confident in designing outdoor learning experiences. Local experts in science and stewardship were often tapped to lead staff outings and workshops. Teachers even received backpacks and other gear so they could feel and look more like an "Outdoorsy" Mountain Teacher. All these structures, from the outdoor classrooms to the teacher support, were crucial in building a culture that embraced PBL and meaningful outdoor learning experiences.

Also crucial for building a PBL culture was the district's adoption of the Next Generation Science Standards (NGSS) in November 2014. The California Science Framework formally integrated NGSS with already approved environmental literacy goals, called the California Environmental Principles and Concepts (CEPC), encouraging teachers to use their local environments to develop understanding about the issues and dynamics between the environment and society. Science inquiry around local phenomena and issues, coupled with engineering design as defined by NGSS, encourages students to solve local problems and take action to make their community a better place, naturally and culturally.

PUSD's commitment to teach NGSS pretty much sealed the deal when it came to PBL. District leaders were ready to invest more deeply in a comprehensive PBL program. With leadership buy-in secured, I worked with Nicholle Crowther, a fourth-grade teacher-leader, to design a concept that became Outdoor Core Mountain Kid, a 36-week, 180-day approach to learning and living in Plumas County for K-6 students. The program officially launched during the 2016–2017 school year after a two-year pilot with the staff at Chester Elementary School.

The name "Outdoor Core Mountain Kid" encapsulates the method and impact of the program. "Outdoor Core" embodies our commitment to engage every student in local, outdoor PBL throughout their education as part of their core curriculum and instruction. "Mountain Kid" embodies the identity, activity, and pride of growing up in a small mountain town. PUSD students are mountain kids who hike the peaks, explore the creeks, learn local stories, and begin to understand the web of life that weaves it all together. Knowing their place and caring for it with a full head and heart makes each student a Mountain Kid.

A Progression of Place: How Outdoor Core Fosters Mountain Kids

Grade-Level Themes Ground Students in Place

Under Outdoor Core, every grade level is assigned a year-long, place-based theme (see sidebar). Each year builds through the exploration of science inquiry – using NGSS and CEPC standards as benchmarks – and culminates in student-designed projects that support the stewardship of that year's focus. While these thematic years are life science-centric by name, they also integrate physical, earth, and space science with principles of engineering design. Every year is an intentional rite of passage of place, one that is fully inclusive of the habitat, ecology, and cycles of which they are a part.

Outdoor Core Mountain Kid Grade-Level Themes

Kindergarten – Garden Year

First Grade – Year of the Invertebrate

Second Grade – Year of the Reptile and Amphibian

Third Grade – Year of the Mammal

Fourth Grade – Year of the Trout

Fifth Grade – Year of the Bird

Sixth Grade – Watershed Year

We deliberately chose the grade-level themes to reflect a student's place in the world at that point in their lives and how their understanding of place expands and deepens as they get older. In kindergarten, students focus on "the world around me" using their school garden and "nature's garden" as a way to explore and touch on each of the themes they will cover throughout their Outdoor Core experience. First-graders study little creatures like ladybugs, butterflies, bumblebees, and other pollinators and learn the importance of caring for very small beings – something that is relatable to students who are still small themselves. This animal theme carries through fifth grade before shifting back to a broader, environmentally framed focus on earth and space science in sixth grade. Sixth grade is the capstone year of Outdoor Core – students start the year with their four-day residential outdoor school experience and end with the "Plumas to the Pacific" rafting trip. These experiences are a culmination of everything students have learned throughout elementary school and set the tone for the coming shift to secondary education.

Using a yearly thematic focus has been fundamental to Outdoor Core's success. The themes provide a structure for conducting research and exploration in the forest, creek, and meadow habitats of a school's Learning Landscape, using the same land each year for inquiry and stewardship but viewing it through a different lens.

A "Trinity of Learning"

Our grade-level themes are built around a three-part structure I like to call the "trinity of learning" – education, recreation, and restoration. These three elements carry over from year to year and are embedded in every Outdoor Core learning experience and project.

- **Education:** This is the reason schools exist. We want students to deepen their understanding of subject matter and broaden their areas of curiosity and mastery.
- **Recreation:** When kids are having fun, they are HOOKED! I saw this firsthand with our initial sixth-grade Adopt-a-Watershed camping experience. Having adventures like this develops a student's place-pride and social-emotional identity – the deeply embedded knowledge that they can know a place and belong to a place, just by deciding to care.

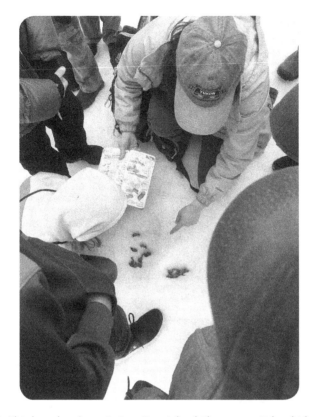

Photo 8.2 Third-graders from C. Roy Carmichael Elementary School identify scat on a Winter and Wildlife field trip as part of their Year of the Mammal studies. Credit: Rob Wade.

- **Restoration:** If education does not have an actionable end, it loses power. When students know that they will be taking action to help solve a problem they have observed all year, they become more invested in the learning process.

The following example shows how the "trinity of learning" is woven into the fifth-grade focus on birds. Students begin with foundational learning punctuated by weekly forays outdoors that include regular bird counts. They follow the passage of the year through the lives of local birds with each student mastering knowledge of and advocating on behalf of an adopted species. Using birds as the unifying theme, students study grade-level science concepts that include the Earth's solar transit (seasonal changes and

Photo 8.3 Fifth-grade students from Quincy Elementary School work with local biologists to trap and record data about local raptors as part of their Year of the Bird studies. Credit: Rob Wade.

constellations overhead with bird migration navigation); the natural history of local birds (life cycles, energy, and matter flow); forces and gravity (bird flight and migration); hydro-, geo-, and biosphere interactions (relationship to bird habitats); and engineering design (bird stewardship and conservation). NGSS field journals are maintained throughout the year to track student learning and support their metacognition. As a summative project, students design a habitat restoration or community education project to change environmental and cultural conditions for a species of identified concern. Fifth-grade students also participate in an overnight experience to prepare them for their sixth-grade camping and rafting trips.

Field journaling is used as a primary tool of inquiry throughout Outdoor Core. Students are encouraged to use "three languages" on every field journal page: pictures, words, and numbers. We do not rely on a specific curriculum to guide students' use of field journals. These are simply journals with blank pages, supplied to every student each year, to record observations of phenomena from the natural world and explore questions we pose related to the year's focus. This approach makes integrating NGSS pretty seamless. There is no competing agenda. The science standards provide content structure and suggest what topics to explore through a place-based approach.

The Role of Partners

Partnerships are the life-blood of Outdoor Core and are made possible through effective collaboration and relationship building. Partners come from agencies, businesses, and nonprofits in the region. Aside from FRLT, other partners include the Plumas and Lassen National Forests, Feather River Community College, Plumas Corporation, Plumas Audubon, Feather River Trout Unlimited, Sierra Buttes Trail Stewardship, Point Blue Conservation Science, Sierra Institute, and Plumas Fish and Game Commission. These mentors are long-term partners and sources of authentic, real-world connections to PBL. They build trusting relationships with teachers and students by guiding local phenomena study and stewardship problem-solving design. Some organizations even "adopt" an entire grade level, providing financial and curricular support and teacher training resources.

We especially value the partnerships we have with local scientists and stewards, who mentor our teachers throughout the year and help them develop the confidence to lead inquiry and outings on their own. For example, a second-grade teacher at Chester Elementary School works with a biologist from Collins Pine Lumber to support her students' study of Mountain Yellow Legged Frogs and Foothill Yellow Legged Frogs. The biologist shares current studies with students and enlists their help with observation and data collection at nearby ponds. Fourth-grade teachers partner with Feather River Trout Unlimited and the California Department of Fish and Wildlife in their study of native trout. This includes kayaking with Steelhead trout below the Oroville Dam and studying their absence in our region, raising Rainbow trout in the classroom, studying local stream health, and planting willows to improve trout habitat.

Outcomes and Impact

Outdoor Core is evaluated annually by an external evaluator from the California State University System who has found important student impacts and outcomes related to its place-based programming. One hundred percent of PUSD teachers and students participate in the program annually, ensuring equitable access for all students. It did not begin this way 25 years ago, when 20% of teachers self-identified as choosing to teach outdoors. The ease of access and proximity of field sites and the related frequency of activity correlates directly to student environmental self-efficacy – a student's belief in their ability to act on behalf of the environment. In 2018, 74% of fourth- through twelfth-grade students surveyed claimed positive environmental self-efficacy. As students spend more time outside in their local environment, they come to care more about it. It is not about the environment over there but this environment, in this place right here. In the same 2018 survey, 86% of students identified a positive attitude toward and connection to nature and 87% expressed a positive to neutral attitude toward science.

Numbers aside, students simply love Outdoor Core and claim their Mountain Kid-ness whole-heartedly. For example, second-grade students in Mykel Eguiquiza's class at C. Roy Carmichael Elementary School surprised their teacher by choosing a trip to their Kids Creek Forest to look for frogs and lizards over a pizza party after earning a free-time activity of their choice. Local field guides are the preferred book for free reading in Kelli Bainbridge's kindergarten class.

Teachers experience the benefits of Outdoor Core, too. One elementary school teacher stated in the 2018 teacher survey, "I feel more empowered to teach about topics I did not specifically go to school for. I am learning with the students and am very grateful for the experience."

Lessons Learned

Every child must have opportunities to go outside on a regular basis not just for learning, but to support their physical, mental, and emotional health. This becomes a question of equity. The only way to ensure equal access to the outdoors for all students is by understanding and meeting the needs

Photo 8.4 Indian Valley Elementary School third- and fourth-grade students work on a trail stewardship project at their forested Learning Landscape site. Credit: Rob Wade.

and concerns of teachers. PUSD teachers made it clear they needed easy access to natural habitats and outdoor classrooms, and they needed to feel supported and well trained. Putting these resources and supports in place enabled every teacher in our district to accept their responsibility to take students into nature, instead of a few teachers doing so independently. With the right resources, outdoor PBL becomes a powerful way for teachers to teach and embed in everything they do – not an "extra" thing they "have" to do to fulfill some requirement.

Partnerships are essential but can pose challenges. One challenge that might come up is how to develop partnerships between people and organizations with significantly different world views. I have found that asset mapping can be helpful in understanding how different types of partnerships can best support our students. Asset mapping is a process in which you map the human assets of every community in the region. You start with the "bright spots" and connect with those who have a mission-based overlap with the concept of "children in nature." This can help you find neutral common ground with potential partners. In our case, when it came to building partnerships across political and religious lines, our common point of focus was a love of the region, a love of place. This strategy figured prominently in my ability to develop relationships with people and organizations from the early days of the Adopt-a-Watershed program up to the launch of Outdoor Core.

All of our partnerships are symbiotic relationships that provide mutual benefits to all. These relationships are built slowly, person-to-person with purpose. We meet them where they are, train them to be successful in their mentoring role, and maintain the relationship with regular communication, reflection, gratitude, and connection. While not necessarily a formal practice, I do buy a lot of gratitude pints! These partners are people we care about. The students keep them coming back with expressions of thanks, and honestly, this is about community and friendship. People show up for people first, programs second.

Learning from Plumas Unified School District: Creating a Framework for Outdoor PBL in Your District

A committed champion with a vision for implementing a hands-on, broad-scope PBL program was the spark PUSD needed to sow the seeds for Outdoor Core Mountain Kid. Here are some actions you can take to put in place the structures necessary to bring outdoor PBL to your district.

- **Look for the bright spots and start where you are.** At PUSD, we created a groundswell of enthusiasm for nature and outdoor education when we expanded the longstanding sixth-grade two-day camping trip into a year-long rite of passage experience. That Watershed Year, including a week-long camp, whitewater rafting trip, weekly outings, and monthly adventures following their local water drop to the Pacific Ocean, modeled what could be done. Modeling the possibility with one grade opened the door to do the same for every grade.
- **Nurture an equitable culture that values local nature and outdoor education.** Outdoor Core was designed as a culture and a brand for teachers and students across all grades. Every detail was designed to inspire teachers to teach outside and students to see themselves as Mountain Kids. We amplified our PBL model by focusing on fun, local

engagement. Staff training, outdoor gear, outings, mentors, field kits, and a culture of support helped every teacher see themselves as an outdoor educator. Klean Kanteens, etched with the Mountain Kid logo, foster pride in students of who they are and where they live. Every year, students carry Feather River water in their reusable water bottles and accumulate Outdoor Core thematic stickers as they grow their personal and collective scientific and stewardship identity.

- **Identify partners and resources that support your mission.** Asset mapping, mentioned previously, is a deeper way to identify the people, partners, places, phenomena, and problems that can enliven the possibilities of PBL in your given place. Who are the people in your neighborhood who know and care about the things you want to study? What nearby spaces have compelling stories and attributes for exploration? What are the local phenomena and problems you can study and solve?

- **Begin with the end in mind.** Program evaluations do not begin with end-point surveys and measures but rather with front-side design. Identifying short- and long-term outcomes and desired impacts of your PBL endeavor will guide your decision-making. Two essential tools to have in your pocket are a Theory of Change and a Logic Model. These are not dispensable structures – they provide a clear definition of what you are doing, how, and why.

- **The pace and scale of trust.** Moving slowly and moving together allows a program to grow in a way that can be sustained. The promise of Learning Landscapes and Outdoor Core was that we would not take a programmatic step unless we could hold that step for the long term. Roll out your process and implementation so it will build absolute trust and be around for decades and make that a clear communication and commitment.

Synthesis

The wisdom we seek to raise and educate our children into the adults we hope they can become is found in the places where we live and work. By seeing and understanding the land through the eyes of its wild inhabitants, students train their eyes to see like a Mountain Kid, tune their ears to hear like a Mountain Kid, and focus their senses to smell the air like a Mountain Kid. And maybe like Maria, the air will smell like freedom.

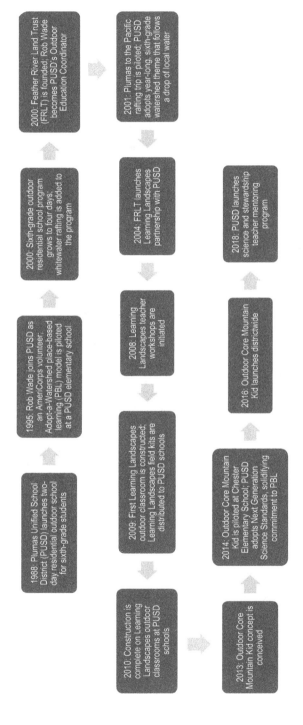

Figure 8.1 Outdoor Core Mountain Kid Program Timeline.

Relevant Websites

Learning Landscapes. Retrieved from: http://www.learninglandscapes-frlt. org/

Outdoor Core Mountain Kid. Retrieved from: https://www.pcoe.k12.ca.us/ apps/pages/OutdoorCore

Plumas Unified School District. Retrieved from: https://www.pcoe.k12. ca.us/

Culture and Climate

A school's culture reflects the values and beliefs of the school community, while its climate is defined by the practices that demonstrate those values and beliefs. You may not be able to see it, but you can get a sense of a school's culture and climate, positive or negative, when you walk in the door. It is evidenced through the everyday actions of leaders, teachers, staff, and students that shape sustainable minds and hearts and foster a belief in an equitable and just future.

Culture and climate infuse all aspects of a school's daily operations and influence the behaviors and attitudes of everyone who leads, teaches, and learns there. They are reflected in the relationships fostered within the school community as well as those between the school and community-at-large. They are reflected in how students engage with the natural world and learn to empathize with people from different cultures or those who hold different perspectives than they do. They are reflected in the food served in the cafeteria and the recreation and fitness opportunities extended to students and staff. And they are reflected in the self-care and wellness approaches that promote the physical, mental, and social-emotional health of every individual in the school community.

DOI: 10.4324/9781003152811-11

This section features four case studies that illustrate how schools and districts are creating the conditions for a positive culture and climate that values and uplifts everyone in the school community.

"Building Resilience through a Trauma-Informed Lens at Codman Academy" describes how Codman Academy Charter Public School adopted a trauma-informed lens as part of its whole-child approach to education. You will learn why Codman Academy adopted its trauma-informed approach and how it is woven into seven focus areas: building design, teacher development, embracing the whole child, safety, community involvement, accountability, and adaptability.

"Adventure and Experiential Learning Take Flight at Evergreen Community Charter School" describes how Evergreen Community Charter School has incorporated outdoor learning and adventure into its curriculum and culture. You will learn how two of the school's teacher-leaders worked with supportive administrators and community partners to put in place structures that support adventure programming and hands-on outdoor learning experiences.

"Fostering Healthy Relationships and Sustainability Mindsets in a Climate of Care" describes how Oak Park Unified School District implemented its Climate of Care, a whole-child approach to well-being and education. You will learn about the components that inform the district's Climate of Care and how this approach is reflected in the district's focus on character development; ethical and compassionate behavior; social and environmental responsibility, service, and global stewardship; and recognizing and embracing all cultures, communities, and people of all abilities.

"Culture Change is the Key Ingredient in Building a Sustainable Food System at Austin Independent School District" describes how Austin Independent School District implemented a districtwide sustainable food system. You will learn about specific steps the district took to build a sustainable food system and be introduced to some of the innovative programs and strategies the district has implemented to bring healthy, nutritious, and sustainably sourced food to its cafés and engage students in learning about healthy eating and local food systems.

Building Resilience through a Trauma-Informed Lens at Codman Academy

Pamela Casna

Codman Academy Charter Public School

Location: Dorchester, Massachusetts

EL Education school with a focus on teaching topics rooted in social justice

Number of students: 345 students

Student demographics: 77.6% Black/African American; 20.7% Hispanic/Latino; 0.9% Multiracial; 0.6% White

"Good morning, Nalia!"
"Good morning, Mr. Marcus!"

This cheerful exchange between a happy young girl and her third-grade teacher may seem like a simple exchange for some. For the staff at Codman Academy, this is an incredible accomplishment. Nalia[1] started at Codman in K/1. In the beginning, the days were long, the interactions were hard, and the concern was real. There were weeks of unexplained tantrums, a lack of learning, and immense stress for everyone – Nalia, her family, and the K/1 teaching team. That was when our school team sprang into action. Nalia was added to our Student Support Team agenda, supports were put in place, her teaching team was further trained, and her family made frequent visits to the school. Slowly

---

1 A pseudonym is used to protect the student's identity.

DOI: 10.4324/9781003152811-12

but surely, things began to change. Our behavioral health partners identified a trauma in Nalia's life through their wrap-around services. The teaching team adjusted its space and identified a set of strategies to support Nalia. Our dean reached out to Nalia's family and started to meet with her parents. Our trauma-informed approach was tested, but with flexibility and grace, the process led to overwhelming success for Nalia.

A Beacon of Hope in an Underserved Community

Codman Academy opened in September 2001 as the first charter high school in Boston's Dorchester neighborhood. Co-located in the William J. Walczak Health and Education Center alongside one of our anchor partners, the Codman Square Health Center, Codman Academy was created in response to a community need for a small, college preparatory high school in the Codman Square neighborhood. Through the granting of a 200-seat expansion by the Massachusetts Department of Education, we added a K-8 program in September 2013.

Throughout our history, we have worked to be a beacon of hope for those needing to build resilience to thrive in society. This includes our most underserved students. Like other urban communities, Dorchester faces high incidences of obesity, mental illness, and poverty. Four of five Codman students come from economically challenged households and almost all are students of color (Ward, 2019). The neighborhood has also garnered an unfortunate reputation as a scary place, and the persistent violence and crime do not help to change that narrative. According to a 2017 article in the Dorchester Reporter, 48 of 56 homicides in Boston happened in Dorchester and its surrounding neighborhoods of Roxbury and Mattapan, neighborhoods that 85% of Codman students call home (Smith, 2017). These statistics, while grim, continue to be today's reality. Some of our students have lost friends and family members to violence on the streets, while others have experienced traumatic events within their families, such as domestic violence and substance abuse. When faced with these daily realities, for many students, getting out and not coming back is the goal.

Codman Academy aims to change that narrative and reclaim the neighborhood as a place where you can be successful, find meaningful employment, and get an education that prepares you for whatever goals you want to reach.

Uplifting a School Community Using a Trauma-Informed Approach

We did not open Codman Academy with the intention of being a trauma-informed school. Our intent was to provide a whole-child approach to education, one that addressed a student's physical and mental health needs along with academics. By improving the physical, emotional, and academic outcomes of our students, we believed that we could simultaneously increase our community's resilience in ways that would begin to break the cycles of poverty and violence that have been replicated for too long.

Our shift to a trauma-informed approach was solidified in response to an additional community need, one just as important as a transformational education: fostering resilience in young people. At Codman, we recognize that while some students enter our doors with some trauma, many enter our doors with much trauma. Conduct a quick Google search and you will find multiple research studies on trauma's effects on a child's brain and their learning. The Center on the Developing Child at Harvard University, the Child Mind Institute, and the National Child Traumatic Stress Center all provide evidence that shows trauma hurts; among other things, it negatively impacts one's ability to form trusting relationships, it interrupts a child's normal development, and it impedes learning.

Trauma-informed education describes a school experience that focuses on the root cause of behaviors rather than the symptoms. Trauma-informed schools invest heavily in developing children's social-emotional skills and using that development to foster strong academic outcomes. Trauma-informed education proactively sets up spaces and experiences that build these skills and allow for character development to remain at the forefront of a child's educational experience. Trauma-informed schools create a safe environment, work on processing unresolved traumatic memories, and promote connections with others.

We understood that it was incumbent upon us as teachers and school leaders to put in place systems and structures that would support and uplift students suffering from trauma. As an Expeditionary Learning (now EL Education) school, our approach to empowering teachers to release their students' potential supports our development and constant refinement of trauma-informed practices. Within EL Education's design principles, words like self-discovery, safety, opportunity, collaboration, diversity, reflection, and service are active. In fostering a trauma-informed environment, these principles keep us grounded in who we are at the core. From the design of our walls to the design of our lessons, Codman Academy ensures that the elements of a trauma-informed education are alive and well far before any student is expected to learn.

Seven Focus Areas of a Trauma-Informed Approach to Education

Trauma-informed education is woven into Codman Academy's fabric; however, the nature of education is fluid. Teachers, students, families, and administrators come and go. To keep that fabric strong, there must be a definitive way to educate all who enter Codman's doors on what it means to be a trauma-informed school, on our terms. To recognize and respond to student needs, we prioritize seven focuses of trauma-informed education: building design, teacher development, embracing the whole child, safety, community involvement, accountability, and adaptability.

Building Design

In a city where many schools resemble prisons, the contrast at Codman is important and intentional. Serene tones and open spaces greet you upon entry. Large windows and unobstructed door designs facilitate transparency throughout. Meeting the windows and reaching down to the pale colored floors, a nature-driven "twig and grass" design persists throughout the school. This is one of many nods to nature you will find at Codman. Walking the halls, you notice they wind softly, and you find yourself stepping on leaf-stamped tiles as you go. Classrooms in this "A Walk in the Woods"

Photo 9.1 Classrooms at Codman Academy include large windows that provide plenty of natural light. Credit: Lindsey Minder.

Photo 9.2 Flexible classroom spaces meet a wide range of learning styles and needs. Credit: Lindsey Minder.

themed school come in different shapes and sizes. Gaping windows are prominent, and natural light fills the beautifully designed spaces. This, coupled with high-quality airflow, lends itself to a relaxed, safe, home-like atmosphere. Speak or stomp in any space and you are immediately aware of the intentional acoustic work, designed to keep noise down within teaching spaces. These design elements are not just about sustainability; they eliminate distractions and discomfort and create spaces that are conducive to learning. Community resilience is evident throughout the school, which is designed to anticipate risks, ensure limited impact, and develop the skills students need to bounce back rapidly. Each space holds these possibilities for the students who enter, first by virtue of design and next by the intentional work of our teachers.

Teacher Development

We cannot expect teachers to guide students to exceed their potential without empowering them with the knowledge they need to ensure that guidance is properly directed. Every year, Codman teachers receive training concerning the latest childhood trauma research to increase awareness and understanding. This education sets them up to successfully weave trauma-informed practices into the flow of the school day. Through Ted Talks, readings, and student testimonials, our staff is exposed to what trauma looks like and how it shows up in our school and community. Staff members then work closely with coaches to ensure their schedule, curriculum, lessons, and specials (art, music, movement, and recess) are responsive to this awareness. We work together to ensure we are transparent about who we are – a school that works with children who have experienced levels of trauma – so we can be transparent about what we are doing: building trusting relationships, helping students reach developmental milestones, and fulfilling our mission of fostering academic achievement.

Our school provides our staff with flexible and well-designed spaces that support their use of trauma-informed practices. From dedicated "cozy caves" to individual student toolboxes, teachers exercise flexibility in their use of practices to identify which work best for students in their spaces. Classrooms have clear, posted schedules, and changes to those schedules are avoided. Adults in classrooms are familiar to the students and spend a significant amount of time building trust and understanding among the classroom community. As much as possible, our staff reflects our diverse student body so students see themselves in roles that are respected, honorable, and consistent. Lessons and their content help students make

Photo 9.3 Codman Academy staff reflect the school's diverse student body so students see themselves in roles that are respected, honorable, and consistent. Credit: Lindsey Minder.

A **responsive space** is a proactively designed space that supports a trauma-informed educational experience. All spaces at Codman Academy are actively designed through a trauma-informed theme to support flexibility for students and teachers. We have a sensory room that allows students to release energy and supports self-regulation, a counseling room with play therapy materials relatable to our students, and a backyard with a soothing pebble harp and sand table.

connections and often include characters who look like them. Each of these methods allows us to build on our physical space to ensure that students feel valued, safe, and can thrive.

Embracing the Whole Child

Educating our staff on trauma and its adverse effects is incredibly important to the growth of our students and community. It is also important that we take a holistic view of our students. We support the whole child at

Codman: physically, socially, emotionally, and academically. Through an active partnership with the Codman Square Health Center, students have access to health care, screenings, dental care, vision care, mental health services, and sexual health education. At our local YMCA, students take classes and learn about exercise and nutrition in a hands-on way that supports their development while keeping our community involved. Our seventh- and eighth-graders start their day at the YMCA and our ninth-graders go there in the early afternoon. The remaining high school students have active passes and are required to spend a specific amount of time in the gym taking classes, playing sports, or using the weight room each week. Partnerships like these have allowed us to expand our social-emotional guidance for students, offering in-school group and individual counseling along with consultation for our staff and student support teams. Our Open Circle curriculum, the targeted program our teachers use once a day to tackle social-emotional health issues, helps teachers increase consistency and ensure students across all grades are developing their social-emotional skills simultaneously with their academics.

Open Circle is a social-emotional learning curriculum developed by Wellesley College that is designed to teach, model, and reinforce prosocial skills in K-5 students. The program supports developing skills for recognizing and managing emotions, empathy, positive relationships, and problem-solving while helping schools build safe environments for students to learn.

Safety First

Experiencing trauma contributes to feeling unsafe. The only way to break that feeling is to offer ongoing opportunities for students to feel safe. We do this in many ways at Codman Academy, explicitly and implicitly, all with the knowledge that relationships are vital to successful schools. As previously mentioned, predictability is important. From consistent schedules to consistent adults, classrooms must be places that students can picture in their minds and see what they expect when they walk in the door. At Codman, we complete comprehensive student intakes to increase this level of predictability for students and their teachers. During intakes, families answer a series of questions related to their child's physical health, emotional well-being, and academic history. These questions are used to support the teacher in planning their classroom set-up and curriculum structures as the school year begins. Many teachers make important choices around classroom "tools" based on this information. Teachers will adjust desks to provide students with seat cushions or leg bands in response to sensory needs, they will work with support staff to develop academic scaffolds for students with interrupted education, or they will contact the health center to schedule a vision screening for a student identified as having struggles with sight. These are just a few examples that show how student intakes are used to set up safe, trauma-informed spaces.

Community Involvement

Enter Codman Academy on any given day and a warm and engaged woman at the front desk will greet you. She is not only a Codman employee but also a Dorchester resident who applied with excitement when presented the opportunity to work in her community. Her desire to work at Codman and support its growth is becoming more common as community members, parents, board members, and alumni join our staff in meaningful ways. Our High School Dean of Culture is a parent of four current students and a 2017 alumnus. Hailing from Dorchester and developing much of his skill as a Boston Police Department Street Work and Boys and Girls Club Director, he brings endless insight and vital support to our students and families. Our ninth-grade Inclusion Associate, a role that supports students with disabilities in the general education classroom, is the parent of two current students and a 2018 alumnus. She is working toward a degree in Secondary Education while gathering valuable learning from the teachers she supports. Our library and lower school classrooms are constantly buzzing with board members shelving books and alumni offering a hand with organized games. Our extensive tutorial program includes many alumni who are putting to work what they learned at Codman and in college to ensure current students have access to high-level content instruction outside of class.

Bringing the community into our school is an intentional move in responding to the trauma experienced by students who enter our space. Going out and connecting with the community is just as important. We use neighborhood parks for recess and community-building events. We complete "service days" by cleaning the streets, beautifying gardens, and supporting local businesses. In 2021, we installed Boston's first micro-healing forest in a vacant lot across from our upper school as both an outdoor classroom and a gift to the community we call home.

Accountability

Developing our teachers, ensuring a holistic view of students, maintaining safety, and getting our community involved all contribute to Codman Academy's trauma-informed approach. It is also vital that our school be held accountable, and we hold our students accountable, in ways that allow for growth. At Codman, we uphold our accountability to our students through a shared understanding of restorative practices. Restorative practices help us engage with students in predictable, growth-oriented practices in response to undesired behaviors, rather than relying on punitive measures. Proactive practices, such as rotating clean-up duties in the dining hall and holding classroom jobs like line leader and technology support, remind students that we are part of a community and must work to support that community. These same practices are employed when we work to restore our community following a misstep.

Clear and consistent accountability is also needed to address situations that arise in the community. Following an undesired behavior or situation that does not fit with our school's culture, students work through a reflection process in a quiet space that focuses on our Five Habits of Scholarship (effort, responsibility, critique, compassion, and collaboration) and reflect with support staff through pictures, silent conversations, and/or verbal responses. This process encourages students to be accountable, self-identify ways to "fix it," and have a trusted adult's support as needed. In addition, logical and predictable consequences allow the entire community to make sense of any steps taken to repair our school following an undesired behavior or situation. Older students follow the restorative circle process, which allows students and adults to come together, reflect, and engage in honest dialogue to work through a community challenge or to support an individual or group within the community who is struggling. The circle has norms and guiding questions that allow the space to remain positive and outcomes to be achieved. This practice, along with others, allows students to see adults as partners in working toward restoring our community as opposed to adversaries working against them.

Adaptability

Perhaps the most important, and most challenging, trait that makes Codman Academy a trauma-informed school is adaptability. Being adaptable AND predictable is an important balance for a trauma-informed space. From the big picture to the granular level, we must constantly be equipped to adapt as needed to best support our students and community. When a child enters school on a Monday feeling happy and excited to learn, but on Tuesday comes in without their homework and following a rough night sleeping on the floor at a cousin's house, we must adapt. At Codman, we encourage our teachers to be a predictable force for that child by doing just that – adapting.

We also recognize that this work is ongoing and must be done together. As a community where 99% of students and over 50% of staff are people of color, we have learned to follow the lead of those we are standing up for and to be active allies in anti-racist work. While we have always been committed to living our mission and supporting social justice, the violence against people of color and subsequent racial reckoning in summer 2020 provided an unfortunate opportunity to dive into this work even more explicitly. Our Equity Team is helping us adapt to ensure our white staff members are working to address their own implicit biases and understand microaggressions and privilege. Most importantly, they are working to make sure everyone shows up for our students as their best, anti-racist self. This work takes time, and being a community committed to adapting to the needs of those it serves, it is time well spent.

Lessons Learned

A trauma-informed approach, when well explained and supported, makes sense to most people. In practice, however, the approach can raise a number of concerns and pushback from those tasked with implementing it.

A common question from staff as we began this journey was, "Does it mean there aren't any consequences?" Many saw the responding, adapting, and repairing as avoiding a real-life truth: there are consequences for unexpected behaviors, some of which are harsh. Our students, young people of color, are not going to get the opportunity to explain or reflect; they are going to be treated harshly. And we, their first experience with authority, must prepare them for that reality. This is a paradigm we are forced to face and wrestle with often. To do this, we go back to what we know: education. When we provide our staff and families with clear and scaffolded learning about our approach to education, we gain their confidence and trust. As we gain more experience and success with this model and see the transfer of trauma-informed approaches from within our walls out into the community, the more confidence and trust we gain in ourselves.

Our staff are not the only ones who ask pointed questions and come with well-informed critique; our families often do the same. For example, a young man consistently removed his shoes after entering his K2 classroom. While a bit of a scene ensued prior to removing the shoes, once off, he was able to reset, focus, and continue learning. Eventually, his K2 team adapted to his need for no shoes and supported him in removing them prior to class starting. His mother entered the space one day for pick up and was confused when she saw him without shoes. "They're the adults! Why would they let him take his shoes off? He's the only one with shoes off! If he thinks he can take his shoes off here, he'll do it everywhere! In the real world, we wear shoes and follow rules!" His mother echoed our staff in that there are rules and standards in life and being flexible is not always an option. While his mother eventually agreed to the value of his learning time being uninterrupted over the value of his shoes being on, she did not change her mind. We had to compromise and there would be non-negotiables her son would have to follow – including shoes on at certain times – regardless of his comfort level. This story, with different characters and details, repeats itself often at Codman, and our best defense in ensuring that we remain true to our trauma-informed approach while remaining true to our community has been a combination of education and collaboration.

Learning from Codman Academy: Bringing a Trauma-Informed Approach to Your School

There is no single right way to implement a trauma-informed approach. Much depends on the students and community you serve. Here are some things to keep in mind as you consider whether to adopt a trauma-informed approach at your school.

- **Know your community.** A trauma-informed approach is not a cookie-cutter approach. You must know your community inside and out to ensure you are truly working in a way that will benefit them and be responsive to their needs. The more you know who you are serving and hear what they want and need for their young people, the more success you will see.
- **Leaders must lead.** As with all school change, leaders must make a trauma-informed approach a priority. They must also have knowledge of trauma-informed practices to advocate for the funding and implementation of this work. Without their commitment, the consistency across grade levels, the professional development needed, and the family engagement will not be strong enough to implement true change.
- **This is the work, not an addition to the work.** Trauma-informed practices must be integrated into every aspect of the school day. No ifs, ands, or buts. This is no small feat as it requires many people, with many different priorities, all agreeing that this is one of those priorities. If you need to start small, such as making it part of one class period, that is an important first step and should not be underestimated or undone.
- **The natural world is your ally.** A trauma-informed approach is not just about what adults and children say and do; it includes what they see. The way we remove barriers to natural light, the tones we use to decorate a space, the frequency of outdoor activities – all of these practices are impactful when adopting a trauma-informed approach. Of course, not everyone has the funding or buy-in to repaint rooms or add twig-design walls; however, everyone can make small changes to remove the stereotypical "prison-style" aesthetics from our urban schools.

Photo 9.4 A natural playground space at Codman Academy. Credit: Lindsey Minder.

Photo 9.5 Two Codman Academy students play in the school's natural playground space. Credit: Lindsey Minder.

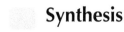 Synthesis

As you enter Codman's kindergarten space, one of the first people you will meet is our mentor teacher, who often quietly greets students at the door as they enter the space. Each morning, she points out the day's schedule and watches as her team gets to work ensuring a smooth transition from home to school. Many days start with a connection to the environment, grounding students in the serene and natural. This strategy, among others, creates a base of trauma-informed practices for students. For some, this base is enough; for others, like Nalia, deeper practices are needed. When it comes to a trauma-informed approach, the work is never done. We will continue to learn from those we serve and change when that learning tells us to do so. Our commitment to and confidence in a trauma-informed approach continues to grow as young people continue to thrive at Codman.

Works Cited

Smith, J. (2017). With 2017 homicides up, communities take to the streets. *Dorchester Reporter*. Retrieved from: https://www.dotnews.com/2017/homicides-communities-take-streets.

Ward, H. (2019, January 04). A safe haven in a world of uncertainty. *Tes Magazine*, 36–43.

Relevant Websites

Codman Academy. Retrieved from: http://www.codmanacademy.org/

Adventure and Experiential Learning Take Flight at Evergreen Community Charter School

Susan Mertz, Marin Leroy, and Jo Giordano

Evergreen Community Charter School

Location: Asheville, North Carolina

Number of students: 444 students in grades K-8

Student demographics: 93% White; 5% Hispanic/Latino; 4% Multi-racial; 1% Black/African American

2012 U.S. Department of Education Green Ribbon School Awardee

2016 North Carolina Green School of Excellence Awardee

Isabel is one of nine students who are certified belayers for Evergreen Community Charter School's climbing wall. Belayers manage the belay line, the rope tied through the climber's harness, and are a climber's saving grace. Should the climber slip from a hold, the belayer can easily stop their fall.

All belayers must complete a certification process and earn their place. For eighth-grader Isabel, that means showing up and being fully present. Isabel joined the belaying team the summer prior to sixth grade and has

DOI: 10.4324/9781003152811-13

belayed almost every Friday since. She enjoys the act of belaying. It is a methodical process that requires strategy: each team member must recognize their niche, identify weaknesses and strengths, and act. But Isabel returns for the human connection.

"I walked past the second-grade class yesterday and half the kids gave me a hug," Isabel says, beaming. "Some kids will make it two feet up the wall, so you'll be like, 'Can you reach that hold up there? You're so close.' Others will climb just for you because they know you can motivate them to get up the harder walls." Isabel's classmate Maya, another student belayer, also notes the human connection. "There's this sense of unconditional togetherness; no matter what happens on the wall or off, we are there for one another."

A Commitment to Outdoor Learning and Adventure Rooted in Purpose and Place

Learning is not a spectator sport at Evergreen Community Charter School. Like Isabel and Maya, our students regularly engage in experiences that encourage them to take risks, persevere through challenges, and develop resilience. It is a hallmark of our culture at Evergreen and what distinguishes us from other schools – public, private, and charter. When we opened in 1999, terms such as resilience and perseverance were not buzz words in the K-12 world. Yet, these are exactly the kinds of values our founders wanted to foster in students. With Evergreen, they sought an alternate approach to a traditional public-school education – one that was holistic, experiential, and prioritized social-emotional learning, environmental stewardship, and social responsibility. They wanted to develop the whole child – mind, body, and spirit – and believed that a strong connection with the natural world was the answer. You could say that our founders were risk-takers themselves!

In 2001, we doubled down on our commitment to root ourselves in the environment, service, and social-emotional learning by adopting what was then known as Expeditionary Learning Outward Bound as our school model. We were inspired by Outward Bound's philosophy of building wilderness and life skills through challenging outdoor experiences – a good match for our focus on social-emotional development and fostering strong connections with the natural world. Much of our Adventure PE programming is shaped by Outward Bound's guiding pillars, which prioritize character development, leadership, service to others, and social and environmental responsibility through active learning. Expeditionary Learning's (now EL Education) ten design principles guide our curricular approach to environmental literacy across all grade levels, specifically the principles that emphasize the natural world, service, and compassion. All ten design principles (see sidebar) inform the creation of our learning expeditions, many of which include an outdoor learning component and focus on the relationship between humans and the natural world.

EL Education Design Principles

1. The Primacy of Self-Discovery
2. The Having of Wonderful Ideas
3. The Responsibility for Learning
4. Empathy and Caring
5. Success and Failure
6. Collaboration and Competition
7. Diversity and Inclusion
8. The Natural World
9. Solitude and Reflection
10. Service and Compassion

Our culture is also deeply influenced by our physical location. Evergreen's ten-acre campus is nestled in the foothills of the Blue Ridge Mountains on the outskirts of Asheville, North Carolina. The region is a popular destination for outdoor sports enthusiasts, and the City of Asheville is known for its environmental ethos and progressive culture. The forests, fields, rivers, and creeks that surround Evergreen offer ample opportunities for outdoor adventures, physical activity, and hands-on learning experiences. On any given day, you can find students walking and riding bikes on campus trails, making their way through our ropes course, digging in our school gardens, or conducting group projects on our pond systems.

Yes, outdoor learning and adventure are a natural fit at Evergreen. However, it takes more than a purpose and a place to make adventurous, experiential experiences possible. It takes intention and passion from dedicated teachers and the administrators who support them. At Evergreen, our teacher-leaders have created programs and learning experiences that immerse students in the natural world in ways that encourage them to grow – physically, mentally, and emotionally.

People Bring Outdoor Learning and Adventure to Life at Evergreen

Brain science might not be the first thing that comes to mind when you think of adventure programming, but Jo Giordano would beg to differ. As Evergreen's Adventure PE teacher, Jo takes pride in incorporating the latest science into her PE curriculum to challenge students' minds and bodies. Jo came to Evergreen in 2004 after spending three years with Outward Bound. Her deep knowledge of and experience with Outward Bound has uniquely shaped our adventure and PE programming, prioritizing character development and health and wellness in addition to physical activity.

When we hired Jo, Evergreen's adventure programming was in its infancy. We were looking for someone who could create more opportunities for students to engage in challenging outdoor experiences, during and after school. Jo embraced her role as Adventure PE teacher from the very beginning and, over time, transformed what could be considered a traditional, standards-driven PE curriculum into a more sophisticated and creative program that is guided by choice and intrinsic motivation.

Jo started our PE curriculum's transformation by reviewing the standards. For each grade level, she synthesized five national PE standards, four state essential standards, and 15 state objectives into ten power targets to guide classroom instruction and lesson planning. She researched everything from relay races to risk management, attended workshops, and interviewed professors and specialists to build a knowledge base which she used to shape her 40-minute PE enrichment classes. She aligned much of her curriculum with the SPARK program, a widely regarded PE model that provides high-quality lesson plans and opportunities to maximize social-emotional learning in the classroom.

While team sports are a mainstay, Jo deliberately includes a variety of non-contact physical activities to keep students moving throughout class time. For example, she opens class with a section called ASAP (as soon as possible movements), a rotating set of ten moves to get students primed for warm-ups and stretches. Students are tapped to lead their peers through these moves and the warm-ups and stretches to follow and are often allowed to choose the moves they want to perform. Jo occasionally introduces a new move or two to keep things fresh and encourage students to exercise different parts of their bodies.

PE classes include activities that exercise the brain as well as the body. A student favorite, called Trivia, challenges students to answer questions about brain science and the reasons we need exercise for mental health. Jo created this activity to merge core subjects with PE and reinforce key concepts for students in a less formal context. Students receive tickets for correct answers, which are drawn later in class for opportunities such as leading a round of shout-outs and compliments for their peers.

In addition to reformatting our PE curriculum, Jo drew on her Outward Bound experience to create a robust adventure program that includes clubs

Photo 10.1 First-graders in Adventure PE class learn how to lead four of their peers in stretches and discuss why our brains need exercise. Credit: Brittany Keeler.

for climbing, mountain biking, skiing, snowboarding, wilderness skills, and our ropes course. These adventure clubs are offered in addition to traditional sports like flag football, volleyball, basketball, ultimate frisbee, and soccer. True to our school's mission, our adventure program is centered on developing the whole child and fostering important life skills and traits, such as leadership, resilience, risk-taking, confidence, and respect. Many clubs are suggested by students, and we make every attempt to turn a student interest or passion into a club.

To build more adventure experiences into the school day, Jo created team-building blocks that engage teachers and their students as active participants in a variety of activities. During these two-hour blocks, Jo facilitated trust falls, low ropes course elements, ice breakers, and other team-building initiatives. She role-modeled Outward Bound instructional and debrief techniques and demonstrated to teachers the potential of adventure programming in fostering social-emotional development. These activities eventually became part of our Crew program and are now overseen by our Crew Coordinator.

Students have voice and choice when it comes to engaging in PE and adventure activities. Evergreen's Adventure PE is a Challenge by Choice program. That means that we give students all the tools, knowledge, and motivation they need to complete an activity, but respect a student's decision to opt in or opt out of participating in the activity. For example, during climbing wall day in PE class, all students are expected to move through the line, get tied into the rope, and go through the commands to prepare to climb. If a student says, "I prefer not to climb," the teacher says okay, and then the student goes through the commands to release themselves from the rope and moves to the back of the line. When it comes to adventure at Evergreen, we want students to succeed in the adventures of their choice, which means giving them freedom to make decisions about risk that best meet where they are.

Creating a culture of physical activity and adventure is important, but so is our commitment to providing students with meaningful outdoor learning experiences. We took a big step to shore up our environmental education-focused curriculum by establishing a dedicated Environmental Education Coordinator (EE Coordinator) position during the 2005–2006 school year. The EE Coordinator oversees our outdoor learning assets (e.g., gardens, ponds, nature playscapes, and forest trails) and keeps a birds-eye view on how the teaching and learning of environmental literacy and social justice are being integrated into the curriculum and classroom practices across the grades. Marin Leroy, our current EE Coordinator, assumed the position in 2012 and has played a significant role in expanding social-emotional learning opportunities in the outdoors, including the development of our woodland playscape and forest playground. She also works directly with students as an enrichment teacher, helps educators plan grade-level appropriate learning expeditions, and nurtures community partnerships to support expeditions and bring learning to life for students.

Outdoor Learning and Adventure PE in Action

Movement and learning go hand-in-hand at Evergreen, whether students participate in a team sport during PE class, engage in nature play, conduct on-campus field work, or trek through the wilderness on a multi-day excursion. Here is just a taste of how our programming has evolved to keep students on the go and learning.

Adventure Programs at Evergreen and Beyond

Our adventure program has blossomed thanks in large part to Jo's dedication and persistence as well as some key partners who helped us develop the infrastructure needed to implement several of our adventure clubs. Our climbing wall is a great example. We spent six years taking students off campus to a local climbing gym before we secured funding in 2012 for our own wall. We built our climbing wall from the ground up – it was a true grassroots effort and Jo was often left figuring out the final touches. She spent many late nights on ladders and scaffolding painting the wall to her vision and specification. She volunteered through weekends and summers to create forms and procedures, attend personal certification courses, train interns, and fundraise for gear. Her efforts got the attention of Beanstalk Journeys and The American Adventure Service Corps. We already had a personal connection with these organizations and had supported their programs for over a decade. We requested a consultation for a climbing wall manual and waivers and assistance with evaluations and inspections. To our delight, both organizations went above and beyond, helping build structures, collaborating on training modules and yearly inspections, and providing moral support. Not long after our climbing wall was up and running, Beanstalk Journeys donated a ropes course to expand our adventure programming.

Another strong partnership is with Specialized Bikes. In 2016, Evergreen was selected as one of ten schools to receive a bike fleet through a national pilot program called Riding for Focus. The purpose of the program was to get more students engaging in vigorous exercise during and after school. Upon receipt of our bike fleet, Jo created an early morning program called Dirt Squad where students could come to school at 7:30 am and ride bikes for 40 minutes, three days a week. Dirt Squad eventually evolved into our mountain bike club and is now overseen by our Adventure Coordinator.

Adventure programming is not limited to PE class and after-school activities. When we hired Jo, one of our goals was to provide students with more opportunities to participate in multi-day outdoor adventure trips. Jo got the ball rolling, working with administrators and teachers to plan and execute a suite of trips for all grades. A scaffolding approach was

Photo 10.2 Middle school students teach lessons to younger students as part of their checklist for becoming an Evergreen Ropes Course Guide. Credit: Evergreen Community Charter School.

used to create a calendar and program to ensure trips were developmentally appropriate. Our kindergarteners and first- and second-graders stay on campus and learn camping basics, such as pitching a tent and taking turns talking around a fire. Third-graders go on a three-day camping trip in the Pisgah National Forest. Fourth-graders spend three days at Mountain Trail Outdoor School in Hendersonville, North Carolina. Fifth-graders spend four days hiking and whitewater rafting in Great Smoky Mountains National Park. Sixth-graders spend three days exploring the area around Asheville and visiting a local zipline and ropes course. Seventh-graders spend three days whitewater rafting and doing service projects in West Virginia. Eighth-graders complete a four-day Outward Bound course in the Pisgah National Forest. Many trips include student-led workshops where students are assigned a topic to teach their peers. Past topics have included Leave No Trace principles, edible plants, campfire cooking, and animal track identification.

Taking students off campus for several days requires someone to oversee risk management. Jo delivered teacher training and encouraged teachers to take their personal learning further. Some chose to complete a Wilderness First Responders course, and some chose to attend a summer Outward Bound Educators course. Administrators networked with local agencies to offer discounted or free courses to our teacher-leaders. It took approximately five years to run 20 teachers through professional development courses in adventure sports. Through school and some personal funding, we slowly established our own consultants right on campus. We still outsource most of our liability to adventure companies for end-of-year trips, and now with confidence, we have built-in knowledge and expertise on each grade-level team.

Nature Play in the Forest Playground and Woodland Playscape

In August 2009, a group of educators held a discussion concerning woods play at Evergreen. Running, recess-type play, and fort building had gone unchecked for several years and undermined the integrity of our woods and trails, resulting in erosion and long-term loss of herbaceous plants. The educators wanted to create a place for creative and imaginative play that would allow us to maintain the integrity of the natural landscape surrounding our campus. This discussion continued within our Environmental Education Leadership Team, who eventually came up with a set of recommendations for woods play and trail use at Evergreen. We opened our forest playground several months later as a space for exploration, free play, and quiet observation of nature. The space is also used for hands-on learning opportunities as part of science and environmental education lessons.

Our forest playground is not the only space dedicated to nature play at Evergreen. In 2016, some of our K-1 teachers expressed a desire to give students more opportunities for imaginary play and sensory engagement in the outdoors. Working with Marin, our EE Coordinator, teachers and parent volunteers brainstormed and decided to create an outdoor space for kindergarten through second-graders called the woodland playscape. The playscape opened for student use in April 2018. What makes the woodland playscape unique is the variety of natural materials that are available for building, balancing, climbing, and pulling. There is even a mud kitchen adjacent to the playscape where students can create "delicious meals" from things like acorns, pinecones, and hickory nuts. Teachers noticed an immediate, positive shift in their students' learning and behavior after spending time in the playscape. They were calmer, more focused, and collaborated better with their peers.

Outdoor Learning through Expeditions and Field Work

Environmental literacy is best taught through hands-on, outdoor experiences. At Evergreen, we equip students with the skills, knowledge, and dispositions to be environmental stewards through learning expeditions and field work.

Learning expeditions are the primary way of organizing curriculum and content at EL Education schools. Generally speaking, expeditions are long-term, interdisciplinary, in-depth studies that engage students in real-world topics and issues using compelling themes and guiding questions. At Evergreen, our expedition themes are often environmental or community-focused and include developmentally appropriate field work, community education, and service learning. All expeditions culminate with products or performances that have authentic audiences.

Over the last ten years, our expeditions have shifted to focus more on environmental literacy and social justice, with a greater emphasis on community, partnership, and the relationship between humans and the natural world. A perfect example is our fifth-grade expedition, Conversations with Local Farmers, which uses an agricultural lens to study concepts related to ecology and sustainability. Students visit different kinds of local farms, such as a creamery, a cattle farm, and a vegetable farm, to learn how each operates and compare and contrast farming practices. They read the novel *Esperanza Rising* to explore various perspectives around human relationships and agriculture and learn about migrant farmers and the history of the labor movement. Working in small groups, they use primary documents to research sustainable practices, tour the school garden, and develop an educational product, such as a poster or a presentation, on a sustainable practice of their choice. The expedition culminates with a student-led garden workday, where students teach parent and community volunteers about their chosen sustainable practices and then work in small teams in the school garden to clean out and lay down compost and pull plants, among other maintenance tasks. We typically conduct this expedition during the fall so students can help put the garden to bed for the winter.

Another great example is our second-grade Life Cycles expedition, which we typically conduct in the spring. Volunteers from a local river advocacy organization called Riverlink come out and take students down to Haw Creek, which runs just below our campus. Over a series of three visits, volunteers introduce students to different kinds of larvae and macroinvertebrates found in Haw Creek and teach them how to collect and use the larvae to gauge the creek's health. Students also collect spring peeper eggs from the pond behind our school and create a classroom terrarium where they place and observe the eggs as they wait for them to hatch. Meanwhile, they learn about the life cycles of other animals and, for their final product, create short videos about the life cycle of a chosen animal, complete with narration and pictures they draw themselves.

Not all field work is conducted as part of learning expeditions. Students venture outside daily to learn about the flora and fauna that call our campus and the surrounding region home. Second-graders learn to take measurements from our weather station and use the data they collect to make predictions about the weather. Third-graders roam our campus

Photo 10.3 Evergreen fourth-graders build nest boxes with community volunteers on Earth Day. Fourth-graders build, maintain, and collect data on 26 nest boxes on Evergreen's campus as part of the Cornell Lab of Ornithology's Nest Watch citizen science program. Credit: Evergreen Community Charter School.

trails in search of different kinds of plants during a study of plant communities and track seasonal changes by observing trees in their phenology plots. Fourth-graders maintain our school's nest boxes and track the types of birds that visit throughout the school year. They also help lead a whole-school birding day each February for Audubon's International Backyard Bird Count. Fifth-graders collect water quality data from five local streams each spring and work with Riverlink to care for a stretch of stream that our school officially adopted.

Lessons Learned

Building a program from scratch is no easy feat. Sustaining a program is even harder. That is one of the biggest challenges we have grappled with concerning our adventure program. As we adopted the progression of overnight trips, we engaged teachers in planning and implementation, which made these experiences sustainable and embedded. However, as we gradually added sports and clubs to our menu of choices for after-school activities, we did not plan for building our coaching and coordinating capacity. Similarly, as eager and grateful as we were to engage with partners in creating our climbing wall, mountain bike, and ropes course components, we did not consider a long-term plan for maintaining equipment, training instructors, and teaching and coordinating the clubs. What became a full slate of adventure clubs and activities and a full class schedule was more than we had the capacity to sustain. In response, we hired a dedicated Adventure Coordinator in 2017 to oversee our adventure clubs, manage the purchasing of gear and equipment, maintain our equipment, and instruct students during in-school enrichment classes and after-school clubs.

Learning from Evergreen Community Charter School: Bringing Outdoor Learning and Adventure to Your School

Inspired pedagogy, passionate teachers, and a supportive administration make it possible for outdoor learning and adventure to thrive at Evergreen. Here are a few steps your school can take to incorporate outdoor learning and adventure as part of your curriculum and culture.

- **Have a plan in place.** Define a vision, short- and long-term goals, and resource needs for your program first so you can set appropriate milestones and expectations.
- **Remain flexible.** Your plan may need to change occasionally. Keep your eye on your long-term goals but allow yourself to take a different path when needed.
- **Identify a champion.** Find that one person who has the passion and vision to implement your program and give them the time and support they need to move forward and succeed. Evergreen's champions are supported by numerous community partners – individuals and organizations who have shared visions for students engaging in outdoor learning and adventure.
- **Be persistent with fundraising.** Jo wrote many grants over the years to secure funding for our climbing wall and ropes course. Once funders saw the commitment and tenacity Jo had to implement these programs, they followed through with funding and donations to support implementation.

- **Start small when implementing new experiences.** When it comes to preparing students for adventure excursions, ease them into the experience in developmentally appropriate ways. For example, our kindergartners start out by having a sleepover in the classroom. As first-graders, they progress to camping in the gym. In second grade, they camp on the field.
- **Provide training and support.** Teachers need to feel comfortable teaching and adventuring outdoors so they have the confidence to do so on a regular basis. Give them opportunities to take professional development courses focused on outdoor teaching and learning, risk management, and wilderness skills.
- **Hire the right people.** When making hiring decisions, prioritize individuals who have experience in outdoor settings, risk management, environmental literacy, and your school design model (if applicable).

Synthesis

Outdoor learning and adventure can be relentless. Mountain trails are uncompromising, weather is unpredictable, and practice does not always make perfect. But perfection is not the goal. At Evergreen, outdoor learning and adventure are all about becoming a better person and an impassioned environmental steward, and helping others do the same. "Because of these experiences," says middle-school belayer Maya, "I know when I go out in the world, I can lead."

Relevant Websites

Evergreen Community Charter School. Retrieved from: https://www.evergreenccs.org/

SPARK program. Retrieved from: https://sparkpe.org/spark-family

Fostering Healthy Relationships and Sustainability Mindsets in a Climate of Care

Jay Greenlinger and Brendan Callahan

Oak Park Unified School District

Location: Oak Park, California

Number of schools: Seven schools

Number of students: 4,426 students

Student demographics: 55% White; 25% Asian; 10% Hispanic/ Latino; 6% Multiracial

2013 U.S. Department of Education Green Ribbon District Sustainability Awardee

2018 Best of Green Schools School System Awardee

"Hi David! So good to see you. Did you have a chance to work things out with your friends since we last spoke?" asked Maddie. David walked over to where Maddie and her fellow Advanced Peer Counselors were creating a series of signs to advertise their high school's upcoming Awareness Week. David had sought Maddie's advice the week before after having a disagreement with several of his classmates. "Yes! Things are much better now. We

DOI: 10.4324/9781003152811-14

worked it all out. In fact, we decided to partner up for a water quality project we are doing in chemistry class." Maddie smiled widely. "I'm so glad to hear that, David. Do you want to help us create some signs for Awareness Week? Our theme is Compassion this year." David put down his bookbag and picked up a marker. "I'd love to. You helped me. I will help you."

David and Maddie's conversation may not be earth-shattering or life-changing, but it is representative of the culture at Oak Park Unified School District (OPUSD). Our students have a passion for caring for each other and the environment. That passion is nurtured, thanks to our Climate of Care.

Can a School District Be High Performing AND Care Deeply About Its Students?

OPUSD has a long-held reputation as an award-winning, high-achieving school district. Our schools and district have won numerous awards for high levels of student achievement. In fact, we are one of the few districts in California that is a District of Choice, meaning that some students come to our schools from areas outside of district boundaries. Approximately 50% of our students are from outside the district, some driving long distances to access what has become a more diverse and inclusive community.

However, academic results alone do not define our success as a school system. Ask any student or parent, past and present, what makes OPUSD a great district and they will tell you it is the culture of caring that sets us apart. All students are loved and cared for, and everyone is treated with dignity and respect. This culture of caring extends beyond the human community and applies to the actions we take to reduce our district's environmental footprint and foster an ethos of environmental stewardship among our students.

We call this approach our Climate of Care, and it is at the heart of all we do. Policy decisions, economic decisions, all choices we make as a district are held to the standard of what is best for our students and staff. This work is highly intentional and not always easy. We have received our fair share of pushback and criticism. But, at the end of the day, our commitment is to our students and providing them with the knowledge, resources, and support they need to become active global citizens and environmental stewards.

Creating the Conditions for a Climate of Care

Tony Knight was already a district veteran when he stepped into the role of superintendent in 2004. Dr. Knight joined OPUSD in 1982 as a teacher, and he chose to spend his career here because he was drawn to the district's moral purpose. Not long after becoming superintendent, Dr. Knight worked with students, staff, and our Board of Directors to codify this moral purpose into four moral imperatives that guide every aspect of our work. Launched in 2010, our moral imperatives include:

- **Teaching and Learning:** All students can exceed California State Standards, become lifelong learners, and reach their potential.
- **Moral Character:** All students can grow to be compassionate and creative global citizens.
- **Organization and Shared Leadership:** Oak Park's success depends on the support of all of our stakeholders, self-reflection, and a culture of continuous improvement.
- **Finance, Budget, and Facilities:** Oak Park must conduct school district business with integrity.

Once our moral imperatives were in place, we started to move away from a strict focus on student achievement data and take a more global and holistic approach to whole-child learning and development. We looked closer at the social-emotional development of our students and started to measure things such as school connectedness and engagement. We altered our school-year calendar so the end of each semester aligned with longer vacations, ensuring students and staff had minimal workloads over summer and winter breaks. We asked our teachers to find ways to incorporate authentic world issues into their instruction and assess student learning through alternative forms of assessment. Talk about the world being "flat" was common, and our schools needed to prepare students for a global society and economy.

An equally important part of our shift to a whole-child approach was developing a motto that reflects who we want our students to become. In fall 2014, we used a collaborative community process – including students, teachers, parents, alumni, and community members – to develop our motto, *Educating Compassionate and Creative Global Citizens.* The three Cs of our motto – compassion, creativity, and citizens – summarize the essence of what it means to be a learner in our district. Compassion and creativity are the qualities that drive skillful, productive, and informed citizens who will shape a healthy and just world.

As our moral imperatives and motto took seed in the community, a groundswell of enthusiasm blossomed from teachers and students throughout the district. They recognized that it was rare for school districts to embrace such a caring, student-centered approach to education. Simultaneously, we started to deepen our focus on sustainability with the understanding that the foundation for a successful school district starts with student and staff well-being. Having clean, well-maintained campuses landscaped with native plants showed that we care about our buildings and grounds, and the people who learn and work there every day. This attitude of care rippled throughout our facility management practices, curriculum, and governance. We established the phrase a "Climate of Care" in spring 2015 as a way to encapsulate our whole-child approach to well-being and education. The goal is to ensure that all students feel cared for and valued for who they are, and that each student is connected to their school and the adults who teach, care for, and interact with them every day. Maintaining this type of learning and growing environment is possible due to the engagement of our entire staff, our parents, and our families.

Photo 11.1 Outdoor learning areas, shipping container classrooms, and the school garden at Medea Creek Middle School. Credit: Natural Pod.

Engaging and Supporting Students in a Climate of Care

Dr. Knight often states that our schools have 'soul.' Although it is not easily defined, you can feel whether a school has a soul just by walking in its doors. It is that certain something that makes a school unforgettable. Our Climate of Care is the soul of our schools and our district. It defines who we are as a school community. Most importantly, our Climate of Care gives students an opportunity to joyfully engage in purposeful learning and build meaningful relationships with themselves, their peers and adults, and the natural world. This is made possible through our focus on character development; ethical and compassionate behavior; social and environmental responsibility, service, and global stewardship; and recognizing and embracing all cultures, communities, and people of all abilities.

Character Development

Character development begins in kindergarten, where students are introduced to the character traits (e.g., respect, determination, responsibility, kindness, cooperation, and acceptance) that embody our school culture. These traits are taught and reinforced throughout all grades, from elementary school to high school.

Our district counseling program plays a significant role in teaching and modeling positive character traits through social-emotional learning and interpersonal relationship building. Our program has evolved from one of 'acceptance' to 'appreciation,' meaning that students learn to identify and value the individual differences of their peers. At the elementary level, each school is assigned a counselor who addresses student needs and concerns through group activities and individual sessions. For example, our elementary counselors offer a Character Education class during the first week of school where they engage students in discussions and activities that highlight what it means to care about the people around us as well as review caring behaviors and responses to different scenarios. At the middle and high school level, our program is led by teams of counselors who focus on students' social and academic needs. Oak Park is a community that looks highly upon higher education, so our counselors spend a great deal of time working with students and parents to find the right fit for college applications and selections. We take pride in the fact that our student-to-counselor ratios (270:1 in grades 6–8 and less than 300:1 in grades 9–12) are well below the average ratio for California (more than 600:1) and in line with those suggested by national counseling organizations (The American School Counseling Association recommends 250:1). This staffing strategy facilitates more meaningful connections between counselors and students.

Peer mentoring is another way we foster character development at OPUSD. Our Where Everyone Belongs program pairs in-coming sixth-graders with eighth-grade mentors to ease their transition from elementary school to middle school. This includes participating in 'Camp Medea,' a two-day introduction to middle school for incoming sixth-graders where they get to know the teachers, students, and culture of their new school. At our high schools, students can take an active role in promoting a positive school culture by serving as Advanced Peer Counselors (APCs). APCs serve as a conduit between students, faculty, and administration. They help mediate peer issues, conduct schoolwide presentations to enhance school culture, and address issues of concern for the student body. To be eligible, students must have a history of exemplary conduct and have served as a peer counselor in a previous year. All APCs are co-enrolled in a mental health class called Mind Matters that prepares them to lead mediations and be available as a positive influence for their peers.

Photo 11.2 Oak Park High School's Advanced Peer Counselors gather for a group photo. Credit: Oak Park High School.

Ethical and Compassionate Behavior

At OPUSD, we believe that it is important to guide and support students as they develop their own set of beliefs and standards that will lead them to become engaged and accountable citizens. Our commitment to promoting an ethical and compassionate environment for all students won us recognition from the Anti-Defamation League, which designated OPUSD as a 'No Place for Hate' in 2018.

One way we encourage students to model ethical and compassionate behavior is through participating in units and projects that challenge them to develop a sense of justice. These lessons are not reserved for high schoolers. Students in all grades all equipped with the knowledge and skills needed to take action, from fourth-graders learning about historical and modern-day genocide, to middle school students studying contemporary

Photo 11.3 Advanced Peer Counselors participate in team-building activities at a local park. Credit: Oak Park High School.

social justice reformers, to high school students giving presentations to community groups on climate justice.

Another way we encourage (and celebrate!) ethical and compassionate behavior is through Awareness Week at our high schools. APCs are the leads for this event, while hundreds of students participate in selecting a "big theme" for the week such as "Compassion," "Diversity," or "Appreciation." Students coordinate a series of events and activities that express the theme in different ways to normalize talking about feelings, showing compassion, and acting with empathy. Guest speakers are invited to present on topics related to mental health and social well-being, and students create large art installations around campus as permanent reminders of these themes. Students also organize and participate in games and activities on the Great Lawn to build community and provide respite from the stresses of academic life.

Photo 11.4 Advanced Peer Counselors participate in team-building activities at a local park. Credit: Oak Park High School.

Social and Environmental Responsibility, Service, and Global Stewardship

At OPUSD, being a good global citizen means having a sense of social responsibility for the people around us and caring for the environment we share and will pass on to future generations. Through curriculum and extra-curricular activities, we encourage students to engage in their community and take an activist approach to social and environmental issues.

When fifth-grade students visit the nearby Channel Islands National Park and Marine Sanctuary, they have opportunities to interact with and discover concepts such as natural selection, endemic and invasive species, biodiversity, the experiences of Indigenous people, and what goes into restoring and protecting wild places. On Santa Cruz Island, or *Limuw*, as it is known in the native Chumash language, students learn about the Chumash people and the island's important ecosystems. They also learn how the Chumash people have been caring for this land for thousands of years and how it is our duty to continue this care and stewardship. Teachers extend the learning once they return to the classroom by inviting guest speakers from local nonprofits that care for the island, the Chumash tribe, and the National Park Service to come and speak with students. This transforms the island from a fun destination to visit into a classroom that teaches the cultural and scientific history of the local environment.

At Medea Creek Middle School, students engage in projects in and outside the classroom that address the 17 United Nations Sustainable Development Goals (SDGs). For example, the seventh- and eighth-grade elective course, Environmental Explorers, examines topics such as food, water, energy, and biodiversity through hands-on lab investigations and team projects. The class annually participates in EarthEcho International's OurEcho Challenge, a national competition that challenges middle school students to identify a local biodiversity issue and propose a solution that will address the issue and improve the local ecosystem. In 2020, a trio of seventh-graders submitted a project proposal to address the spread of Red Swamp Crayfish throughout the Medea Creek watershed. Calling themselves Team Crayfish, the students worked with scientists to design and prototype low-cost traps made from recycled materials to trap the invasive crayfish with little to no by-catch. The team was selected as one of

Photo 11.5 Principal Erik Warren joins fifth-graders in collecting ocean water samples off the coast of Santa Cruz Island. Credit: Jay Greenlinger.

ten finalists and eventually was named a grand-prize winner, receiving a $10,000 award to expand their invasive species project in Medea Creek.

Oak View High School, our district's continuation high school, shifted to a nature-based program in 2018 to provide an alternate way to engage students whose needs were not being met at our comprehensive high school. Many students who attend Oak View have difficult life circumstances or need to work to support themselves. One of the things that make Oak View special is its focus on getting students out into the community and engaging in ecosystem restoration projects. On any given day, you can find Oak View students removing invasive plants on Anacapa Island or hiking the trails of Yosemite National Park, activities not usually found in alternative high school programs.

Recognizing and Embracing all Cultures, Communities, and People of All Abilities

At OPUSD, we are very intentional in our efforts to value and celebrate the diverse cultures, identities, and abilities of our students. One way we celebrate our district's cultural diversity is through our food program. Food is a great way to introduce students to cultures from around the world as well as honor the many cultures represented by our student body. We serve a variety of culturally diverse dishes each day, including Korean Bibimbap, Indian curries, and lentil tacos. We even offer a Halal cart! Daily menus always include vegetarian and vegan options for students who choose to abstain from meat for religious or personal reasons. Cultural celebrations are held throughout the school year where students, staff, and families have opportunities to share music, food, and traditions from their cultures and countries. Periodic schoolwide lessons are also held to introduce the school community to celebrations such as Lunar Year, Nowruz, Black History Month, Asian Heritage Month, Hispanic Heritage Month, and Indigenous Peoples' Day.

Another way we celebrate diversity in our student body is through the books we select for our libraries and curriculum. It is important that all our students can relate to and see themselves in the literature we stock on our library shelves and assign in our classrooms. We take great care to introduce students to authors of different nationalities and gender identities and expose them to books that offer different perspectives and ways of thinking about the world. For example, we offer a twelfth-grade English course called Environmentalism and Literature that explores the role of literature in the environmental movement, from the writings of Henry David Thoreau up to Greta Thunberg. Our Voices is another English course that highlights the role of youth writers in the social and cultural movements of the last century.

Celebrating and valuing diversity also means helping our students and staff empathize with and respect people of different identities, religions, and perspectives. In 2019, several parents brought to our attention that their children who identify as non-binary – assigned a gender at birth, but not identifying as that or any other gender – were being bullied. We also learned that our teachers and staff were confused and unprepared to help these students navigate the issues they were encountering at school. We were already aware that gender non-conforming students face a higher rate of mental health concerns, suicide, and at-risk behaviors, and that education and modeling of acceptance by supportive adults decrease bullying and harassment. So, we tapped our Director of Student Support and School Safety, Stew McGugan, and our elementary counselors to create age-appropriate gender diversity lessons that could be integrated into our monthly social-emotional lessons. After months of research and discussion, the elementary counselor team developed a series of lessons using children's books to help students better understand gender, gender stereotyping, self-expression, and uniqueness. Each lesson begins with an age-appropriate book that is read aloud to students. Afterward, students are led through a discussion of the topics presented in the book and finish up with a shared art activity. The elementary counselor team also led trainings at staff meetings to help teachers and staff build empathy for students across the gender spectrum.

Over the course of two months in fall 2019, our elementary counselors visited every elementary classroom and presented the gender diversity lessons to students. The lesson schedule was shared widely with parents, so everyone was informed about when the lessons would take place. Some parents used this information to foster discussion with their children. A few parents used the information to keep their children home. After the lessons were presented, we received a lot of feedback from parents about the lessons and their impact on their children. At our December 2019 board meeting, one parent commented that "for the first time [his child] came home from school having felt seen by their school." We learned a lot about compassion and empathy over those months. What resulted was a greater appreciation for the uniqueness of students and families in our schools, and a meaningful statement from the district about the values we are committed to upholding as a school community in our Climate of Care.

Lessons Learned

One of the most important questions we continue to ask ourselves is, "How can we make sure that our Climate of Care extends to each child?" Commitment to the vision is important as well as intention – everything we have done, and continue to do, to implement our Climate of Care comes from both. This is not to say we have not faced pushback. When we rolled out our gender diversity lessons, we encountered angry and confused parents who felt the topic was not age appropriate or that it went against their religious beliefs. Dr. Knight and the district leadership team listened and were receptive to their concerns. In the end, they decided that "doing what was best for our students" meant staying the course and moving forward with the gender diversity lessons. Parents were not given the option to opt out of the program on behalf of their students. We did create a webpage on our student wellness website, #OakParkConnects, with information about the lessons to make our work on the topic more transparent to the school community. Ultimately, the lessons were a success, and a group of district educators is working on a plan to bring similar lessons to our middle school students.

Our work on gender identity taught us that doing the right thing for students is never the wrong thing. We learned that engaging with those who question your work adds to transparency. While we could not 'convince' everyone, we made our intentions and motivations clear and understandable. Most of all, we believed in what we were doing. With the stoic support of our school board, superintendent, administrators, and teachers, we were able to make our schools more supportive and accepting for all students.

Learning from Oak Park Unified School District: Bringing a Climate of Care Approach to Your District

Vision, intention, and buy-in from the school community all play a role in making our Climate of Care possible. Here are a few ways you can leverage our experience to bring a Climate of Care to your district.

- **Set specific goals.** It may seem strange to set goals around school culture and climate, but as the saying goes, what gets measured, gets done. Start simple – what is one or two things your district can do to enhance the ideals you want to embody? What needs to happen to turn them into actions? When district and school leadership set and own these goals, so too will teachers, staff, and students.
- **Identify shared values and beliefs.** What makes your school and community unique? Talk to students, families, staff, and teachers and find out what they value and believe in. Make those values and beliefs part of your culture, whether it is through your mission or vision statement or a motto.
- **Share and celebrate.** Students and families are some of our best teachers when it comes to celebrating cultures, traditions, and identities. We are always looking for new ways to share and celebrate what makes our students and families unique so our district feels like 'home' to everyone.

- **Accept the work is never done.** Upholding our Climate of Care is a continuous process. We are constantly evaluating our goals, learning from mistakes, and identifying next steps. Do not be afraid to admit where you fall short. Continuous improvement and self-evaluation will help you reach your goals.

Synthesis

OPUSD is a community because we foster a Climate of Care that extends to everyone. We set high expectations for our students when it comes to academics and their role within the community. When students graduate from our schools, we hope that they take with them a sense of responsibility to care for themselves, the environment, and the people around them.

Relevant Websites

Oak Park Unified School District. Retrieved from: https://www.oakparkusd. org/

#OakParkConnects. Retrieved from: https://sites.google.com/opusd.org/ oakparkconnects/home

Cultural Change Is the Key Ingredient in Building a Sustainable Food System at Austin Independent School District

Darien Clary, Anne Muller, Anneliese Tanner, and Lindsey Bradley

Austin Independent School District

Location: Austin, Texas

Fifth largest school district in Texas

Number of schools: 125 schools

Number of students: 74,988 students

Student demographics: 55% Hispanic/Latino; 30.1% White; 8.3% Multiracial/Other; 6.6% Black/African American

Growing up in the urban core of Austin, Texas, Ari believed that the food on his plate came from the grocery store. Then Ari became a student at Small Middle School and his whole perception of food changed. Ari learned about the interconnectedness of land and food and the many

DOI: 10.4324/9781003152811-15

factors (e.g., availability, seasonal/environmental influences, and economics) that impact food systems. This new perspective grew in the school garden, where Ari got his hands dirty planting and harvesting vegetables. He remembers being fascinated to learn that carrots could be found hiding in the dirt beneath wispy green stalks. Firsthand exposure to the roots and shoots of his food, paired with a nature-based curriculum, nudged Ari to choose a salad at lunch so he could enjoy the fresh kale he recently harvested.

Serving over 13 million meals a year, Austin Independent School District (AISD) works to bring healthy, sustainable food to all children, regardless of socioeconomic status. The importance of feeding Austin's schoolchildren and engaging them in sustainable food systems cannot be underestimated, especially in a city where access to healthy food can be a challenge.

The Reality of Food Insecurity

Food is a basic need and access to healthy food is a right of all Austin students, regardless of where they live in the city. Yet, over 60% of AISD students live in a food insecure household and rely on the district for food. Over the past decade, the supply of local, fresh food in Austin and surrounding communities has steadily decreased. Twelve zip codes do not have a grocery store and are designated as healthy food priority areas by the city. The area has also lost 25% of its farmland over the past 11 years to unprecedented urban growth (City of Austin, 2018). Recognizing the threats of food insecurity, food deserts, lost farmland, and related impacts on the local population, the City of Austin introduced programs in 2015 to expand local food production, increase demand for locally grown food, improve access to nutritious food, and reduce food waste (City of Austin, 2018). This initiative helped set the stage to transform AISD's school food program into a model of nutrition and sustainability for its students.

"As the largest restaurant chain in the city, we play a critical role in determining how food is sourced, prepared, and served," notes Nicole Conley, AISD Chief of Business and Operations. "The bottom line is, developing a sustainable food strategy is good business and the right thing to do" (Conley, 2019). A sustainable food program at a school district can increase family participation and purchase of school meals. More importantly, it is an investment in students to support their success. AISD is committed to growing a culture of sustainable food systems that will increase access to nutritious, sustainable food in the cafeteria, classroom, and schoolyard through education, infrastructure, and community partnerships.

Creating a Districtwide Sustainable Food System

A Vision Is Realized

AISD's vision for a sustainable food system was inspired by feedback received via the district's School Meals Survey, which was first administered in 2015. Through the survey, parents, students, and staff voiced a preference for local and sustainably sourced foods. Sensing the time was ripe, AISD leadership developed a plan to create a sustainable food system.

First, AISD recognized its buying power as a catalyst for change. In 2015, Food Service Director, Anneliese Tanner, was hired and went to work on a strategic procurement plan to transition AISD into sourcing more sustainable food products. Conley recalls, "we began to create a sustainable food strategy under Anneliese Tanner, who has done a fantastic job of expanding menu choices and dining options, while bringing scratch cooking and clean label initiatives to district menus" (Conley, 2019).

Defining Scratch Cooking at Austin Independent School District

AISD uses the School Food Innovation Lab's working definition of scratch cooking: using fresh, whole ingredients to prepare meals that capture original flavors. This approach supports using ready-made products when necessary, such as broths and breads, and combining those with fresh ingredients (Chung, 2019). Ready-made products should meet clean label standards as outlined in the Ingredient Guide for Better School Food Purchasing by School Food Focus.

In 2016, AISD became a member of the City of Austin's Good Food Purchasing Program coalition and began to align with the Center for Good Food Purchasing framework. The framework considers factors such as local economies (for AISD, this means food produced in Texas), environmental sustainability, valued workforce, animal welfare, and nutrition (Center for Good Food Purchasing, n.d.). In 2019, AISD Superintendent Dr. Paul Cruz approved a districtwide regulation to formally adopt the Good Food Purchasing Program, becoming the first Texas school district to do so. Strategies for a sustainable food system were also integrated into AISD's sustainability plan, which includes actions to increase student engagement with food systems through gardens and composting.

Pathways to Change

The adoption of new ways to feed students came about mainly through communication, feedback, and collaboration. Lessons learned regarding how to bring about such change are worth sharing.

A small but significant piece of building a supportive food culture and engaged school community has to do with the language used to talk about school food. This starts with the very place where students eat their meals every day. AISD uses the term "café" instead of "cafeteria" to describe where meals are served and experienced to elevate the perception and reflect the quality of the food served. Then there is the menu. AISD changed its menu to include icons that denote scratch-cooked items (allowing for seasonal, fresh ingredients and fewer preservatives), plant-based meals, and locally procured foods. Other icons show whether a food is gluten-free or contains pork, the latter of which helps families who avoid pork for religious or cultural reasons. In addition to its menu, AISD's Food Service website contains information about their Good Food Purchasing goals, clean label food, and the phase-out of Styrofoam in favor of reusable, recyclable, and compostable serve ware, trays, and utensils.

Surveys are another tool used by AISD to build a supportive food culture. In the past, end-of-year feedback surveys were used to assess menu preferences for students, parents, and staff, helping AISD plan for the school year ahead. Now, these surveys are also used to inform families about AISD's sustainable food initiatives. Feedback consistently shows that families want healthy, local, and organic foods served in district cafés. Student voice and choice remain important when it comes to menu options. When students requested that AISD's food truck include more locally sourced foods on its menu, the district added another food truck and now both serve local and sustainable scratch-cooked meals.

Interdepartmental collaboration is also key to AISD's successful approach to a sustainable food system. At the helm is the Food Service Director and 700 department staff who make sustainable food strategies a priority in their procurement, operations, food preparation, staff training, communications, waste minimization, and innovative programming. The Construction Management Department facilitates the integration of outdoor learning and food gardens into design specifications for new or renovated campuses. The Outdoor Learning Specialist identifies and reviews outdoor learning specifications, ensures that gardens and other outdoor connections are integrated into the curriculum, and ensures that teachers have professional development opportunities relevant to outdoor learning and partner agencies have a route to help schools increase green schoolyard features. The AISD Sustainability Manager tracks initiatives districtwide, integrates them into the district's long-range planning, and encourages cross-sector collaborations to achieve sustainability goals. The AISD Zero-Waste Specialist ensures that all cafés have composting and recycling programs to keep food and packaging waste out of the landfill.

Integration of Intentional Design

Intentional design is integrated into AISD's kitchens to reinforce behaviors related to a sustainable food system and position cafés to function as learning environments for food literacy. For example, all cafés have waste stations with compost and recycling bins so students can divert food and packaging waste from the landfill. After their meal, students sort remaining food scraps and compostable paper goods from recyclables and landfill trash. Compostable trays are stacked near the waste station and carted to the dumpster by café staff. Stacked trays take up less space in a dumpster than haphazardly placed trays, ensuring that the dumpster fills less quickly. This helps minimize the frequency and added cost of dumpster hauls. Zero-waste-themed curriculum is available to teachers who choose

Photo 12.1 AISD offers composting and recycling at all cafés. Credit: AISD Food Service.

to use the café and facility as a living lab for lessons related to resource use, recycling, composting, and advocacy.

Implementation and Impact of a Districtwide Sustainable Food System

The move to a sustainable food system and the accompanying culture shift at AISD has earned the district renewed trust in the quality of its school meals. Administrators and teachers now dine with students in the cafés rather than bringing meals from home or fast-food restaurants, and many campuses encourage parents to eat lunch with their children. This supportive culture is sustained and enhanced through active engagement. Programs, including the ones featured here, foster experiences and leadership that reinforce the café's role as a classroom.

Garden to Café

With more than 90 school gardens growing fresh produce, AISD plays an active role in connecting students to the local food system. One example is the district's Garden to Café program, which extends lessons learned in the garden to the café. Campuses can apply for approval to have café staff prepare and serve garden-grown produce in school meals. To be eligible, campus gardens must follow a set of standards developed by the City of Austin and AISD, in compliance with the Texas Department of State Health Services, related to sustainability and food safety. Gardens that follow these standards are considered to be approved food sources by the Texas Department of State Health Services' Food Establishment Rules. This creates a unique and student-generated route to healthy, fresh, garden-grown foods through school meal programs.

Photo 12.2 AISD café manager accepts a garden-grown harvest through the district's Garden to Café program. Credit: AISD Food Service.

Photo 12.3 AISD offers a Garden to Café program which provides guidelines for campuses to safely serve garden-grown food. Credit: AISD Food Service.

Modernized Presentation

Since students "eat" with their eyes first, a focus on presentation and quality creates positive experiences with nutritious, sustainably sourced food. AISD chefs prepare recipes and pairings that maximize the visual appeal of healthy foods. At elementary schools and newly constructed secondary schools, the salad bar is first in the serving line, so students encounter a colorful array of produce at the start of their lunchtime experience. This arrangement encourages students to make vegetables the literal and figurative center of their plate. It also allows them to make a physical connection to the food they choose which increases consumption and decreases food waste.

Bulk Milk Dispensers

During the 2019–2020 school year, AISD started to replace single-serve milk cartons with milk dispensers and reusable cups to reduce product waste and the costs associated with disposal of cardboard milk cartons.

189

Photo 12.4 AISD offers daily salad bars which often feature local vegetables.
Credit: AISD Food Service.

This has become a design specification for new construction and major renovations and will be phased in at existing schools through 2026.

Share Tables

To expand food access and decrease food waste, all AISD cafés have share tables where students can place unwanted, uneaten, and unopened food and drinks and whole produce for other students to take. Any items left at the end of the service period that meet food safety guidelines are brought back into the kitchen to be served at a later time.

Vegetable Tastings

Several times a year, AISD hosts districtwide local vegetable tastings of items not usually on the menu, such as fennel, kale, beets, and eggplant, to educate students about the variety of vegetables grown in and around Austin. Since tastings require a smaller volume of produce than menu items, AISD works with local farms to provide heirloom varieties that represent "taste of place" and teach students about seasonality and nutrition.

Photo 12.5 AISD share tables keep unopened food and milk from being wasted. Credit: AISD Food Service.

Recipe Samplings

AISD cafés conduct around 15 recipe sampling events each school year to test new ingredients, plant-forward dishes, and global flavors. Samples are offered the day before a new or potentially unfamiliar recipe, like vegan lentil chili, Frito pie, or Indian vegetable curry, appears on the menu. This allows students to try the entree before choosing it as part of their meal. Café staff are instructed to conduct active versus passive samplings, which include displaying corresponding signage, talking with students and staff about the featured sample, and positively encouraging them to try it.

Internships in AISD Kitchens

The Food Service Department works closely with the Career and Technical Education Department to offer semester-long internships in campus kitchens to culinary students at Clifton Career Development School and Travis Early College High School. Café managers work closely with interns, guiding them in mass food production, knife skills, food safety, and sanitation. Interns gain hands-on learning opportunities, competitive job market skills,

Photo 12.6 AISD provides education about the food system with local vegetable samplings throughout the school year, such as mixed organic radishes from Johnson's Backyard Garden, a farm located in Austin. Credit: AISD Food Service.

and a platform to showcase their talents, preparing them for careers in the culinary and hospitality industries.

Diced and Sliced Student Chef Competition

Each year, middle school culinary students participate in focused learning sessions with the District Dietitian and Executive Chef to develop themed recipes. During these sessions, the District Dietitian shares strategies for preparing nutritious meals, and the Executive Chef teaches students food safety, culinary skills, and how to build flavorful dishes. Finalists from each school compete for the title of "Ultimate Dish," and the winning recipe is featured on the following year's menu during National School Lunch Week.

Food Trucks

AISD operates four food trucks under two district brands, the Nacho Average Food Truck and Food 4 Thought. Three of the trucks visit a different high school each day and are available for elementary and middle schools by request. The fourth food truck has a permanent residence at a high school.

The food trucks feature global flavors that emphasize vegetable-centered meals that are nutritious and sustainably sourced. This modern take on the school lunch experience allows students to participate in one of Austin's iconic cultural foodways – eating from a food truck. Students can purchase food with their student meal account (free/reduced-price/paid), just as they would in the café.

Professional Development

AISD provides professional learning opportunities through the Office of Academics to help teachers build skills and confidence to teach a variety of subjects in gardens and on school grounds. Past workshop topics included how to start and maintain a successful garden, school garden leadership, community gardens, and integration of gardens into the curriculum. Teachers can also receive professional learning credit for attending trainings from approved partners, such as EcoRise; Partners for Education, Agriculture, and Sustainability (PEAS); National Wildlife Federation; and the University of Texas – Lady Bird Johnson Wildflower Center.

Photo 12.7 AISD has a fleet of food trucks that travels to schools daily and offers local, sustainable, and scratch-cooked menu items. Credit: AISD Food Service.

In-Person Outreach

AISD welcomes opportunities to educate the community on the district's sustainability initiatives. The District Dietitian and Executive Chef visit classrooms, campus events, and parent meetings to share successes, future plans, and how each meal served brings better food to all students. This has proven successful in increasing meal participation, with one campus serving 500 more lunches and 80 more breakfasts the month following a presentation during the 2018–2019 school year.

Partnerships

AISD partners with many local agencies and nonprofits that support the district's sustainable food initiatives. One way partners can engage is through AISD's Environmental Stewardship Advisory Committee. With over 30 members, including parents, teachers, non-teaching staff, businesses, nonprofits, and local government representatives, the committee's role is to build a culture of environmental awareness and action at AISD schools through teaching and learning, infrastructure and operations, and community. Members receive regular updates about sustainability initiatives, including those related to food systems and food gardens.

Several organizations on the advisory committee serve as implementing partners in AISD's sustainable food system, creating an ecosystem of support that brings food-system education to life for teachers and students. PEAS provides outdoor and edible programming to students while empowering teachers and activating school vegetable gardens. EcoRise, National Wildlife Federation, and Out Teach provide professional development, grant opportunities, curriculum, and support for a range of sustainability topics, including food systems and food justice. The City of Austin's Bright Green Futures Grants program funds school-based sustainability projects that include food gardens. Collaboration with these partners has resulted in food-system education and professional learning at over 32 district schools, engaging 50,490 students and 878 teachers during the 2019–2020 school year.[1]

---

1 Some students and teachers have been involved in programming from multiple partners and are counted more than once in these totals.

Lessons Learned

Equitable access to healthy, sustainable food is a top priority for AISD. As such, finding sources for local products that can supply and deliver the volume of food required to make 72,000 meals a day can be a challenge. With its buying power, AISD works with local farms to plan menus and ensure farmers plant crops to meet volume requirements. This provides farmers with assurance that they have a guaranteed buyer for their produce. AISD also connects smaller-scale local producers with current distributors, allowing the distributor to work as an aggregator to bring local products into schools.

Another challenge of procuring local and sustainable food is the cost. Here, AISD has boosted its communications to help the community understand the impact that collective effort can have on the ability to purchase more sustainable food. When families purchase school meals, more funds are available for sustainably-minded programming and procurement.

Parents and students have a significant but unrealized role in their purchasing power to bring these preferences to their plates. Since the National School Lunch Program is federally funded, AISD is reimbursed for each meal served. Thus, the more students who eat school lunch, the more funding the district receives to invest in its food-service program. Using economies of scale, if more students ate school meals, AISD could afford higher cost products and ingredients. Currently, 54% of students regularly consume school lunch. However, records show that "if every student not currently eating school lunch made the choice to do so once a week, all beef served in AISD could be grass-fed. If every student not currently eating lunch ate it twice a week, AISD could serve entirely organic produce. If students who aren't eating school lunch now ate it three times a week, AISD could serve organic milk at every meal" (Broyles, 2018). Through an increase in student meal participation, AISD has made progress in all three areas and continues its commitment to these goals.

Finally, the greatest challenge has been educating the school community about the quality of food available in the cafés. Changing the negative perception of "cafeteria food" is an ongoing issue that AISD continues to work on to overcome. Parents often do not realize the amount of local and sustainable products that are on the menu or that fresh, scratch-made meals and salad bars are offered every day.

Learning from Austin Independent School District: Bringing a Sustainable Food System to Your District

Interdepartmental collaboration and support from the school community were key ingredients in AISD's efforts to bring a sustainable food system to fruition. Here are some steps your district can take to implement a sustainable food system of your own.

- **Hire like-minded leaders and staff.** AISD's efforts to build a sustainable food system started with hiring Anneliese Tanner as Food Service Director, specifically for the innovative ideas she brought to the table. Anneliese then built a team of like-minded professionals to support the mission. When hiring food-service staff, applicants are asked to highlight their knowledge, skills, and experience related to sustainable food systems.
- **Implement staff training.** As AISD adopted more sustainably driven operations and menus, it was important that café staff understood the whys behind these changes. Many team members were unaware of what defined sustainability and the benefits of sourcing locally. During training, local vendors or community partners are invited to share how the work being done in the cafés impacts the greater food system.
- **Garner districtwide support.** Innovation is fueled within AISD's Food Service Department; however, successful implementation is attributed to support from upper administration down to the school level. This support manifests in many ways. For example, food-service initiatives, such as breakfast in the classroom, are included as action items in the AISD 2015–2020 Strategic Plan.
- **Explore external funding opportunities.** Funding is often the biggest barrier standing in the way of change. AISD actively sought out and developed relationships with organizations that shared similar interests in local and sustainable food. These organizations played a key role in funding and supporting efforts to introduce and expand programs

like the district's food trucks, salad bars, and school gardens. Every opportunity is unique, with different guidelines and requirements, so be open to conversations with potential partners. Equipment grants through the U.S. Department of Agriculture and School Nutrition Foundation can fund cafeteria upgrades that encourage more efficient operations to support scratch cooking. These grants can help offset expenses and allow more dollars to be allocated toward sustainable purchasing.

- **Plan diligently and have patience.** It takes extensive planning to develop and implement successful food-service programs. AISD typically takes a multi-year approach to implementation, taking volume, logistics, and labor into consideration. For example, an effort to feature local carrots on school menus began with a conversation with a local farmer. That conversation led to fields of carrots being planted specifically for AISD, and those carrots appeared on spring lunch menus the following year.

Synthesis

It has been ten years since Ari first visited Small Middle School's garden. Now, with a young child of his own, Ari is inspiring others to get involved in the local food system. His family recently adopted a garden plot at a school in their neighborhood. When Ari's daughter becomes a student at the school in several years, she will have already formed connections and memories with garden-grown food. These are the kinds of outcomes AISD wants for all students who are touched by the district's sustainable food efforts.

By reinventing its school food system, AISD is affecting real change in the district and the broader Austin community. By 2025, AISD aims to dedicate 65% of its food budget to purchasing local products and at least 25% to supporting additional categories of the Good Food Purchasing Program. Unpublished data show that 20% of families who responded to a recent AISD Food Service survey report that the healthy and sustainably sourced food options available at school have encouraged them to make healthier and more sustainably-minded choices at home. This shows that action taken within the school setting has a ripple effect, one which AISD believes will transform communities – one meal at a time.

Works Cited

Broyles, A. (2018). What would it take for AISD to serve organic milk, produce? More kids eating school lunch. *Austin American-Statesman*. Retrieved from: https://www.austin360.com/article/20180807/ENTERTAINMENT/308079743

Center for Good Food Purchasing. (n.d.). The program. Retrieved from: https://goodfoodpurchasing.org/program-overview/

Chung, J. (2019). Personal communication.

City of Austin Office of Sustainability. (2018). *2018 state of the food system report*. Retrieved from: https://www.austintexas.gov/sites/default/files/files/Sustainability/COAOS-0106_FoodReport_ForWeb_1_.pdf

Conley, N. (2019). Personal communication.

Relevant Websites

AISD's Food Service website. Retrieved from: https://www.austinisd.org/nutritionfood-services

Austin Independent School District. Retrieved from: https://www.austinisd.org/

Center for Good Food Purchasing. Retrieved from: https://goodfoodpurchasing.org/

Facilities and Operations

Schools that practice whole school sustainability strive to achieve the highest industry standards for building design and energy efficiency while minimizing the environmental impact of their facilities. These schools have policies and procedures in place that influence purchasing, transportation, design, construction, operation, and maintenance of the school's building and grounds. They have facilities managers who actively collaborate and communicate with district and school leaders, teachers, students, and community members to achieve their school's sustainability goals.

Building, operating, and maintaining sustainable school facilities that integrate the latest green-building design principles is only one piece of the puzzle. Just as important is building capacity within the school community to understand how the building's systems work and how they can participate in maintaining and enhancing its sustainability features. Using the building and grounds as teaching tools is a hands-on way to get teachers and students involved and engaged in green building design. Facilities become living laboratories that bring concepts like energy to life, grounding classroom learning in real-world examples while demonstrating how sustainability practices contribute to reducing our environmental footprint.

This section features four case studies that illustrate how sustainable facilities and operations can contribute to smaller environmental footprints

DOI: 10.4324/9781003152811-16

and reduced costs and serve as teaching tools, engaging students in real-world learning.

"Discovery Elementary School: A 3D Textbook Comes to Life" describes how Discovery Elementary School was designed to serve as a 3D textbook for experiential learning. You will learn about the collaborative design process, how Discovery's building features were intentionally designed to serve as teaching tools, and how teachers are integrating the school building and grounds into the curriculum across all grades.

"Waste Not, Want Not: Boulder Valley School District's School Food Project Leads the Way in K-12 Food Waste Reduction" describes how Boulder Valley School District implemented a districtwide food waste reduction program. You will learn about key structures and partners that supported program implementation and strategies the district has adopted to reduce food waste and involve students in waste reduction efforts.

"Academy for Global Citizenship's Living Campus Reimagines Public Education" describes how the Academy for Global Citizenship has set out to design and build a net-positive school campus. You will learn about the visioning process and why school leaders decided to pursue the Living Building Challenge, take a "tour" of the new campus and its notable features, and learn how the buildings and grounds will be used as a 3D textbook.

"From LEED to Leader: Virginia Beach City Public Schools Sets the Bar for Divisionwide Sustainability" describes how Virginia Beach City Public Schools (VBCPS) adopted a holistic, divisionwide approach to sustainability. Told from the perspective of the division's Sustainability Officer, you will learn about VBCPS's sustainability journey and how the division uses the triple bottom line of sustainability to guide its efforts in three key areas – building assets, transportation, and food.

Discovery Elementary School
A 3D Textbook Comes to Life
Keith David Reeves

> ### Discovery Elementary School
>
> First net-zero energy school in Virginia and the Mid-Atlantic region
>
> Location: Arlington, Virginia
>
> Number of students: 600 students
>
> Student demographics: 68% White; 11% Hispanic/Latino; 14% Multiracial; 5% Asian; 2% Black/African American
>
> 2017 U.S. Department of Education Green Ribbon School Awardee

On July 17, 2018, the Washington, D.C. area experienced its most severe storm and most significant rainfall in generations, flooding the nearby community of Arlington, Virginia. On the campus of Discovery Elementary School, this once-in-a-century rainfall was so severe, it floated the top layer of the turf athletic field that covered the geothermal wells below. The recycled crumb rubber that supports the field began to float on the runoff. A giant river formed, carrying hundreds of pounds of black pellets toward the low-lying southwest area of the school grounds. The rain stopped. The skies cleared. At that storm drain, hundreds of pounds of rubber pellets that would have certainly entered the drain and ended up in the Chesapeake Bay watershed were shoveled up and carefully replaced on the field from which they came.

The unique filter system that prevented those rubber pellets from ending up in the region's waterways was not designed and built by a group of

DOI: 10.4324/9781003152811-17

stormwater professionals. No, that system was designed and built by a group of Discovery fifth-graders. Over a series of weeks in spring 2018, these students took measurements to define the topography of the southwestern part of campus, tested runoff patterns, and, with adult help, constructed a filter from wood and mesh that would fit into the storm drain in question. On that fateful July day, the students' filter system not only helped preserve the cleanliness of the region's water system but saved Arlington Public Schools a significant expense.

People often cannot believe that Discovery is a public neighborhood school. Surely, the school must belong to a special program or a public–private partnership that supports its efforts to maintain such a revolutionary place and practice revolutionary pedagogy. Surely, it is not possible to create a public school where experiences like this are everyday occurrences for the brilliant kids and amazing teachers who make up the school community. But Discovery is the real deal, and every kid should have an opportunity to attend a school just like it.

Can a Building Teach Sustainability?

Traditional school design has often been predicated upon social structures of control, such as factories and prisons. You may recall instances from your school experience of not being allowed in the hallway outside of class time or requiring a hall pass to use the restroom. Cramped, narrow corridors, very few windows, and restrictive elements that prevent one class from seeing another were common features of early 20th-century school design. These physical structures mirrored outmoded pedagogy, which focused on controlling students, restricting behaviors, engendering compliance, and compartmentalizing curriculum.

Current, research-based pedagogy places more of an emphasis on student-centered learning and acknowledges that the building and the curriculum are inextricably linked. There is also heightened awareness of the need to design schools that are more sustainable and have smaller environmental footprints.

When Discovery opened in 2015, the 97,588 square-foot facility was the largest certified net-zero energy school in the U.S. (International Living Future Institute, n.d.). The school was designed from the outset to give teachers new tools for teaching through its seamless integration of design, sustainability, and learning. The story of Discovery's design and how these tools are used by teachers serves as a model for other school leaders looking to transform their buildings into 3D textbooks.

What is a net-zero energy building?

A net-zero energy building is one that produces as much or more energy than it needs to function, measured annually.

Designing Discovery to be a Teaching Tool

A key factor in Discovery's successful outcome was its integrated design process. VMDO Architects, CMTA Consulting Engineers, and Iconograph (environmental graphic design) all had significant experience in designing buildings as teaching tools. They were also incredibly open when it came to listening to Discovery's educators and learning about their needs and challenges. Uncertain future enrollment and organization? Create modular walls and select modular furniture to reconfigure the school on the fly. Looking to eliminate grade levels? Use wayfinding graphics and language to define neighborhoods within the school community that are not "grade levels," but common spaces.

Discovery also benefited from having a district administration and school board open to breaking new policy ground. The school board took the extraordinary step of hiring Discovery's new principal, Dr. Erin Russo, in 2014, a full year before the school opened. This allowed her to pull together a team of educators and leaders who shared a common vision and had the right skills to bring Discovery's building and grounds to life. Immediately, Dr. Russo dove into learning about green schools and networking with experts familiar with sustainable best practices. Bridging building design and curriculum design, she worked with the building design team and alongside district staff and educators to ensure Discovery's features were robust and integrated into the curriculum at all grade levels. She hired coaches and leaders with deep operational knowledge in their respective fields and then supported them in learning more about Discovery's net-zero energy building.

By working directly with Discovery's teacher-leaders, the building design team was able to gather the best ideas and develop tools, like the Solar Lab and Discovery's custom-built energy dashboard, that aligned with educator needs. These collaborations facilitated widespread literacy and buy-in, so the intention and use of the building were not tied to one or two leaders but rather the entire school community. These collaborations also encouraged the development of curriculum that embedded the use of building systems, educational graphics, and the energy dashboard within the lessons themselves.

Building Design

Many building design strategies employed at Discovery were piloted in previous VMDO projects. Outdoors, bio-retention ponds, a butterfly garden, and native tree, shrub, and flower plantings serve a dual purpose, providing food and shelter for a variety of local animals and authentic spaces to teach about plant systems, biomes, habitats, and earth science. An outdoor learning space, designed and built by students in 2019, allows students to explore an older-growth forest, from examining tree rings and animal habitats to observing insects and birds. Located on a roof deck accessible from the second floor, Discovery's Solar Lab consists of three individually metered solar panels that can be manipulated by students and teachers, enabling hands-on experimentation. A fourth exemplar solar panel is connected to an onboard dual-axis controller, allowing it to track the sun. Coupled with nearby solar water heater collectors and an outdoor digital screen, the lab allows students to experiment with powering technologies up close, enabling the building's design and curriculum to work hand-in-hand.

Moving indoors, you will notice that Discovery's classrooms are flexible, designed to be reconfigured as needed. With writable, modular, lightweight, and diverse seating and work surfaces, students and teachers can rearrange their physical classroom spaces to meet diverse learning needs. Each themed hallway or "neighborhood" features a Studio Classroom, with foldable walls that can open to accommodate small- or large-group work. Beyond classrooms, the large, open, and flexible hallways and common areas lend themselves to collaborative learning and encourage movement throughout the day. Some spaces have large open hard floors, ideal for robotics activities, and others are more intimate and carpeted, lending themselves to small-group collaboration. Art classrooms feature roll-up garage doors, allowing the entire corridor to become an open, fluid workspace. This was particularly useful when fifth-graders designed and constructed a two-story seating and "hangout" structure they call "The Nest," featuring rope swings, two levels of seating, and semi-private spaces for students to read.

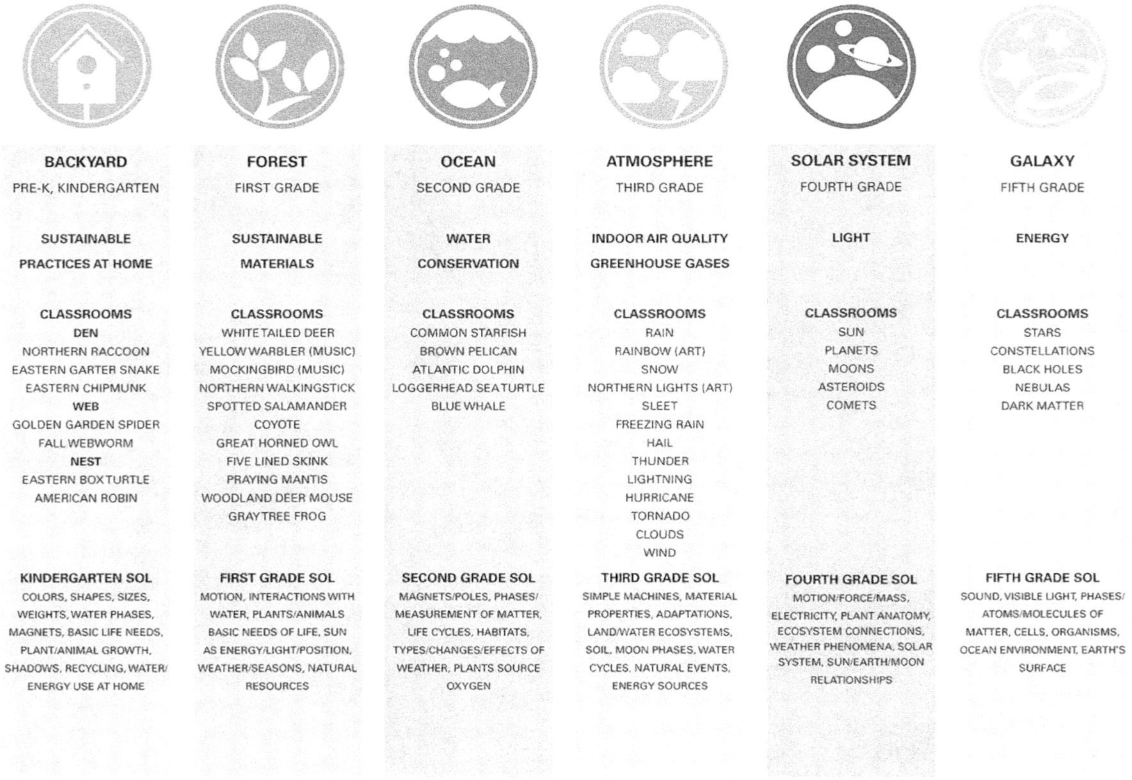

BACKYARD PRE-K, KINDERGARTEN	FOREST FIRST GRADE	OCEAN SECOND GRADE	ATMOSPHERE THIRD GRADE	SOLAR SYSTEM FOURTH GRADE	GALAXY FIFTH GRADE
SUSTAINABLE PRACTICES AT HOME	SUSTAINABLE MATERIALS	WATER CONSERVATION	INDOOR AIR QUALITY GREENHOUSE GASES	LIGHT	ENERGY
CLASSROOMS DEN NORTHERN RACCOON EASTERN GARTER SNAKE EASTERN CHIPMUNK WEB GOLDEN GARDEN SPIDER FALL WEBWORM NEST EASTERN BOX TURTLE AMERICAN ROBIN	**CLASSROOMS** WHITE TAILED DEER YELLOW WARBLER (MUSIC) MOCKINGBIRD (MUSIC) NORTHERN WALKINGSTICK SPOTTED SALAMANDER COYOTE GREAT HORNED OWL FIVE LINED SKINK PRAYING MANTIS GRAY TREE FROG	**CLASSROOMS** COMMON STARFISH BROWN PELICAN ATLANTIC DOLPHIN LOGGERHEAD SEA TURTLE BLUE WHALE	**CLASSROOMS** RAIN RAINBOW (ART) SNOW NORTHERN LIGHTS (ART) SLEET FREEZING RAIN HAIL THUNDER LIGHTNING HURRICANE TORNADO CLOUDS WIND	**CLASSROOMS** SUN PLANETS MOONS ASTEROIDS COMETS	**CLASSROOMS** STARS CONSTELLATIONS BLACK HOLES NEBULAS DARK MATTER
KINDERGARTEN SOL COLORS, SHAPES, SIZES, WEIGHTS, WATER PHASES, MAGNETS, BASIC LIFE NEEDS, PLANT/ANIMAL GROWTH. SHADOWS, RECYCLING, WATER/ENERGY USE AT HOME	**FIRST GRADE SOL** MOTION, INTERACTIONS WITH WATER, PLANTS/ANIMALS BASIC NEEDS OF LIFE, SUN AS ENERGY/LIGHT/POSITION. WEATHER/SEASONS, NATURAL RESOURCES	**SECOND GRADE SOL** MAGNETS/POLES, PHASES/MEASUREMENT OF MATTER, LIFE CYCLES, HABITATS. TYPES/CHANGES/EFFECTS OF WEATHER, PLANTS SOURCE OXYGEN	**THIRD GRADE SOL** SIMPLE MACHINES, MATERIAL PROPERTIES, ADAPTATIONS, LAND/WATER ECOSYSTEMS, SOIL, MOON PHASES, WATER CYCLES, NATURAL EVENTS, ENERGY SOURCES	**FOURTH GRADE SOL** MOTION/FORCE/MASS, ELECTRICITY, PLANT ANATOMY, ECOSYSTEM CONNECTIONS, WEATHER PHENOMENA, SOLAR SYSTEM, SUN/EARTH/MOON RELATIONSHIPS	**FIFTH GRADE SOL** SOUND, VISIBLE LIGHT, PHASES/ATOMS/MOLECULES OF MATTER, CELLS, ORGANISMS, OCEAN ENVIRONMENT, EARTH'S SURFACE

Figure 13.1 Themed signage and educational graphics are integrated with grade-level Standards of Learning at Discovery. Credit: VMDO Architects.

205

Indoor air quality at Discovery is facilitated by air sampling "sniffers" in each classroom and major space that connect back to the building's automation control system. When carbon dioxide levels exceed 900 parts per million, the level at which student cognition can be impacted, fresh outdoor air is pumped into that space. Angled ceilings facilitate powerless convection of air currents within learning spaces, helping to increase circulation and promote equal distribution of cooled and heated air. An energy recovery wheel in the HVAC system can extract a portion of the energy spent on conditioning the air without mixing air flows, facilitating even greater efficiency. This entire system, which serves as the "lungs" of the school, is visible through a large window, and each system component is labeled using child-friendly language.

Signage and Educational Graphics

Discovery's signage and educational graphics were designed around a narrative thread, "Your Expanding World." The idea was to develop distinct themes for each grade level that would connect wayfinding, environmental graphics, and curriculum (represented by Discovery's Standards of Learning in Figure 13.1). These themes expand in scale as students progress grade by grade at Discovery.

Photo 13.1 Circulation spaces and common spaces double as teaching spaces, offering a range of collaborative learning environments outside of the typical classroom. Credit: Lincoln Barbour.

The building's physical layout reinforces this approach. The first floor is themed around Earth ecosystems, and the second floor is themed around the skies above. Students start out as Backyard Adventurers in kindergarten and scale up to Forest Trailblazers (first grade) and then Ocean Navigators (second grade). Educational graphics in the Forest and Ocean cover sustainable materials and water conservation. Expanding outward and upstairs, third-grade Atmosphere Aviators focus on air quality and carbon footprints, and fourth-grade Solar System Pioneers and fifth-grade Galaxy Voyagers explore space and conservation of light and energy.

A variety of icons, colors, words, and illustrations were incorporated throughout the building to engage students, parents, teachers, and visitors of all ages and learning abilities. Many educational signs feature real-world facts related to grade-level themes, transforming wayfinding features into creative educational opportunities relating students

Photo 13.2 The "garden wall" reinforces the kindergarten's "Backyard Explorer" theme, with unique reading nooks named after animal habitats that can be found right outside. Credit: Alan Karchmer.

Photo 13.3 Students sign their names on large-scale graphics that identify each grade level. Credit: Lincoln Barbour.

and their actions to environmental stewardship. Learning takes place at all scales of the building from large-scale graphics down to classroom signage that highlights native flora and fauna. Animals depicted on each classroom entry can be found in Arlington's backyards, and all silhouettes throughout the area are life-size. In the Forest, sustainably harvested woods emulate trees, complete with species-corresponding leaf silhouettes to match leaves students may bring in from outside. The Atmosphere's blue sky is filled with life-size silhouettes of flying creatures great and small, which are denoted by a key that describes their biological qualities. Signage throughout Discovery's outdoor spaces provides information on everything from tree species to the operation of the geothermal wells beneath the athletic field.

Building Dashboard

Discovery's building design team worked with educators to develop a custom, cloud-based energy dashboard, so anyone can access data from any device at any location. The dashboard displays real-time energy use and

Photo 13.4 Educational graphics present information at different scales from the individual to the building to the planet, mirroring students' expanding curriculum as they progress through Discovery. Credit: Lincoln Barbour.

production data, performance data such as carbon emissions and equivalencies, and the building's net-zero energy goals – all of which are actively integrated into lessons across grade levels. For example, students can see how solar productivity is affected by the clouds outside their window, or how building energy demand drops when they turn the lights off or change their thermostats. Recent enhancements to the dashboard include integrated trash and recycling data and transportation modality data, which is collected by students on Discovery's Eco-Action Team. Dashboard data tell a story about the school building and how well it is working from a sustainability standpoint. This makes it a tremendous teaching tool, providing authentic data points that can be used by students to ask questions and drive further study.

The dashboard also provides a virtual experience for visitors, with 360-degree views of a typical Discovery classroom, the kitchen, roof, Solar Lab, mechanical room, and HVAC room with sustainability features highlighted and links to relevant graphics and graphs, expanding the school's educational resources far beyond its walls.

Photo 13.5 A screenshot of Discovery Elementary School's digital dashboard displays real-time energy use and production data. Credit: VMDO Architects.

Discovery's 3D Textbook Comes Alive

While Discovery's net-zero energy building is impressive, in the end, its features must translate into effective learning experiences. This is where Discovery's teachers make all the difference. The building thrives as a teaching tool not just because of how it was built, but because of how it is used.

Maximizing Energy Production

Discovery is not only net-zero, but net-positive – the building produces far more power than it uses on an annual basis. As a result, students are often challenged to identify ways to maximize energy production. For example, a group of third-grade students wondered if the school's solar panels should be cleaned more often. A representative from the district's facilities department and a solar-panel cleaner assisted these students in investigating the cost of cleaning the panels more frequently, and the extent to which a slight decrease in transparency and increase in opacity, due to a layer of dust or pollen, impacted power production. By placing various levels of transparent and opaque materials on the Solar Lab's three experimental solar panels, they determined that the increased risk to the system and expense of cleaning would not significantly improve power production. Even though

Photo 13.6 The Solar Lab enables hands-on experimentation to understand the effects of orientation and weather on energy production. Credit: Lincoln Barbour.

the answer was "no, that doesn't work," the answer nevertheless was a fantastic discovery by students and a valuable lesson for the school, informing leaders and staff where to concentrate for further improvements.

Reducing Waste

Discovery is a National Wildlife Federation Eco-Schools USA Green Flag School. One of the ways Discovery teachers use the program's Pathways structure to advance student learning and school sustainability initiatives is by having students conduct waste audits. Working with the school's custodial and nutrition teams, students weigh recycling and food waste to better understand how much waste is produced daily. These measurements are tracked using the G Suite for Education platform, and the data is available on Discovery's dashboard. These waste audits have helped the school community modify its behaviors to have a lighter impact on the environment. For example, students used their findings to redesign the "trash line" in the Dining Commons to promote recycling and the donation of leftover food to the local food assistance program as well as to eliminate single-use plastics and promote the use of reusable lunch containers.

Growing Food with Hydroponic Systems

Around 2018, the first of three indoor hydroponic systems were installed at Discovery by a teacher and a group of students. The system, a hydroponic wall, was constructed to grow lettuce and other greens for use in school meals. It also provided an authentic, hands-on way for students to observe and participate in the plant life cycle. Since then, Discovery's teachers have worked to integrate hydroponics in the curriculum across all grade levels. That way, every student gets to participate in the process by engaging in developmentally appropriate and standards-aligned learning experiences. Kindergarteners plant and germinate seeds in seed trays in their classrooms. First-graders nurture the young plants and troubleshoot issues that arise. Third-graders transplant the sprouts into the hydroponic systems, while fourth-graders measure, monitor, and adjust pH and nutrient levels in the various tanks. Fifth-graders monitor and record data trends to improve the systems and collaborate with other grade levels to teach them about the systems – for example, working with second-graders to harvest the crops and move them to the kitchen for food preparation.

Preserving Biodiversity

Caring for and learning about the plants and animals that make up the local ecosystem is an integral part of environmental stewardship and Discovery students have many opportunities to do so without leaving campus. As part of the Eco-Schools USA program, first-graders engage in a lesson called Learning About Our Forests. In this lesson, students count and measure the size of various tree species around campus and then "adopt" a tree. They name their adopted trees and care for them throughout the season. Second-graders use Discovery's pollinator garden to learn about the life cycle of insects like the Monarch butterfly. The garden includes milkweed specifically to attract Monarch butterflies, and through floor-to-ceiling windows, students can observe the butterflies and learn about their migration patterns. Fifth-graders study biodiversity by examining the insects, amphibians, and mammals that thrive in and around Discovery's biofiltration gardens. They also set up a trail camera to monitor the various nocturnal species that call Discovery home.

Impact on Teacher Practice

By involving educators early and often in the planning and use of the campus as a teaching tool, Discovery's leadership team has fostered a culture that empowers educators to take initiative in creating an innovative environment for creative and effective teaching. Discovery is not a place that likes to say no; it is a school that leans hard into saying "yes." Educators are encouraged to think big and realize big because of the resources provided to them, notably by the building itself. When a second-grade teacher wanted to play a version of the game Settlers of Catan to teach her students the principles of currency, supply, and scarcity, she did not settle for playing the board game in her class. Instead, she translated the idea into a life-size version that was played on the massive vinyl tiles in the school's atrium. Teaching in a building that facilitates collaboration, openness, and teaching efficacy encourages educators to rise to its example and continuously improve their practices.

Photo 13.7 Each neighborhood's color palette, educational graphics, and themed signage reinforces the grade's "identity," which ties back to Discovery's Standards of Learning. Credit: Lincoln Barbour.

Lessons Learned

A common challenge for any school, but especially at a school like Discovery, is ensuring everyone knows how to take full advantage of its resources, including how to use the available spaces and technology. Discovery has a full-time educational technology administrator – someone who is a qualified and experienced classroom teacher first and foremost, but who has a strong background in integrating technology into learning – to help teachers navigate the building's tools and technologies. Discovery has also assembled a robust coaching team to ensure teachers are fully supported as they integrate not only devices but the entire learning environment into their work. Comprised of full-time educators who do not have classes of their own, the coaching team "pushes in" to classes and works directly with staff as on-site professional developers, helping to co-plan and co-teach instruction and facilitate Collaborative Learning Teams made up of grade-level educators. The team includes two English Language Arts coaches, a mathematics coach, a gifted education coach, the technology coach, the school counselor, the Special Education lead teacher, the Instructional Lead teacher, and the school librarian.

 ## Learning from Discovery Elementary School: Leveraging Your School Building and Grounds as a Teaching Tool

Discovery Elementary School offers many lessons and much inspiration for schools looking to use their buildings as teaching tools. Its building design features and concepts can be applied, at some scale, to any school – new or existing, large or small. Here are some tips for getting started.

- **Look for project champions.** Each project must have a champion (or two!) who will spend time and effort making connections and cultivating consensus and integration between design and curriculum. Dr. Russo's efforts in the early stages of Discovery's design were crucial in ensuring that the building's features could be leveraged by teachers in the curriculum. Also, having a "resident expert" on how the building works has helped Discovery's teachers maximize use of the school's facilities as teaching tools.

- **Provide coaching and professional development.** An innovative, revolutionary school by definition has features and opportunities that educators have not encountered elsewhere or learned about in teacher preparation programs. Having a powerful coaching staff and an ongoing culture of professional learning will equip all educators, new to veteran, with pedagogical, assessment, curricular, and planning skills to take full advantage of a building's learning features. Integrating the building into learning, as a learning tool, must be directly and regularly instructed and supported for maximum effectiveness.
- **Prioritize students and learning.** A school is not "for" adults, not even teachers. A school is for students. Consequently, reconsider structures, physically and organizationally, that are designed for control and consider how to replace them with open accessibility, freedom of choice and movement, and opportunities to enhance curiosity and exploration. If a large wall looks promising for painting or displaying, ask how that wall can be used to enhance student learning, reinforcing content and skill mastery.
- **Look at existing spaces with new eyes.** Redesigning a space may involve knocking down a wall or pulling off a door, or it may simply involve rearranging or reassigning a space's use. Take time, as a school leader, to dwell within underutilized, ineffective, old, large, or confusing spaces and consider how they can be reorganized, repurposed, or retrofitted. Many schools are built, furniture is placed, and things never move again. Instead, challenge yourself and your colleagues to ask key questions: Is this space the best it can be for students? What learning takes place here and what features would enhance that learning?
- **Be flexible.** Giving students voice and choice over how to structure their spaces facilitates creativity and the learning process. Discovery abandoned single desks and chairs in favor of more flexible seating arrangements. Students can choose from chairs, wobble stools, benches, beanbag chairs, and carpet spaces. Just as important, students know that they can and should rearrange their spaces as needed to meet their learning needs.

Synthesis

American school design and construction has changed somewhat, but the underlying principles of school design remain largely traditional in many quarters. Discovery encourages communities, educators, designers, and thought leaders to reconsider their priorities and revisit the basic underlying principles of everything from how a school is laid out to how to make a space student- and learning-centered. As we reconsider the schools of today and design and redesign schools for the future, we must situate environmental responsibility and stewardship at the center of our work, both behind the scenes in the building's physical plant and on the surface where students interact and dwell. In doing so, we can and must create schools that are themselves learning technology, and Discovery demonstrates that both priorities are symbiotic, relevant, and useful.

Discovery's leaders and educators not only want their school to thrive; they want every student in every school in America to thrive. The key to making that happen is building schools, like Discovery, that foster a reciprocal relationship between the content that is taught and where that content is taught – where educators help design the environment in ways that allow the environment to educate students.

Thank you to Robert Winstead of VMDO Architects and Brittney Butler of Iconograph for their contributions to this story.

Works Cited

International Living Future Institute. (n.d.). Zero energy certified Discovery Elementary School. Retrieved from: https://living-future.org/lbc/case-studies/discovery-elementary-school/

Relevant Websites

Discovery Elementary School. Retrieved from: https://discovery.apsva.us/

Waste Not, Want Not

Boulder Valley School District's School Food Project Leads the Way in K-12 Food Waste Reduction

Laura A. Smith

Boulder Valley School District

Named first REAL Certified school district in the country in November 2016

Location: Boulder, Colorado

Number of schools: 56 schools

Number of students: approximately 31,000 students

Student demographics: 67.8% White; 19.1% Hispanic/Latino; 6% Multiracial; 5.7% Asian; 1.0% Black/African American; 0.3% Native American; 0.1% Native Hawaiian

2014 U.S. Department of Education Green Ribbon District Sustainability Awardee

DOI: 10.4324/9781003152811-18

Uneaten sandwiches. Ripe, red apples. These items, among other perfectly edible food, were ending up in Douglass Elementary School's trash cans after lunch. Frustration was growing, action needed to be taken. So, a small band of students, with support from an invested parent, formed a Food Waste Club to educate their school about food waste and ways to reduce waste during the school day. Club members surveyed their peers to gauge which foods students did or did not like and to get their thoughts on portion size, hot versus cold lunches, and how hungry they were at lunch time. They then conducted a waste audit, weighing discarded food from the cafeteria to see how much food their school was wasting. The students discovered that many of their peers were throwing away untouched fruits and vegetables. In response, they created an "untouched food bin," where students can place uneaten fruits and vegetables to be washed and used in future lunches.[1] The data was also used to increase awareness among students and to promote the idea of "take what you want and eat what you take." Club members prepared a video about food waste and how to be proactive in the lunchroom to share with classes and on the school's website. Their efforts received national attention in 2016 when the U.S. Environmental Protection Agency recognized the Food Waste Club with the President's Environmental Youth Award.

These student-led efforts show what is possible when students organize around an issue they are passionate about. They also reflect a broader commitment to curb food waste across Boulder Valley School District, an initiative that originated with the district's sustainability plan.

The Challenge of Food Waste

Colorado's Boulder Valley School District (BVSD) is not immune to the challenges posed by food waste and is aware of the consequences of not taking action. In 2019, 35% of 229 million tons of food available went

---

1 Untouched food bins, also known as share bins or share tables, became an acceptable food waste reduction effort at BVSD in 2017. The USDA recognizes share bins as an ideal way to return uneaten food to the meal program, provided that proper food safety precautions are taken (Kline, 2016). School districts should contact their state and local health departments for further guidance and approval before implementing their own program.

Photo 14.1 A poster created by elementary students now hangs in all BVSD cafeterias. Credit: Douglass Food Waste Club.

unsold or uneaten in the U.S. Most became food waste – approximately 54 million tons – and ended up in a landfill or a waste incinerator or was left to rot in a field. The environmental impact is enormous – agricultural and energy resources are wasted, and millions of tons of greenhouse gases are released into the atmosphere (ReFED, n.d.). Schools see a significant amount of food end up in the compost and garbage, which impacts the environment and wastes school resources. As one of the largest institutional buyers in a community, a school district's procurement and waste practices can have a profound impact. Nearly 100,000 schools and institutions serve meals to 29.6 million students each day (School Nutrition

Association, n.d.). Federal nutrition guidelines require schools to provide five meal components – fruit, vegetable, protein, grain, and fluid milk. Serving sizes are dictated by the U.S. Department of Agriculture (USDA), leaving school food-service operations with limited flexibility to reduce food waste. But this is where innovation can happen.

As a sustainability leader within the larger community, BVSD's Food Services department, also known as the School Food Project, is always looking for ways to improve existing sustainability efforts. By closely monitoring food preparation, reducing food waste at various points throughout food production and service, and educating staff and students, the School Food Project is creating a more sustainable program, reducing food waste, and lowering food costs.

Partners and a Plan: Laying a Foundation for Food Waste Reduction

BVSD's sustainability work began in the 1990s with a districtwide recycling program and a focus on making energy-efficient upgrades, such as installing LEDs, motion sensors, and a few small solar photovoltaic systems. These programs were driven internally by an Energy Manager and supported by local partner Eco-Cycle, the community's recycling and compost processor. Over time, these programs became stronger and more embedded in the district's schools.

In 2008, BVSD hired Ghita Carroll to serve as its Sustainability Coordinator. One of Ghita's first tasks was to create a sustainability plan. Ghita worked with an advisory committee made up of staff, parents, community members, and students to develop BVSD's Sustainability Management System (SMS). First drafted in 2009, and updated in 2015, the SMS is a master plan that serves as a comprehensive road map for the district's sustainability efforts. The plan is divided into four categories: buildings, materials, transportation, and education. Each category includes long-term "stretch" goals, five-year goals, and recommended strategies for achieving those goals. Food waste lives under the materials category, which includes goals for green purchasing, sustainable food, and waste diversion. The holistic integration of the SMS's values and practices into daily operations has allowed BVSD to move forward with increasingly innovative solutions.

In 2009, BVSD hired Chef Ann Cooper as its Food Services Director. In addition to emphasizing healthier, scratch-cooked foods in school meals, Chef Ann introduced a holistic approach where schools function as part of a sustainable food system. This meant moving away from disposable plates, trays, utensils, and cups in favor of reusables and introducing commercial dishwashers into school satellite kitchens. Regional production kitchens were established to streamline food production for BVSD schools. Local and regional food vendors and products were prioritized, and school gardens were further integrated into farm-to-cafeteria and nutrition education programs offered by BVSD and its nonprofit partners.

When it comes to addressing food waste, one of the most influential programs is the Green Star Schools (GSS) program, hosted by Eco-Cycle. GSS provides recycling and composting opportunities in schools, while helping students to better understand the relationship between waste and environmental issues such as pollution, resource depletion, and deforestation. GSS also targets large-scale waste diversion in school kitchens and cafeterias to meet their goal of zero-waste schools throughout the community.

Building on 25 years of waste reduction efforts courtesy of GSS, the School Food Project formally launched its food waste reduction program in 2012, starting in the regional production kitchens. Long before technology was introduced, production kitchen staff saved food scraps to get a sense of the amount of waste created. Staff training included a review of the GSS program, how to maximize the edible parts of fresh produce, waste reduction efforts students were learning about outside the cafeteria, and trips to partner farms to gain a better understanding of and appreciation for the products used in school meals. Around 2012, School Food Project staff started working directly with students to help them understand portion sizes and taking only what they intend to eat. Posters hang in cafeterias and kitchens to remind students and staff of how they can reduce food waste, while school GSS champions support waste-reduction messaging and education.

The collaboration between GSS and the School Food Project was a natural fit. GSS became an advocate for and champion of BVSD's waste reduction efforts in cafeterias and kitchens, and the School Food Project helped GSS prepare presentations for students. Each year, GSS hosts a Waste-Free Lunch Contest that challenges students to bring waste-free meals from home and reminds students who buy school lunch that food scraps can be composted, while reusable trays and utensils should be returned to the kitchen instead of thrown away. Today, GSS and the School Food Project continue to work side by side empowering students and staff to make a difference in their school's waste reduction efforts.

A Sustainable Food Leader

BVSD has built a reputation as one of the country's foremost school food programs. The School Food Project serves nearly 17,000 fresh, nutritious, scratch-cooked meals every day, using locally sourced and organic ingredients whenever possible and avoiding highly processed foods, high fructose corn syrup, chemicals, dyes, and food additives. Salad bars are offered daily at every school and are stocked with local, farm-fresh fruits and vegetables. Students provide regular input on menu items and create their own as part of BVSD's annual Iron Chef-style competitions.

The Many Facets of Food Waste Reduction at BVSD

There is no simple, single fix to reducing food waste in school cafeterias. Rather, it requires a multi-pronged approach that considers everything from the food that is purchased to the dinnerware it is served on. Here are some of the most impactful strategies BVSD has adopted to reduce food waste and involve students in waste reduction efforts.

Salad Bars and Cycle Menus

Self-serve salad bars play an important role in reducing food waste because they offer a high degree of flexibility when it comes to fruit and vegetable offerings. This flexibility allows BVSD to purchase whatever farmers have available and respond to opportunities in cases of severe weather events. For example, in August 2018, many farmer partners were devastated by a series of hailstorms. Severe weather destroyed 80% of the tomato and pepper crops at one farm, making these crops less marketable at farm stands, CSAs, and farmers markets (Covington, 2018). BVSD's focus on local

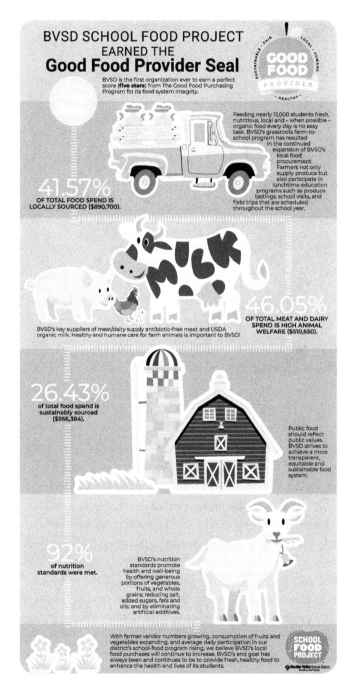

Photo 14.2 Credit: Boulder Valley School District.

Photo 14.3 BVSD cafeteria staff prep ingredients for a scratch-cooked meal.
Credit: Boulder Valley School District.

procurement and built-in procurement flexibility allowed orders to react to unique events like this. Damaged tomatoes are great for tomato sauce while hail-pocked peppers and cucumbers can be chopped up for use on salad bars. A salad bar's flexibility extends to students, too. The variety of fruits and vegetables found on a salad bar allows students to choose what they want to eat, instead of being served something they may not like (and throw in the garbage).

While maintaining flexibility on salad bars, BVSD's lunch menu follows a regular six-week cycle to ensure predictability, projections, and tracking of procurement and meals served. Using a cycle menu makes it easier to predict the quantities of food needed each time a menu item is served. Kitchen managers track the number of servings ordered versus the number of meals served and use that data to adjust their orders for the next time that same menu mix comes up. BVSD's procurement manager and chefs also depend on the cycle menu to identify areas of overlap and multiple uses for ingredients. With this information, procurement managers can aggregate purchases, receive items in bulk, and reduce over-purchasing of items or ingredients that will not be used before they expire. Cycle menus can allow school districts to project purchasing needs for the entire year, reducing "guesstimates," over-purchasing, and resulting waste.

Reducing Food Packaging Waste

There is more to food waste than food. It is just as important to eliminate the amount of packaging that is wasted as well. One of the first changes the School Food Project made to shift to a more sustainable operation was to introduce bulk milk dispensers in 2010. While all school food-service operations are required to serve white milk, BVSD chooses not to rely on it as a food item to create a reimbursable meal under USDA guidelines.[2] Students can take a full eight ounces of milk, but are not required to. Instead, they can opt for three of the four other meal components – fruit, vegetable, meat/meat alternate, and grain. As such, students only take as much milk as they will drink.

In addition to cutting down on milk waste from unfinished eight-ounce servings, bulk dispensers reduce waste generated by milk cartons. In a medium-sized school district like BVSD, that keeps nearly 1.5 million single-serve milk cartons out of the waste stream each school year! The cost savings are tremendous, allowing BVSD to serve organic 1% milk in all cafeterias. The organic bulk milk is less expensive per serving than conventional milk served in individual cartons or plastic containers (Chef Ann Foundation, n.d.).

BVSD took its waste reduction efforts a step further in 2015 with the introduction of reusable plastic containers (RPCs) to replace cardboard packaging. Through a grant from StopWaste, BVSD purchased 660 RPCs

---

2 USDA School Meal Program guidelines for breakfast and lunch dictate that certain meal components (grains, fruit, vegetable, meat/meat alternate, milk) must be available during mealtimes; however, students are only required to take two of three components at breakfast and three of five at lunch (U.S. Department of Agriculture, 2015). Some schools rely on eight ounces of milk as a required meal component for all students to ensure they meet the guidelines for a reimbursable meal. This can lead to large quantities of wasted milk among students who cannot or do not want to drink milk.

and 350 fish tubs to rotate through the food delivery process. In its inaugural year, the program yielded a savings of $4,581 in packaging and eliminated 4,587 pounds of cardboard from the district's waste stream (Reusable Packaging Association, n.d.). As full RPCs are delivered, empty containers are made available to suppliers for use the following week when another shipment is delivered. After piloting the program with apples and beef patties, BVSD expanded the program to include all local produce, local beef patties and ground beef, local bone-in chicken, and local tortillas.

BVSD has also reduced its dependence on disposable serve ware in its cafeterias. In 2010, the district shifted to using reusable trays, plates, bowls, cups, and utensils for school meals. This move nearly eliminated polystyrene and paper products from its cafeterias. Moving from disposable to reusable serve ware does require additional resources, including commercial dishwashers and the staff to run them. If schools can afford the upfront costs of installation and plumbing, over the life of a dishwasher, the cost savings and positive impact on the environment can be a no-brainer for sustainability-minded school kitchens.

Tracking and Measuring Impact

The School Food Project targeted food waste reduction as a priority in 2017. To reduce food waste within the department, staff members first needed to understand the amount and type of waste being created during daily operations. After receiving a grant from Boulder County's Resource Conservation Division, BVSD installed LeanPath machines in the district's three regional production kitchens. In 2020, the School Food Project moved into a central production kitchen and now uses the LeanPath machines to measure food waste in three different areas of the facility.

Using the LeanPath food waste tracking system, each time an employee goes to throw away food, they place the food waste in a compost bin that sits on a floor scale. The employee selects the food type and specific item to be tossed and the reason for its disposal (i.e., overproduction, spoilage, and trimming). The system also tracks the employee's name and estimates the cost associated with each item's disposal. The LeanPath system then generates a series of reports that detail the pounds of food thrown away by day, week, month, or year; estimated food cost lost; trends indicating type of food most often wasted and employees responsible for the majority of food waste; increases and decreases in waste over time; and more. These analytics have helped BVSD chefs and procurement managers introduce food waste reduction strategies, adjust future food purchases, and create awareness among employees of food waste. Tracking allows for further comparisons by production method, food vendor and dish being prepared, and inferences about food costs and food waste estimates.

Having a better understanding of waste generated during meal production informs new, creative strategies to divert waste from the compost bin. For example, while broccoli stems are not ideal for salad bars, they can be repurposed for use in dishes like the ever-popular Broccoli-and-Cheese-Stuffed Potato where pretty florets are less necessary. The LeanPath system also introduced opportunities to recognize staff for their efforts to track food waste and is set up to incentivize staff for recording their waste. By tracking their waste, staff create opportunities to learn new techniques for reducing food waste and to understand the financial and environmental impacts of food waste and food waste reduction.

BVSD is now home to 11 LeanPath machines – three in the central production kitchen, two in school satellite kitchens, and six in school cafeterias

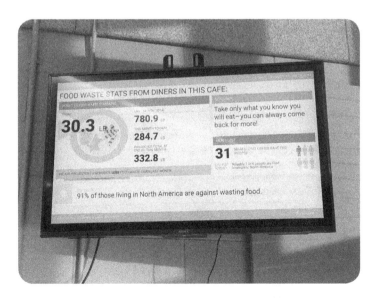

Photo 14.4 LeanPath Spark food waste tracking systems provide real-time feedback in BVSD cafeterias. Credit: Boulder Valley School District.

– with plans to add two more in fall 2021. BVSD's central production model and scratch-cooking operation mean that there are many opportunities to reduce food waste throughout the production process. Capturing data from initial production to final preparation allows for refinement of procedures, additional team training, and implementation of best practices across the district.

Using the LeanPath Spark system in cafeterias is another one of BVSD's food waste reduction strategies. In the five schools with Spark systems, students scrape their plates into a compost bin that has a large floor scale underneath to weigh every piece of organic waste generated in the cafeteria. Each transaction is recorded, generating a report similar to the ones produced by the LeanPath machines, while real-time data is displayed in cafeterias and translated into kid-friendly statistics and equivalents, such as the number of meals lost, swimming pools of water wasted, and cars on the road. So far, the program has only been piloted as a passive communication display, with a 30% noticed reduction in post-consumer food waste. As such, the School Food Project is working to introduce a food-waste toolkit with additional classroom and practice-based learning opportunities for teachers and students to implement using data generated in their schools.

Sample BVSD LeanPath Reports and Observations

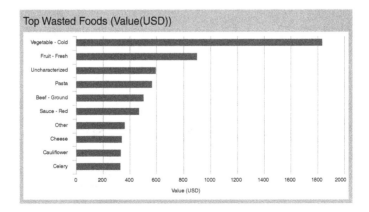

Figure 14.1

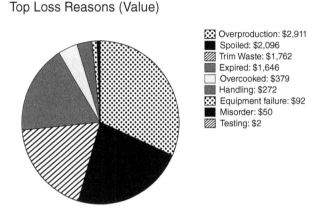

Top Loss Reasons (Value)

Overproduction: $2,911
Spoiled: $2,096
Trim Waste: $1,762
Expired: $1,646
Overcooked: $379
Handling: $272
Equipment failure: $92
Misorder: $50
Testing: $2

Figure 14.2

Cold vegetables, like those prepared for salad bars, present the best opportunity for more detailed analysis. While some vegetables have a high AP (as purchased) to EP (edible portion) ratio, others have inescapably low AP:EP ratios. For example, there is little waste with tomatoes which only need the stem removed before washing and serving. Winter squash, however, must be deseeded and skinned prior to serving.[3]

Overproduction and spoiled or unusable food are the categories to target first with new reduction strategies. In analyzing the product types that are often overproduced, marinara sauce appears to be the highest value product. BVSD produces hundreds of gallons of marinara sauce almost every week for spaghetti and pizza dishes. This presents an opportunity for creative reuse strategies. When implementing reuse strategies, it is important to train staff on proper storage practices and ensure kitchens have enough storage space, which is already a challenge.

---

3 "Uncharacterized" is a default category for foods that are not entered under a more descriptive category.

Engaging Students as Food Waste Warriors

Involving students in their school's waste stream supports efforts to educate them on waste reduction and how they can make a difference. Thanks to a World Wildlife Fund (WWF) grant, in spring 2019, BVSD schools were invited to participate in a districtwide food waste audit program to collect data and implement strategies to reduce food waste at schools and throughout the district. BVSD and eight other communities across the country collected data on the amount of food thrown out in school cafeterias. The aggregated dataset was used by WWF's policy team to make a business case for reducing school-generated food waste.

In association with the audit, WWF provided BVSD with a Be a Food Waste Warrior toolkit, a three-part science and math lesson that can be adjusted in complexity depending on grade level. The toolkit included food

Photo 14.5 Students at five BVSD schools completed audits of their cafeteria lunch waste as part of a 2019 grant from the World Wildlife Fund. Credit: Boulder Valley School District.

waste audit log sheets, discussion questions, a companion PowerPoint, and teacher resources and materials. Teams of students at five BVSD schools conducted a series of food waste audits in their cafeterias. With these Food Waste Warriors as peer leaders, students separated post-lunch waste into nine categories – fruits, vegetables, reusable fruit, composed entrees, fluid milk, other liquids, non-edible compostables, recycling, and landfill. Led by science and practice-based learning teachers, students weighed the waste after each lunch period over the course of six school days and recorded their data. Students then converted food waste weights to water used and greenhouse gases emitted and calculated the difference in greenhouse gas emissions depending on whether food waste is landfilled or composted. These calculations helped students better understand the ramifications of wasted food in their school's cafeteria. Backed by data and observations, Food Waste Warrior teams designed communication campaigns and implemented new school-based strategies to further reduce waste in their schools.

As part of the Food Waste Warriors program, teachers developed lesson plans based on Colorado Common Core Standards and aligned with BVSD's 3D learning model, integrating eight student-driven scientific approaches to examining a problem or inquiry and applying crosscutting concepts for students to use as they make sense of and solve issues related to core ideas in the disciplines of earth and space science, life science, physical science, and applied science. The lesson plans developed for and by BVSD teachers will allow other educators to meet curriculum standards through sustainable food systems and food waste reduction projects. In addition, the School Food Project actively works with teachers to incorporate classroom discussions and activities around local food systems, social studies, ecology, and economics into their lessons.

Lessons Learned

BVSD's School Food Project has experienced a variety of challenges in addressing food waste over the years, but none more so than time and money. From the production kitchen to meal service and clean up after lunch, ensuring students and staff follow best practices for food waste reduction takes time until it becomes part of the daily routine. BVSD continues to seek grants and partnerships to ease the cost and training burden associated with its food waste reduction program. Grant funding from state and private programs was used to purchase LeanPath machines and partnerships supported food-service staff and teachers in learning to implement best practices and engage students in championing the work. Time devoted to learning about food waste reduction was built into staff back-to-school training, professional development opportunities were provided for teacher champions, and ongoing technical assistance was provided to custodial staff partnering with School Food Project activities.

Another big challenge is engagement. Reducing food waste in schools is a team effort, and every individual in a school has a part to play. When the School Food Project kicked off its food waste reduction program, it was only mildly successful because administrators, teachers, staff, and students had not yet made a commitment join the effort; they were bystanders, not active participants. Since then, everyone has stepped up and embraced the challenge of reducing food waste across the district. There is still work to do. Educating students, especially young ones, on what to compost, recycle, or toss in the trash can be time-consuming and frustrating. However, space needs to be made for students to make mistakes, learn, and develop good habits. And students have a responsibility to encourage each other, to understand their role in producing waste and its impacts on the environment, and to feel empowered as part of the solution.

Learning from Boulder Valley School District: Reducing Food Waste at Your District

BVSD's food waste reduction work is possible thanks to the dedication of their food services department and support from partners and the school community. Here are some steps your district can take to start or ramp up a food waste reduction program of your own.

- **Cafeteria as a classroom.** There is an ongoing need to educate students, parents, and staff about food waste and how to reduce it. Having volunteers in the cafeteria to talk with students and help them understand waste diversion is vital. Learning does not stop in the classroom and teaching should not either.

- **Get students involved in the solution.** The food waste reduction practices and procedures implemented in a school affect students every day. Allow them to play a role in creating solutions so they feel a sense of ownership and responsibility for their ongoing success.
- **Measure.** You cannot manage what you have not measured. Start tracking food waste in your school kitchen or cafeteria. A simple log paired with your school meal schedule can reveal areas for improvement.
- **Start small.** There are many facets to food waste reduction; it can feel important yet daunting to tackle them all. Start with solutions that will work best and be most sustainable for your school community. Build off the momentum generated through small wins to tackle bigger issues. Every step to reduce food waste is a step in the right direction.
- **Look at your policies and contracts.** Policies such as the length of each lunch period and contracts detailing individual versus bulk packaging of food products can make a big difference when it comes to waste generated in schools. Talk to your team and your vendors about ways to ingrain waste reduction into everyday operations.
- **Partner up.** Food waste and waste reduction in general is applicable to many subjects, careers, and focuses. Partner with your school's environmental science teacher to develop an experiential learning project. Collaborate with municipal waste haulers to help students and staff understand what waste their school is generating. Team up with local beekeepers and farmers to educate students about the impact waste has on food production and ecosystems.

Synthesis

Food waste is not an easy issue to tackle, especially in schools. Students and staff come and go, so there is an ongoing need to educate and model best practices to keep engagement high and progress on track. The School Food Project remains committed to finding new areas for innovation and efficiency and empowering students, staff, and teachers to be collaborators in reducing food waste. If Douglass Elementary School's Food Waste Club and BVSD's Food Waste Warriors are any indication, the message is coming through, loud and clear.

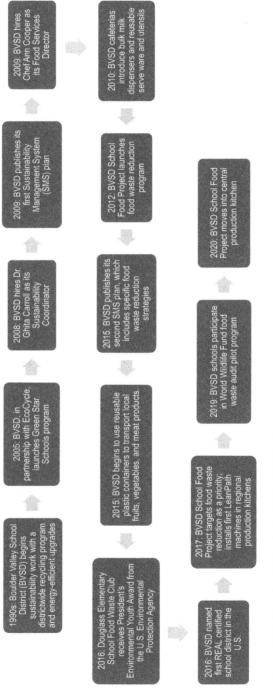

Figure 14.3 Boulder Valley School District Timeline.

Works Cited

Chef Ann Foundation. (n.d.) Bulk milk. Retrieved from: https://www.thelunchbox.org/procurement/bulk-milk

Covington, L. (2018). Late hail proves devastating for some small family farms. *Westword*. Retrieved from: https://www.westword.com/restaurants/when-hail-takes-out-the-farm-10709988

Kline, A. (2016). The use of share tables in child nutrition programs [Memorandum]. *U.S. Department of Agriculture*. Retrieved from: https://fns-prod.azureedge.net/sites/default/files/cn/SP41_CACFP13_SFSP15_2016os.pdf

ReFED. (n.d.). Food waste: The challenge. Retrieved from: https://refed.com/food-waste/the-challenge

Reusable Packaging Association. (n.d). *Going green in school food service*. Retrieved from: https://reusables.org/wp-content/uploads/2016/06/Boulder-Valley-Case-Study_FINAL.pdf

School Nutrition Association. (n.d.). School meal trends & stats. Retrieved from: https://schoolnutrition.org/AboutSchoolMeals/SchoolMealTrendsStats/

U.S. Department of Agriculture. (2015). Updated offer vs serve guidance for the NSLP and SBP beginning SY2015–16. Retrieved from: https://www.fns.usda.gov/cn/updated-offer-vs-serve-guidance-nslp-and-sbp-beginning-sy2015-16

Relevant Websites

Boulder Valley School District. Retrieved from: https://www.bvsd.org/

BVSD's Sustainability Management System. Retrieved from: http://bvsd.org/green/Pages/sms.aspx

Green Star Schools (GSS) program. Retrieved from: https://www.ecocycle.org/schools/gss

School Food Project. Retrieved from: https://food.bvsd.org/

Academy for Global Citizenship's Living Campus Reimagines Public Education

Katherine Elmer-Dewitt and Amanda Hanley

Academy for Global Citizenship

Location: Chicago, Illinois

Number of students: 620 students in grades preK-8

Student demographics: 91.8% Hispanic/Latino; 4% White; 3.6% Black/African American; 0.6% Native American

2012 U.S. Department of Education Green Ribbon School Awardee

"Do you think we'll have enough room to grow tomatoes?"

Ruler in hand, a young boy gingerly kneels in the rich soil of a raised-bed garden while his classmate stands nearby, notebook and pencil in hand. He methodically measures out a large square plot, shouting out measurements as he goes. Together, eyes squinting in concentration, they sit on the edge of the garden bed and work through the math to figure out the perimeter and area of the measured plot. Their teacher approaches and squats down in

DOI: 10.4324/9781003152811-19

front of them, shading her eyes from the bright sun shining down overhead. The boys look up, smiles on their faces. "Yes! Can we grow some basil, too?"

A former barrel factory in the industrial heart of Chicago's southwest side seems like an unlikely place to find students learning math concepts like perimeter and area in an organic garden. However, pay a visit to the Academy for Global Citizenship (AGC), which occupies this space, and you will find students learning in our schoolyard chicken coop, well-loved garden beds, and other non-traditional spaces. Look a little closer and you will also find a small solar array and a demonstration wind turbine. These are small symbols of the prototype sustainable campus our community has been planning since we first opened.

An Opportunity in Disguise

AGC is a public charter school in the Chicago Public Schools system. We were established in 2008 with an audacious vision to reimagine public education. Our mission is to develop mindful leaders who take action now and in the future to positively impact their communities and the world beyond. As an International Baccalaureate school, we are rooted in whole-child education and an inquiry-based approach to learning. Central to our mission is a commitment to holistic wellness, social justice and equity, and sustainability. Students study sustainability concepts throughout their core subjects in an experiential, transdisciplinary learning environment that is contextualized for their specific place and time. Our Sustainability Education Coordinator helps educators integrate hands-on environmental education throughout various subjects. Our curriculum is guided by the Sustainable Schools Project's Education for Sustainability standards and the Cloud Institute for Sustainability Education's Education for a Sustainable Future: Benchmarks for Individual and Social Learning.

Foundational to our vision to reimagine what is possible in public education is a commitment to incubating, scaling, and sharing best practices to empower all students to lead positive change in their communities. Over the years, we have refined how we use our buildings and grounds as essential teaching tools in our inquiry-based approach to sustainability education. We have welcomed thousands of educators from around the world to observe and learn from our approach. Our current facilities – two rented

Photo 15.1 An International Baccalaureate and Dual Language school, AGC's campus is designed to spark wonder and inquiry. Credit: Eva and Daniel Gillet.

buildings, one a converted factory space and the other a school built in 1930 – have made this a challenge due to space constraints and a severely restricted ability to adapt our existing learning spaces to meet the needs of nature and inquiry-based education.

Recognizing this challenge as an opportunity in disguise, we set out to design a prototype 'school of the future' that would be a physical embodiment of our sustainability mission and vision, facilitating our inquiry-based learning model and deepening our relationship with nature.

From Green to Net Positive: Designing a Sustainable School for the 22nd Century

Our visioning process for the new AGC campus started in 2008. Students, teachers, parents, community members, and other stakeholders paired up with world-class architects, designers, and sustainability consultants to conduct an iterative school campus design process that centered on community voice.

First, we looked at the unique conditions and critical needs of 21st-century learners. How can we immerse students in nature daily? How can we promote physical and mental wellness? How can we elevate healthy and sustainable foods? How can we enhance collaboration with the world around us? We explored the ways in which AGC has addressed each challenge through our current culture, curriculum, and learning environment. Then, we explored how an intentionally designed learning space could address these needs and serve as a "third teacher."

For this project, we settled on seven essential building blocks for our new campus:

- It should inspire wonder and belonging to encourage lifelong learning.
- It should be open and responsive to student-centered curriculum.
- It should immerse students in nature and the outdoors.
- It should advance sustainability and environmental stewardship.
- It should celebrate food and farming.
- It should facilitate collaboration with the local and global community.
- It should promote well-being of body and mind.

Making no small plans, the AGC team came to an extraordinary decision. We are striving to become the first regenerative school building and community hub project in the Midwest. To do so, we are pursuing the Living Building Challenge (LBC), which includes some of the most ambitious environmental standards in the world. As opposed to other sustainable building certifications, LBC projects are living sites that are designed and operated to reverse environmental damage and have net-positive impacts. These sites consume fewer resources and place a greater emphasis on replenishing and bettering the well-being of occupants, the local community, and the environment. LBC's more expansive approach is defined by seven performance categories or "petals" to maximize impact: place, energy, water, materials, health and happiness, beauty, and equity.

By constructing our new campus to meet LBC standards, we aspire to model emergent living practices that are compatible with our climate region. Living school innovations will demonstrate where the world is heading and equip our students with hands-on, future-forward readiness. By creating a prototype and a destination, we hope to spur others to adopt a regenerative ethos in their communities.

LBC's holistic framework also aligns with our philosophy, values, and commitment to develop healthier humans and ecosystems. Making a net-positive impact on our community is a key driver. Located on Chicago's southwest side, our neighborhood is challenged by racial division and resource disparities, such as a lack of fresh food, green space, early childhood education, and health care. It is also overburdened by polluted air, water, and land; education inequities; unemployment; and poverty. Mindful of fostering equity, AGC's new campus will house a range of community services, including a fresh food market and community garden plots, early childhood education, and an on-site health clinic. Our dream is to offer a welcoming, leading-edge learning center that reflects the history and culture of our place and people and meaningfully uplifts families and the neighborhood. We hope to serve as a job source and green workforce training ground for our neighbors, a catalyst for equitable and sustainable redevelopment of the adjacent barren property, and as a beacon for community revitalization.

In 2018, we took a significant step closer to realizing our dream when we acquired a six-acre parcel a few blocks from our current site. Our ambitious design received approval from the zoning commission in July 2020, and construction is on track to begin during the 2021–2022 school year.

Photo 15.2 AGC's net-positive energy campus will be a hub for community wellness, learning, and sustainability. Credit: Studio Gang Architects.

The project is being funded via an Illinois Department of Commerce and Economic Opportunity capital grant (among others), philanthropic donations, in-kind contributions, and new markets tax credits. Once complete, our new school will house 700 early childhood through eighth-grade students and staff.

AGC 2.0: The Makings of a Living 3D Textbook

Building a Living Campus

Students learn best from experiences grounded in place. Our new campus will provide multiple opportunities for students to learn from the built environment in ways that will teach them how to reduce their footprint and live in balance with the natural world. Let us take you on a "tour" of our net-positive campus and highlight the features that will make our school truly one for the 22nd century.

We begin with the building itself. The building's design incorporates a number of biophilic elements, such as the use of natural materials and patterns, to bring the outdoors in. Thoughtfully placed windows will provide daylighting, nature views, and fresh air, and the school's interior will be accentuated with lush green plants and living walls. As for the building's construction, we are prioritizing the use of durable, easy-to-maintain, and sustainably sourced materials such as Forest Stewardship Council-certified wood, locally fabricated steel, and recycled concrete aggregate. Toxic building materials and products – such as halogenated flame retardants, BPA and PVC plastic, formaldehyde, and other harmful chemicals – will be restricted during construction and in maintaining our facilities going forward.

Our building will be all-electric, with no gas hook-up, and powered by clean, renewable sources, primarily an extensive photovoltaic solar array and some demonstration wind turbines. Energy-efficient elements, including a well-insulated building envelope, geothermal heating and cooling, LED lighting, and smart automated controls, will help minimize energy use. To achieve net-positive energy, our goal is to produce more energy (105%) than we will need. Our campus's site design promotes active transportation

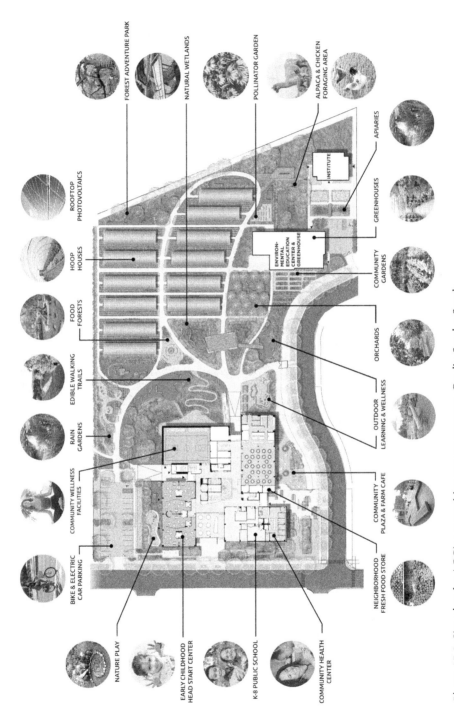

FOREST ADVENTURE PARK

NATURAL WETLANDS

POLLINATOR GARDEN

ALPACA & CHICKEN FORAGING AREA

APIARIES

ROOFTOP PHOTOVOLTAICS

INSTITUTE

GREENHOUSES

HOOP HOUSES

ENVIRON-MENTAL EDUCATION CENTER & GREENHOUSE

COMMUNITY GARDENS

FOOD FORESTS

ORCHARDS

EDIBLE WALKING TRAILS

OUTDOOR LEARNING & WELLNESS

RAIN GARDENS

COMMUNITY WELLNESS FACILITIES

COMMUNITY PLAZA & FARM CAFE

BIKE & ELECTRIC CAR PARKING

NEIGHBORHOOD FRESH FOOD STORE

NATURE PLAY

EARLY CHILDHOOD HEAD START CENTER

K-8 PUBLIC SCHOOL

COMMUNITY HEALTH CENTER

Photo 15.3 Site plan for AGC's net-positive energy campus. Credit: Seed + Spark.

over gas-powered vehicle use with features like improved pedestrian safety measures and covered bike parking. We plan to establish partnerships that will allow us to offer on-site electric vehicle charging stations and bike- and car-sharing options for staff and families.

Water conservation and reclamation on campus will be achieved through a variety of methods. Inside, we will be installing water conserving restroom and kitchen fixtures, such as low-flow faucets and toilets. Outside, rainwater will be harvested for irrigation and toilet flushing (pending approval). An indoor vision panel will show rainwater flowing from the rooftop down to an underground cistern, with a gage indicating how much water was captured for reuse. We also plan to install a number of green infrastructure elements, such as rain gardens and permeable pavers, to slow and filter stormwater runoff.

One of our goals with the new campus site design is to restore the native landscape. Plans include prairie, oak savanna, and wetland (rain garden) habitat zones that incorporate native flowers, grasses, shrubs, and trees. This natural landscape will provide many environmental benefits. For example, the new campus is located near a busy highway, airport, and railway. Trees along the northern border will buffer the highway view and noise and help remove air pollutants. They will also block northwest winter winds and provide shade in the summer. Deeply rooted native prairie plantings will improve biological diversity and soil quality. Most importantly, our living campus will help close the gap for urban kids who tend to have less access to green spaces.

Now that we are outside, let's continue our campus tour by exploring the many features of our learning landscape. In what we call "nature's classroom," an array of structures and unprogrammed experiences will set the stage for students to study, gather, play, and interact with the natural world. Multiple outdoor classrooms will dot our schoolyard, including Council Ring seating around a firepit that can be used for outdoor cooking or as a speaking platform and an Introspective Refuge under a cluster of shade trees where students can go to reflect and de-stress. A learning terrace and two learning balconies will provide easy access to outdoor space from inside the school building. In these unprogrammed platforms, teachers may lead weather-station experiments or guide yoga poses amid soothing birdsongs.

Photo 15.4 Student learning on the new campus will take place outdoors every day, in every type of weather. Credit: Eva and Daniel Gillet.

Numerous play zones will be sprinkled around campus, inviting students to engage in unstructured, age-appropriate nature play. There will be a mud kitchen, an embankment slide, a climbing mound, and sand and water play for preschoolers. Kindergartners and first-graders will have fun playing with a pebble pool and navigating a willow crawl tunnel or log stepper. More adventurous older students will enjoy frolicking along a dead tree net climber and a log balance course.

AGC was founded with a specific focus on engaging children in food and where it comes from. With food and farming as a central teaching tool, students learn the power of daily choices to improve their well-being and the health of their communities and the Earth. Each day, students, staff, and parent volunteers will enjoy organic, locally sourced meals made with love by an on-site chef. Meals will be served in a zero-waste dining café, which will include a community teaching kitchen. Growing as much organic food on-site as possible is a priority. That is why we have dedicated three acres to sustainable urban agriculture, including seasonal raised-bed gardens, 12 hoop houses, a fruit orchard, and a food forest. A Learning Greenhouse will allow students to have year-round gardening experiences, and at the Learning Barn, students will be able to get up close and personal with a variety of farm animals. The barn and its adjacent foraging area will also house rescued farm animals, such as goats, alpaca, pigs, and ducks. Next door is a Food Production Greenhouse that will generate produce for our meal service and a bee apiary that will yield honey harvests and provide pollinators for our farm. An on-site farmers market run by students and parent volunteers will provide fresh produce for our families and others who live in our food-desert community. And our on-site health clinic is planning to offer a FoodRx program that will prescribe fresh produce boxes to those experiencing food insecurity and diet-related illnesses.

Learning from a Living Campus

We believe that it is important to engage students in hands-on, real-world learning that will prepare them to make decisions that will benefit themselves, the planet, and future generations. This is what drives our inquiry-based approach to sustainability education. Our net-positive campus will offer an unparalleled opportunity to build on our curriculum and create more engaging, innovative experiences for students. Let's walk through some examples that demonstrate how our curriculum will evolve as we transition from our current campus to our new one.

Photo 15.5 Meals at AGC are organic, locally sourced, scratch-made, and largely plant-based. Credit: Jason Geil, Humane Society of the United States.

Energy and Water

Renewable energy plays an important role in AGC's commitment to environmental stewardship. As an example, our current campus has a 5 kW photovoltaic solar array that is connected to the building's electrical grid. These panels are a focal point for a unit called "Our Cool School," where students engage in inquiry around how schools are organized and what makes AGC unique. During an outdoor guided inquiry scavenger hunt, students observe the solar panels and learn how they use the sun's energy to do things like power our lights and charge our computers. We use a monitoring system called "Enlighten" that uses many helpful data visualizations to show students how we are making an impact. Through this system, students can see the energy produced by the panels through the equivalent of trees planted, cell phones charged, and much more.

Photo 15.6 Kindergarten students learn about AGC's current on-site solar panels by viewing visualizations of data on a laptop. Credit: Marney Coleman.

On our new campus, students will have access to a solar array and wind turbines to learn about renewable energy. They will also have access to an energy dashboard that will track energy produced by the solar array as well as their consumption patterns. Feedback from the dashboard will give students an opportunity to participate in monitoring the energy it takes to operate a school building and help them make better daily decisions to ensure our school produces more energy than it uses.

Water in and around AGC also serves as a vehicle for learning. On our current campus, second-grade students engage in a science-focused unit of inquiry called "What's the Matter?" where they learn about states and properties of matter. Water and the water cycle are used to make these abstract science concepts more concrete. This unit occurs during the winter months, so students go outdoors on a "water walk" to identify observable properties of water in all its states of matter. One year, students became so impassioned about water usage at our school that they decorated rain barrels, gave a presentation on them to the school, and with the assistance of an adult, installed them in our outdoor garden to water our plants. One rain barrel was already in place, so students were familiar with the concept. The two new rain barrels were installed in the corners of our school greenhouse to capture rainfall.

Photo 15.7 Second-grade students conclude their study of states of matter by decorating a rain barrel to be installed in AGC's current school garden. Credit: Marney Coleman.

On our new campus, students will be able to deepen their understanding of water conservation and use by studying natural methods for water treatment. Permeable pavement can be used to teach lessons on stormwater runoff and infiltration and groundwater tables. Rain gardens can extend this learning and show how different types of native plants can help filter pollution from rain water.

Watersheds and Ecosystems

Teaching students how plants and animals interact in an ecosystem helps them understand that "everything is connected" in a watershed. In our second-grade unit, "Pollinators and Gardens," students engage in a study on pollinators, their interdependence with flowering plants, and humans' impact on pollinators – negative and positive. Students observe how milkweed and dandelion seeds can move without a human planting them and research pollinator-friendly flowers. They also help plan and plant a pollinator-friendly garden in a raised bed in the school parking lot. Students observe their plants daily throughout the spring, hoping to catch a glimpse of a monarch butterfly alighting among the milkweed.

Fifth-graders use our school grounds extensively during their "Sharing the Planet" unit, where they research the various ways in which habitats are impacted by human activity and what they can do to protect Earth's resources. Students are encouraged to be scientists in our outdoor 'laboratory' by participating in various regional and national citizen science programs. They learn how to use dichotomous keys and determine plant species around our schoolyard and then submit their data to BudBurst, an online database focused on climate change and phenology. Students also survey the area for squirrels and submit data to Project Squirrel, a partnership with Chicago's Peggy Notebaert Nature Museum.

Lessons like these will become richer and deeper thanks to the native landscapes and variety of gardens we have planned for the new campus. Learning trails, bird feeders, bat houses, and observation points will encourage students to explore and immerse themselves in a multi-sensory experience. They will hear swishing tallgrass, smell fragrant blossoms, climb prickly tree bark, eye vibrant flowers, and taste delicious berries. They will be able to engage with a wide array of pollinators and watch as they cross-pollinate fruiting trees. They will be able to experience a diversity of habitats without leaving the schoolyard, something our current campus does not provide. And they will all play a role in helping us maintain these spaces as part of their course of study.

Food and Farming

One example of how food and farming are integrated into AGC's curriculum is our first-grade "Farm to Table" interdisciplinary unit where students look holistically at how food is grown, processed, and disposed. The unit opens with students following a piece of fruit from farm to fork. They then dive into the steps it takes to make something like a marshmallow. This exploration leads to discussions around the choices farmers make, the different processes a particular food goes through, and how far a piece of fruit travels to reach a grocery store. Students quickly learn that growing and buying local food is healthy for our bodies and the Earth. For the hands-on part of the exploration, each first-grade class plants a vegetable garden that grows throughout the unit. The garden's produce is used in the unit's final celebration of learning where students prepare a recipe, such as a salad or a salsa, from the garden's harvest.

Another example of integrating the garden and farming into interdisciplinary learning occurs during our fourth-grade's exploration of weathering and erosion in the unit "Change Over Time." As a final summative assessment, students are challenged to create and test a design that will slow the rate of erosion around Lake Michigan. They must use prior knowledge obtained from in-class experiments where they observe how different variables impact the rate of erosion – including vegetation and wind. After multiple iterations of design and testing, students realize that vegetation plays a major role in slowing the rate of erosion. They learn about real-world examples of this in practice (such as the use of maram grass and other native grass plantings around Lake Michigan) and techniques that farms use to slow soil erosion. Armed with this knowledge, students plant cover crops, such as winter rye, in our school garden to help prevent the loss of precious soil in our raised beds.

On our new campus, students will have many more hands-on opportunities to connect with food and farming year-round. They will have access to dedicated experimentation beds, separate from our production beds, where they can test different seeds in different conditions

Photo 15.8 Fourth-grade students apply their knowledge of erosion by planting cover crops in AGC's current school garden. Credit: Marney Coleman.

to better understand what plants need to grow and thrive. Our Learning Greenhouse will be a year-round classroom where teachers can engage students in hands-on lessons on seasonal foods, sustainable farming techniques, and local food systems. Students will be able to learn animal husbandry at the Learning Barn, and our bee apiaries will enrich instruction on pollinators, giving students an up-close look at how bees live and produce honey.

Lessons Learned

Our journey to create a net-positive campus began with an audacious vision that did not always meet expectations for what a school should be. While that was always the intention of the project, we learned that it can be challenging to shift perceptions and, in some cases, regulations, that have been in place for generations. Early on, we spoke with local officials who told us that it would be challenging to gain approval for features like composting toilets, all-gender toilet rooms, rainwater recycling, and an on-site chicken farm. In support of our advocacy to gain an exception to current limits around on-site livestock, two of our school leaders wrote an essay explaining the role of chickens and egg production on our campus, which we lovingly titled "The Chicken Manifesto." We are currently allowed to have 20 chickens and are lobbying for 600. Although it is likely that we will not open our campus with every demonstration feature we had planned for, we learned that ongoing advocacy is a part of sustainability.

Our school redesign process was challenging at times because we had so many ambitions to balance. Our greater aspiration was to serve as a replicable model, and to be replicable, our design must be affordable at

Photo 15.9 A student holds one of AGC's resident chickens. Credit: Elizabeth Gilmore.

the district level. We challenged our design team to stay within the budget allocated for district construction projects. This was an especially difficult task because our district, Chicago Public Schools, has never seen a building project like this. As we balanced trade-offs and value engineering attributes, we looked for smart solutions. For example, square footage is a huge driver of cost. Trading traditional hallways for fluid walking spaces between learning areas will enable more efficient use of space throughout the day. Cutting inefficient space reduced our costs.

We also analyzed upfront and lifetime costs for our innovations. While sustainable options may require higher upfront capital investment, they can improve performance and reduce operational costs. Investments in energy efficiency, water conservation, renewable energy, and food production will ultimately pay for themselves. Fortunately, we will be able to offset some capital costs with grants and rebate incentives. For example, the Illinois Clean Energy Community Foundation provides funding to offset upfront costs for net-zero buildings.

Learning from the Academy for Global Citizenship: Integrating Green-Building Design Principles at Your School

Not every school is ready to make the leap to become net positive. However, there are steps all schools can take to integrate green-building and net-zero strategies into their operations. Here are some tips based on our experiences at AGC.

- **Understand your energy and water consumption patterns.** Scrutinize your electric, gas, and water bills and perform audits to uncover energy and water guzzlers. You may discover simple conservation tweaks and targets for the most effective investments. For example, you may be interested in installing rooftop solar arrays, but an audit may reveal that the payback is better with energy-efficient retrofits since your school is in session during cold winters.
- **Examine your waste stream.** In the cafeteria, trash cans might be overflowing with disposable trays, packaging, and uneaten food. Coordinate your findings with food-service, purchasing, and other staff to

zero in on waste reduction strategies. You might decide to change the menu, switch to reusable serving ware or water dispensers, add more recycling bins with better signage, or compost food waste.

- **Showcase the food cycle.** Growing food offers limitless learning and stewardship potential. In containers or a garden plot, select and plant fruits and vegetables that students will enjoy eating (such as tomatoes or cucumbers), collect stormwater in a rain barrel to water the plants, harvest crops and make an enticing dish (perhaps salsa or pickles), compost fruit and vegetable scraps, and return finished compost to the gardens to nourish the soil. Repeat!
- **Engage students in operations management.** Raise the visibility of your school's energy, water, food, and waste flows. Better yet, encourage students to interrogate these systems in units of inquiry. Signal the importance of protecting and responsibly managing common resources and give students agency to become net-positive changemakers.

Synthesis

The AGC community shares a bittersweet fondness for our current campus. The oft-repaired garden beds, tiny solar array, and parking-lot chicken coop reflect our scrappy determination to show what is possible with limited space and resources. We have shown the value of this learning experience for our students and as an example to others, but it is a small fraction of what we know we are capable of as we dive into the next chapter of our sustainability journey.

The process to realize our vision for a net-positive campus has been long, and there have been many lessons learned along the way. We believe that it was worth this and much more to develop a prototype that will be cost-replicable by public school districts. We are extremely eager to share this model to advance systemic change in education and sustainability and look forward to the day when we can welcome you to our new campus for a tour.

Relevant Websites

Academy for Global Citizenship. Retrieved from: https://agcchicago.org/

Living Building Challenge. Retrieved from: https://living-future.org/lbc/

From LEED to Leader

Virginia Beach City Public Schools Sets the Bar for Divisionwide Sustainability

Tim Cole

Virginia Beach City Public Schools

Location: Virginia Beach, Virginia

Number of schools: 86 schools

Number of students: approximately 67,000 students

Student demographics: 43.6% White; 23.3% Black/African American; 12.8% Hispanic/Latino; 10.4% Multiracial; 6.4% Asian; 0.5% Native Hawaiian/Pacific Islander; 0.2% Native American/Alaskan Native

2016 U.S. Department of Education Green Ribbon District Sustainability Awardee

2018 Governor's Award for Environmental Excellence

Sustainability was not on my mind when I was selected to be an original member of SEAL Team 6 in 1980; nor was it on my mind when I joined Virginia Beach City Public Schools (VBCPS) in 2001. I was originally hired by

DOI: 10.4324/9781003152811-20

VBCPS as a project manager for new school construction. That role eventually morphed into my current position as Sustainability Officer. However, back in 2001, if the cashier at my local grocery store asked if I preferred paper or plastic, I would shrug my shoulders and say it does not matter. Like lots of folks, it simply was not on my radar.

If I had to pinpoint the moment where our school division's sustainability vision came into focus for me, it was outside of Baghdad, where I was serving on active duty in 2006. My "aha" moment happened while I was waiting to be inserted into an operation. It was a fairly peaceful night. I was relaxing and calming my mind. As the sound of small arms fire reverberated off in the distance, I reflected on how I had come to reach the ripe old age of 46. Or, better yet, why? I have survived car crashes, boat crashes, helicopter crashes, parachute malfunctions. I have been shot at and even been drug through the woods by a bear. That kind of reflection can make you ponder your place in the universe and ask "why am I here?" As a special operations guy, you get good at assessing and neutralizing threats. There are the immediate threats you must deal with, like the current operation I was on, and there are the distant threats that require lasting effort and can impose more of a threat. For me, I surmised that the biggest threat facing the future of my children and grandchildren was our collective inability to maintain a symbiotic relationship with one another and the environment. In that moment, I realized that we, as a school division, could have a larger, more significant impact if we adopted a holistic approach that encompassed more than buildings and operations. I knew that it would be a slog to set VBCPS on this path, but, like a Timex watch, we would just keep on ticking.

Winning Hearts and Minds

In 2014, Virginia Beach, Virginia was ranked as the third most conservative city in the country, when comparing cities with populations over 250,000 (Tausanovitch and Warshaw, 2014). Not exactly the kind of place you would expect to find a school division that is a national leader in sustainability. Yet, this has not stopped us from spending the past two decades building a track record of implementing practices that reduce our ecological footprint and operating costs.

It all started with LEED or Leadership in Energy and Environmental Design. When I joined VBCPS in 2001, the division had been building a series of elementary school "prototypes" across the city. LEED was not in the division's vocabulary just yet, largely because the program was so new. I had some experience with LEED. While working at a private practice architecture firm in the late 1990s, I had an opportunity to engage with LEED as a pilot program. Tweaking one of these elementary school prototypes to meet LEED criteria seemed like a logical next step. In private practice, you rarely get an opportunity to have a large-scale impact. With VBCPS, I had an opportunity to impact 86 schools along with all the students who will pass through those buildings in the foreseeable future. Fortunately, I worked for two progressive school leaders. John Kalocay was Assistant Superintendent of Administrative Support Services at the time, and Tony Arnold was Director of Facilities Services. While John had the clout and vision to promote and support new ideas, Tony was, and continues to be, one of the most progressive and fiscally savvy school facility guys you will ever meet. Both would fit right in with military special operators. They are creative and not afraid of risk. Without their support and vision, VBCPS would not be where it is today. John and Tony liked the LEED certification idea and suggested we give it a go.

We started design on our first LEED school, Hermitage Elementary School, in August 2001. The school opened in September 2005 and became the first LEED-certified elementary school in Virginia. Despite being a "sustainable building," Hermitage Elementary School ended up costing less per square foot ($102/sf) than the regional average ($130/sf) (Virginia Beach City Public Schools, 2015). My colleagues were impressed and decided to see if we could build more schools according to LEED standards.

I was not present for the opening of Hermitage Elementary School. I had been called up on active duty and was away for 16 months. It was during that tour of duty that my "aha" moment around sustainability happened. When I returned to the division in June 2006, I was ready to get the ball rolling. However, despite our enthusiasm to explore LEED certification prior to my recall to active duty, it seemed to have lost its focus without someone walking point. Now that I was back, we came up with a unified, comprehensive plan to address sustainability across VBCPS. It would not be easy. How do you create change within a large bureaucracy? Even more daunting, how do you sell sustainability in a very conservative community? Easy, you approach it like a special ops guy. Introducing sustainability into an organization is comparable to guerrilla warfare. You are dropped into a hostile environment. You are severely outnumbered and have limited resources at your disposal. So, you begin to recruit allies. You nurture these relationships, and you steadily win hearts and minds through your successes. Just remember, the only easy day was yesterday.

Adopting the Triple Bottom Line of Sustainability at VBCPS

Laying the Foundation

Every successful plan starts with identifying goals. For our sustainability work at VBCPS, we chose to focus on three goals – develop a sustainable building infrastructure, integrate sustainable practices throughout the school division, and educate the public about sustainability. We already had a head start on the building goal with our foray into LEED with Hermitage Elementary School. Now was our opportunity to cement our commitment to LEED going forward. All new buildings from this point on would meet LEED certification. In February 2009, the VBCPS School Board formalized this process by adopting Policy 3-67, which called for all new buildings to be designed and built according to LEED standards.

Photo 16.1 Rain garden at College Park Elementary School. Credit: Shaleen Wallace.

Meanwhile, we put our heads together around our second goal, integrating sustainable practices throughout VBCPS. One of the first things we did was form a Sustainable Schools Committee in fall 2006. The committee included representatives from every department across the division and provided a means for those departments to share what they were doing around sustainability and determine what steps they needed to take to further integrate sustainability into their practices and culture. One of our first actions was to identify a Sustainable School Liaison at each school to serve as a point of contact for the committee, informing us about VBCPS sustainability initiatives and identifying resources or assistance needed to implement a program or practice. It is no small detail that John Kalocay, Assistant Superintendent at the time, attended all committee meetings and thereby legitimized the process.

At the division level, there were certain practices and programs we wanted to see implemented at every school, such as installing a school teaching garden or starting an environmental club. To encourage our schools to get on board, we started a Sustainable School Recognition Award to recognize schools that implement at least three of the five practices and programs we identified. We handed out the first awards at the end of the 2007–2008 school year. Fifteen schools participated and were eligible for awards that first year. More schools got involved each year since, and by the end of the 2018–2019 school year, 82 of our 86 schools qualified for the award.

Our sustainability work was off to a great start, but a third goal needed our attention – educating the public about sustainability. This was the tricky one, for our division and the surrounding community. First things, first – we needed a common definition and understanding of sustainability. Back when we started this work in 2006, no one in the division really knew what sustainability meant. So, we started by using the United Nations' definition of sustainability: "meeting the needs of the present without compromising the ability of future generations to meet their own needs" (Brundtland Commission, 1987). In 2007, we leaned into a more holistic definition of sustainability that defines it as balancing social, economic, and environmental outcomes. This is the triple bottom line of sustainability, and it is the model we adopted at VBCPS to guide our decision-making and day-to-day operations. We ultimately chose this focus because it views sustainability through a lens that gives everyone a seat at the table. In our case, it allowed us to engage more fully with community members who were traditionally conservative and make the case that the social and environmental practices we were putting in place had a positive impact on our economic bottom line: better buildings, lower costs, and greater energy savings. A win–win–win.

Deepening Our Commitment

By early 2016, we had made great strides to incorporate sustainable practices throughout VBCPS. We had eight LEED-certified schools, 27 EnergyStar-certified schools, and 64 schools with outdoor teaching gardens. Despite these successes, we still had departmental, school, and division leaders who did not see their daily practices through the sustainability lens. To get everyone on board would require a wholesale, divisionwide culture change.

Photo 16.2 Students tend to a garden at Seatack Elementary School. Credit: Marie Culver.

It was around this time that we formally connected with Leith Sharp, Director of Executive Education for Sustainability at Harvard University's T.H. Chan Center for Health and the Global Environment. I had met Leith a couple of times through work with the Center for Green Schools at the U.S. Green Building Council. She taught a course on change leadership for sustainability, and I knew that VBCPS could benefit from her expertise. In July 2016, approximately 50 VBCPS senior leaders – Superintendent Dr. Aaron Spence, his senior staff, and department directors – gathered at the Chesapeake Bay Foundation's Brock Environmental Center for a Sustainability Leadership Summit. The summit was the first time our senior leadership had met in the same room to talk about sustainability. For one and a half days, attendees worked with Leith; Jennifer Seydel, Executive Director of Green Schools National Network; Rachel Gutter, then Director of the Center for Green Schools; and several other experts to identify what our division needed to do to create a culture that values sustainability and supports sustainable practices at every level – from buildings and operations to classroom curriculum. We even invited Jim Spore. Jim had served as Virginia Beach's city manager for over 20 years, and his perspective on how sustainability fit into big-picture goals in a conservative area could not be understated. Many of our senior leaders were very conservative, and we wanted them to hear the business side of sustainability in addition to what was happening in the K-12 arena. As you can imagine, it was no small feat to get a roomful of school leaders to ignore their cell phones for the better part of two days! Yet, everyone remained engaged and by the end of the summit, we had generated over 40 ideas for implementing sustainable practices into our daily operations. Of those 40 ideas, we settled on three big ticket items to focus on – building assets, food, and transportation.

Putting the Triple Bottom Line of Sustainability into Practice

Following the summit, we immediately got to work on the focus areas identified as priority one for our sustainability efforts. It has been five years since the summit, and we have made significant progress in all three areas. While we still have work to do, here is what we have accomplished so far.

Managing Building Assets

Our commitment to build to LEED standards has not waned since we began in earnest in 2006. We finished construction on our 13th LEED building in September 2021, which put us at just over two million square feet of LEED building space. Plans are in the works to begin design on our next high school, which will add another 350,000 square feet, and another elementary school has been funded. Once those are on the books, we will have 15 LEED buildings in our school division, ranging from LEED-certified to LEED Platinum.

Despite increasing our square footage by 9%, we have managed to decrease our energy consumption by close to 27%. Using 2006 as our base year, our divisionwide total cost avoidance when it comes to utility costs is $69 million (Virginia Beach City Public Schools, 2021). Our portfolio of LEED buildings and strategies like cool roof systems, LED lights, daylighting, solar photovoltaics, solar hot water, and geothermal systems all contribute to our energy savings in addition to changes in occupant behavior. We also rely on performance contracting to manage our existing

Photo 16.3 Atrium at Old Donation School. Credit: Tim Cole.

buildings' energy-efficient upgrades and pay for their services using our energy savings.

So, we have built these great LEED buildings and introduced a bunch of new technology and systems to support their sustainability. This is all great, but buildings cannot take care of themselves. Realizing that we needed to do a better job managing our building assets, we created a program in 2017 that placed craftsmen from our school plant maintenance facility as building managers at our school sites. Building managers handle every aspect of maintenance, inside and outside of buildings, and address concerns before they become full-blown issues. They take the load off assistant principals, who were previously in charge of building maintenance, and allow them to focus on the job of educating students. Now, fewer work orders are submitted, problems are solved faster, and everyone can rest easy knowing that there is a subject matter expert in each school, each day, walking the halls to see what needs to be fixed. We have 60 building managers spread out across our building inventory – one per high school and large middle schools and one serving two elementary schools or an elementary school and a middle school.

Managing our buildings is important, but so is managing our grounds and sites. In Virginia Beach, sea level rise and how we handle flooding from storm surge is a big deal. Since 2010, we have been going beyond code requirements to design new school sites to manage a minimum ten-year storm on-site; some sites are even designed to manage a 100-year storm. People have asked us, "why are you spending extra money to install underground chambers to handle stormwater?" Our answer is, we are constructing buildings that are built to last for 80+ years, and we know the burden that will be placed on these sites by sea level rise in the coming decades. We might as well plan and design for that future now to preserve the integrity of our school sites.

Lowering Transportation Emissions

Greenhouse gas emissions were not top of mind for VBCPS until we formed our Sustainable Schools Committee in 2006. Since then, we have published two greenhouse gas emissions inventories (in 2011 and 2019); both

Photo 16.4 A solar wind array at Ocean Lakes High School. Credit: Nathan
Botwright.

show that transportation is the division's second largest emissions source,
behind building electricity (Moseley Architects, 2019). With approximately
735 buses in our yellow fleet and 314 white fleet vehicles, this finding is
not too surprising. But how do you go about managing such a large fleet in
a more sustainable way? We had an anti-idling policy in place, but obviously, we needed to think bigger. So, we set some ambitious goals. Two
of these include reducing fuel consumption by 50% for the entire vehicle
fleet by 2030 and reducing our transportation emissions by 50% by 2050
(Moseley Architects, 2019).

One way we are looking to achieve these goals is by shifting to newer,
lower emission vehicles and vehicles that operate on propane and electricity. We have acquired 50 propane buses so far and are looking into expanding our propane fuel capabilities. Electric vehicles, however, appear to be
the technology that will take us where we need to go from an emissions
perspective, so we are wrapping our heads around what that will look
like for VBCPS. In 2020, we completed a long-range study that looked

at electric vehicle charging infrastructure for our entire vehicle fleet. We currently have eight electric school buses and nine charging stations and are working to expand our fleet and charging capabilities. We received our electric buses through a partnership with local utility Dominion Energy, which is paying to offset the cost of the electric buses as compared to diesel buses. Dominion Energy recognizes the potential in vehicle-to-grid capabilities, and we hope to help expand these capabilities.

Another way we are looking to meet our goals is by optimizing how we transport students. In the past, bus routes were figured out using pencil, paper, and a lot of institutional knowledge. In 2019, VBCPS started to use a routing software package to map out bus routes. This process will prove to be much more efficient over time.

The shifts we have made thus far in our transportation department are bearing fruit. According to our 2019 Greenhouse Gas Inventory and Emissions Reduction Plan, between 2006 and 2016, we reduced our division's overall emissions by about 47,520 metric tons of CO_2. That is equivalent to removing 10,089 passenger vehicles from the road for one year! In addition, gas consumption within our white fleet has decreased 39%, and diesel consumption within our yellow fleet has decreased 4%, both since 2006 (Moseley Architects, 2019).

Adopting a Sustainable Food System

When I was growing up in the 1960s and 1970s, all cafeteria food was cooked from scratch. I still remember how school rolls smelled and tasted. It is a fond memory for me. Unfortunately, many students today cannot relate to my experience with cafeteria food. Up until 2017, VBCPS, like many school divisions, primarily served heat-and-serve meals, and our school meal numbers reflected student (and staff) dissatisfaction.

This was by no means our food-service workers' fault. They receive no funding from the division, so they must buy food, pay salaries, and purchase equipment, among other expenses, with the money they earn from breakfast and lunch sales. If pizza and fries are the big sellers, then so be it, pizza and fries will be the staple. And, given we removed most of the equipment used to cook food in our kitchens over the last 30 years, heat and serve became the default cooking style and the chicken biscuit wrapped in plastic became the culinary gold standard.

We did make some positive shifts in the 2000s. During the 2009–2010 school year, VBCPS started a farm-to-school program and our Office of Food Services began to map the sources for local produce (harvested within 400 miles). However, our biggest shift came after the 2016 summit when we decided to implement a divisionwide scratch-cooking program. Aside from providing healthier, more nutritious meals, we believed that this was a great opportunity to connect our school gardens with the cafeteria and show students how the two systems are interconnected as well as educate the school community on the benefits of buying local and the impact that has on reducing emissions.

We kicked things off with a year-long pilot program at Old Donation School in 2017. We worked with Beyond Green Sustainable Food Partners to train our food-service workers in scratch-cooking skills and techniques and help them feel comfortable cooking in the kitchen. We discovered that the pilot was not that painful to implement, and we learned something else valuable, too. Up to that point, our food-service workers did not feel valued in their roles. This was leading to low self-esteem and high absenteeism rates. So, empowering our food-service workers as educators and respected members of the school staff became an additional goal for us as we continued to roll out our scratch-cooking program.

In 2018, not long after the pilot ended, we hired a division chef to lead our scratch-cooking efforts. We built a team dedicated to scratch cooking and created a "from scratch" menu that is being scaled up across the division. We are installing equipment in our school kitchens that will allow workers to cook from scratch. The plan is for all 86 school kitchens to be retrofitted for scratch cooking by 2024. We also created baker and cook positions within our schools to give food-service workers another pathway to advance their careers and build their self-esteem as valued members of our school community.

We continue to focus on using local produce in our school meal program. Our goal is to increase local procurement by 30% over 2009 levels. We are getting a boost in this area through our participation in the Department of Defense's Fresh FFAVORS program and from our school garden clubs, which are coordinating with the division chef and growing food in their gardens that can be harvested and used in their schools' scratch-cooked meals. Everyone in the school community is responding positively to the changes we have been making. More students are buying breakfast and lunch at school, and food-service workers are taking on a larger role in planning and supporting school gardens.

One area we want to improve on in the coming years is food waste. VBCPS does not currently have a comprehensive food composting program, and cafeteria waste is a significant part of our waste stream. The biggest barrier is a lack of infrastructure in Virginia Beach to support food waste compost collection. We continue to have discussions on this topic but will likely need to engage the city in a larger program to ensure it is cost-effective for us. In the meantime, we are exploring better ways to serve condiments and the use of reusable trays and real silverware in our cafeterias in an effort to move toward net-zero waste. The latter of the two is posing a challenge for some schools, especially our middle schools where students are accidently throwing the silverware away with their trash. An education component is clearly in order to make use of reusables more efficient and sustainable.

Lessons Learned

A big challenge we face at VBCPS revolves around communication and getting the word out to a broader audience regarding our sustainability initiatives. It is a three-part challenge. First, there is the need to get everyone across the division – teachers, staff, and others – to understand and buy into the triple-bottom-line mindset. We have a long way to go before the triple bottom line is ubiquitous across the division. Second, we need to communicate the triple bottom line to our students and help them understand that there is a social, environmental, and economic impact to everything they do. Some schools do this really well, but we have much more work to do before all students have a firm grasp of the concept. This is especially true when we talk about equity issues and how to increase diversity. Sustainability is a great tool for engaging students in discussions around the importance of diversity in the natural environment and how we, as humans, are an extension of that environment.

Photo 16.5 Sustainability Officer Tim Cole reviews building plans with students at Old Donation School. Credit: Ara Howrani.

Finally, we need to get better at self-promotion. In the past, we kept our heads down and figured that our successes would speak for themselves. However, we have come to realize that if you are not out there promoting what you are doing, you are missing a critical educational opportunity. We must remind ourselves – it is all about winning hearts and minds.

Learning from Virginia Beach City Public Schools: Adopting a Triple-Bottom-Line Mindset at Your District

When it comes to adopting a triple-bottom-line mindset, slow and steady wins the race. We are fortunate at VBCPS to have committed champions for sustainability lending support along the way. Here are a few ways your district can learn from our example.

- **Pilot key initiatives.** Start small and grow your programs through their success. Our LEED buildings, propane and electric vehicle initiatives, and scratch-cooking program began as pilots. Everything starts small.

- **Develop allies across departments.** Identify like-minded folks in departments and schools, cultivate relationships that have potential, and slowly develop your team.
- **Get senior leadership on board.** Our sustainability summit is a great model for accomplishing this. People are more inclined to listen to third parties and welcome their help in navigating topics like the triple-bottom-line mindset.
- **Constant reinforcement is key.** Introducing everyone to the triple bottom line of sustainability is important, but so is the need to keep the conversation going. It is a given that people will stumble around what sustainability means and what is involved in the triple-bottom-line mindset.
- **Implement at a grassroots level.** It is easy to get buy-in at the division level, but when it comes to implementation, most of the work happens in schools. Our Sustainable School Liaisons have been a tremendous help in getting sustainability initiatives off the ground in our schools and our Sustainable School Recognition Award incentivizes schools to participate, allowing VBCPS to meet its school-level goals.

Synthesis

We are at a critical juncture in our evolution as a species. Our current trajectory, if unaltered, does not bode well for future generations. Our success depends on how well we educate students on the interconnectedness and interdependencies of all systems. Whether we just survive, or thrive, will depend on our ability to exist in a symbiotic relationship with every other carbon-based life form on this spaceship we call Earth.

A buddy of mine was fond of saying "people don't follow the plan; they follow the man." So, I encourage you to be the person that people can follow. It does not take much; all you have to do is lead by example.

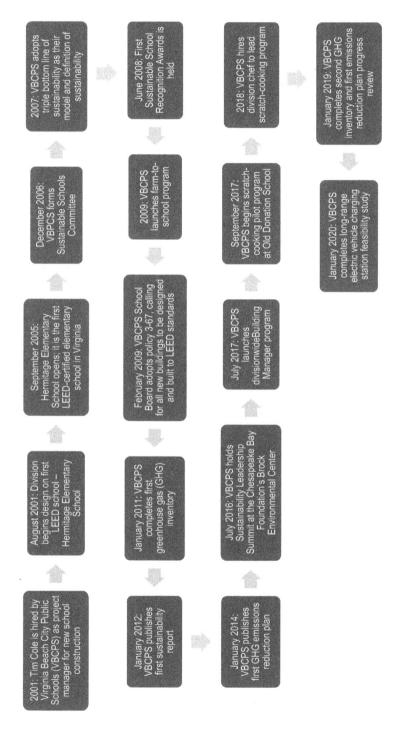

Figure 16.1 Virginia Beach City Public Schools Timeline.

Works Cited

Brundtland Commission. (1987). *Our common future.* Oxford: Oxford University Press.

Moseley Architects. (2019). *Greenhouse gas emissions inventory + emissions reduction plan progress review.* VBCPS Sustainable Schools Committee.

Tausanovitch, C. and Warshaw, C. (2014). Representation in municipal government. *American Political Science Review, 108*(3), 605–641. Retrieved from: https://www.jstor.org/stable/43654395

Virginia Beach City Public Schools. (2015). *2015 sustainability report.* Retrieved from: https://www.vbschools.com/UserFiles/Servers/Server_78010/File/About%20Us/Our%20Leadership/Our%20Departments/Construction/Sustainable%20Schools/SustainabilityReport.pdf

Virginia Beach City Public Schools. (2021). *Facilities update school board briefing* [Presentation]. Office of Facilities Services.

Relevant Websites

Virginia Beach City Public Schools. Retrieved from: https://www.vbschools.com/

Notes on Contributors

Sarah Anderson is an educator and author specializing in place-based education and curriculum design. Anderson served as a middle school humanities teacher for nine years, first in Annapolis, Maryland and then at the Cottonwood School of Civics and Science in Portland, Oregon. She is currently the Fieldwork and Place-Based Education Coordinator at the Cottonwood School, where she leads workshops and mentors teachers in place-based curriculum design. Anderson has also worked extensively with the Oregon Historical Society, where she has written local history curricula for grades K-12. She is the author of *Bringing School to Life: Place-based Education across the Curriculum* and has written for Teaching Tolerance, Educational Leadership, Education Week, and more.

Lindsey Bradley is the Marketing Specialist for Austin Independent School District (AISD) Food Service. Born and raised in Michigan, Lindsey received her BS in Journalism from Central Michigan University. Following graduation, she moved to Texas where she began her marketing career in the beverage distribution industry. Lindsey joined the AISD Food Service team in 2015, pursuing a personal passion to create healthier communities. Through graphic design, social media management, and community outreach, her work has helped to bring national recognition to the district's innovative approaches to expanding healthy food access and redefining the student dining experience.

Brendan Callahan is Director of Bond Programs, Sustainability, Maintenance, and Operations at Oak Park Unified School District (OPUSD). He received a BS in Business Administration from Boston University, an MBA from Georgetown University, and an MEd from The Broad Center. Before joining OPUSD, Brendan worked at Green Dot Public Schools, managing finance and operations for schools in South Los Angeles. He also led process improvement at Lockheed Martin as a Lean Six Sigma Black Belt. While in college, Brendan founded a nonprofit that constructed a Tanzanian rural village's first secondary school. Outside of work, he can be found hiking local trails with his wife Alyssa; their pit bull/mastiff mix, Ellie; and their lab/shepherd mix, Joy.

Pamela Casna is the K-12 Principal of Codman Academy. Prior to joining Codman, Pam worked in the New York City Public Schools, first as an English as a Second Language teacher and then moving into administrative roles, supporting language development of all learners. At Codman, Pam started as Director of Student Services, overseeing a comprehensive department including Special Education, English Language Learners, Literacy, and Social Work. She earned her BS in International Relations with a minor in Spanish from Hofstra University, her MEd in TESOL from Long Island University in Brooklyn, New York, and her CAGS in Educational Leadership through the Commonwealth Leadership Academy at Endicott College in Beverly, Massachusetts.

Tim Cole is the Sustainability Officer for Virginia Beach City Public Schools. Tim was instrumental in the promotion and development of the first LEED-certified elementary school in Virginia – Hermitage Elementary School – and the first K-12 LEED Platinum transportation and maintenance facility in the country. Tim is an original member of SEAL Team 6, which was commissioned within the U.S. Navy in 1980, and is a combat veteran of Operation Iraqi Freedom. Tim holds a Bachelor of Architecture from Virginia Polytechnic Institute and State University.

Darien Clary is Austin Independent School District's (AISD) Sustainability Manager. In this role, she implements and tracks programs for water and energy conservation, recycling and composting, active transportation, green building, nature access and infrastructure, and school engagement. Prior to joining AISD, Darien advanced sustainability at Austin Community College and led community-based conservation and economic growth initiatives in the Dominican Republic for Columbia University's Center for Environment, Economy, and Society. She holds an undergraduate degree in Biology from Southwestern University and a master's degree in Public Health from the University of Texas.

Katherine Elmer-DeWitt worked in fundraising, communication, and scale at the Academy for Global Citizenship from 2012 to 2019 before transitioning onto the school's Board of Directors. Katherine is a Program Manager at Oak Street Health, a network of integrative primary care centers for adults in low-income communities. She also works as a therapist specializing in the treatment of eating disorders and related mental health concerns.

Jo Giordano has an MA in Physical Education from the University of South Florida and a BA in Elementary Education from Warren Wilson College in Asheville, North Carolina. She is the Adventure PE teacher at Evergreen Community Charter School and has taught K-8 students for 17 years. During this time, she has built Evergreen's adventure and after-school programs while consulting with other schools to help them do the same. She has served on the Evergreen Board of Directors and recently published a book called *Wise From Within*.

Jay Greenlinger is Director of Curriculum and Instruction at Oak Park Unified School District. Jay's education career began when he became a camp counselor at 15. He received a BA in Psychology from the University of Massachusetts, Amherst, an MA in Elementary Education from Pepperdine University, and an MA in School Administration and a Doctorate in Educational Leadership from California State University, Northridge. He is a former teacher, principal, and technology director. When Jay is not at work, you will most likely find him playing outside with his wife Lisa, an elementary teacher; their four children; and their Malteepoo, Wilson.

Amanda Hanley has served on the Academy for Global Citizenship's Board of Directors since 2013. Promoting sustainable solutions for over 30 years, she currently leads a climate justice fund. Amanda co-founded and continues to advise the Hanley Sustainability Institute at the University of Dayton, one of the Sierra Club's Top 20 Coolest Schools of 2018 and 2019. She also serves as a board member of the Global Catholic Climate Movement, working to promote Pope Francis' Laudato Si' encyclical to care for our common home, and As You Sow, focused on corporate accountability.

Naomi Dietzel Hershiser is the Dean of Environmental Learning at Prairie Crossing Charter School, where she works with students and teachers to incorporate sustainability and environmental learning into the daily school experience. Before starting at Prairie Crossing in 2003, Naomi taught environmental education in informal settings at nature centers and museums. She earned a MAT from Dominican University, an Environmental Education certification from University of Minnesota Duluth, and a BA from Carleton College. When she is not working, Naomi enjoys running, gardening, reading, and traveling with her husband Chris.

Amy Illingworth serves as Assistant Superintendent of Educational Services for Encinitas Union School District (EUSD). A lifelong educator, Dr. Illingworth has served as a teacher, literacy coach, and site and district administrator in elementary and secondary settings. Her passion for instructional leadership and coaching led to the publication of her book, *The Coach ADVenture: Building Powerful Instructional Leadership Skills That Impact Learning*. Dr. Illingworth is a prolific reader and has enjoyed learning more about environmental sustainability through her work with EUSD.

Marin Leroy is the Environmental Education Program Coordinator at Evergreen Community Charter School in Asheville, North Carolina. A native of Northern California, Marin obtained a BS in Environmental Biology and Botany from Humboldt State University. After several years of guiding wilderness experiences and facilitating outdoor education programs throughout the west and northeast, she completed an MS in Environmental Studies and secured her high school teaching certificate in biology from Antioch University New England. Marin's graduate work focused on supporting innovations in public education, with an emphasis on integrating the environment and citizenship into the standard course of study.

Francine Locke is Chief Sustainability Officer for Delaware County, Pennsylvania. She served as Environmental Director and Director of Sustainability and Green Schools for the School District of Philadelphia from 2005 to 2021. Francine has a master's degree in Environmental Health and a bachelor's degree in Biology, both from Temple University in Philadelphia. She is a doctoral student at Drexel University, where she is focusing her research on children's environmental health and legacy toxins in older public school buildings. Francine has worked to make Philadelphia schools green, healthy, and sustainable since 2005. Starting out, her role was to ensure the district maintained strict environmental regulatory compliance. Over time, Francine gained the support of district leadership to grow indoor environmental quality, asthma, lead-in-water, and sustainability programs that are deeply rooted in improving student health and academic performance.

Susan Mertz has an MEd in Special Education and a PhD in Curriculum and Instruction from the University of North Carolina – Greensboro. She is the Executive Director of Evergreen Community Charter School in Asheville, North Carolina. Evergreen has a 22-year history of focusing on environmental education and is one of the U.S. Department of Education's 78 inaugural Green Ribbon Schools. Susan has served on the board of Green Schools National Network and the AdvancED State Advisory Council. Prior to joining Evergreen, Susan worked as a School Improvement Consultant with the Southern Regional Education Board, providing consultation, coaching, and professional development to schools across the country.

Anne Muller is Austin Independent School District's (AISD) Outdoor Learning Specialist, where she works to make nature equitably accessible through green schoolyards and outdoor learning. Anne runs the district demonstration habitat, embeds outdoor connections into district curriculum, and supports the right of all AISD students to learn, play, and grow in nature. Anne holds an undergraduate degree in American Studies from Mount Holyoke College and a master's degree in Science Curriculum and Instruction from the University of Texas, Arlington.

Tina Nilsen-Hodges has been an educator for nearly three decades. In 2009, she responded to the call of the United Nations Decade for Education for Sustainable Development by leading the team that founded New Roots Charter School as a whole-school model of sustainability education. Tina has served as the school's leader since its founding, and in 2021, she was a finalist for the Best of Green Schools K-12 Educator Award. Tina lives with her husband Jim, a Montessori teacher, at EcoVillage at Ithaca. Their adult sons Aidan and Niall are pursuing careers that help others create meaningful and lasting connections with the natural world.

Keith David Reeves serves as the educational technology administrator at Discovery Elementary School. He has taught every grade level, preK-12, in underserved and affluent schools in both rural and urban settings, as well as educational methods at the university level. He is the author of several books on education, including *Insurrection: A Teacher Revolution* *in Defense of Children*. He travels across the country as a keynote speaker, conference presenter, professional developer, and expert panelist. He holds diplomas in education from Ithaca College, George Mason University, and The University of Mary Washington and is finishing his doctoral studies and certification at Lamar and Harvard Universities.

Laura A. Smith served as Program and Grants Coordinator for Boulder Valley School District (BVSD) Food Services from 2015 until late 2019. At BVSD, Laura oversaw the department's nutrition education, farm-to-school and sustainability programs, communications, marketing, and fundraising. She now works for Central District Health in Boise, Idaho, addressing persistent community health challenges through policy, education, and promotion. Laura holds a BA in Psychology from Bates College and received her MPH from the Colorado School of Public Health.

Anneliese Tanner began her professional career in finance before pursuing her Master's in Food Studies. She returned from New York to Texas to make change in the food system through school food, where education and volume come together to create change. At Austin Independent School District, Anneliese led a movement to redefine school meals through programs like breakfast in the classroom, food trucks, salad bars, plant-forward menus featuring global flavors, increased scratch-cooking, sustainable purchasing, and zero-waste cafeterias. She is now Director of Research and Assessment at the Chef Ann Foundation, helping school districts across the country transition to scratch cooking.

Joel Tolman is the Lead Teacher for Student Pathways at Common Ground – a high school, urban farm, and environmental education center in New Haven, Connecticut. Joel came to Common Ground as a teacher in 2003 – drawn to Common Ground's commitment to active, authentic learning and environmental justice. Since stepping out of a full-time classroom role in 2008, Joel has helped to develop and grow collaborations and projects including Common Ground's Green Jobs Corps, Teaching Our Cities, the school's four-year pathways plan, and other efforts to root learning in the local community and environment. Before coming to Common Ground, Joel worked for five years in high school reform and youth development in Washington, D.C. He has a degree in Environmental Studies from Williams College and an MEd from George Washington University.

Lauren Trainer is principal at the School of Environmental Studies (SES). Lauren enjoys watching her students collaborate with others and create real-world solutions to environmental and social justice issues that consider a variety of perspectives. One of the most exciting parts about being principal at SES is having experiences in nature with students. From winter camping, to canoeing in the fall, to snorkeling the Great Barrier Reef, Lauren has enjoyed many opportunities to learn alongside her students. Outside of work, she enjoys spending time with her three kids at their home on the St. Croix River.

Rob Wade is a Place-Based Learning (PBL) educator in the Upper Feather River region of northeastern California and has led Plumas County's PBL effort for the past 25 years. His work has scaled nationally, specifically in the land trust community. Rob was the 2016 recipient of the California Environmental Education Foundation's Excellence in EE Award and a 2020 recipient of the Environmental Law Institute's National Wetland Award. He holds a BS in Conservation and Resource Studies from UC Berkeley.

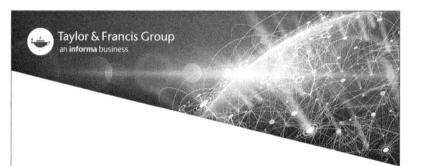

CPSIA information can be obtained
at www.ICGtesting.com
Printed in the USA
JSHW021909180522
26005JS00002B/3